THE CHANGING FACE
OF BRITAIN'S RAILWAYS
1938-1953

The Railway Companies Bow Out

THE CHANGING FACE
OF BRITAIN'S RAILWAYS
1938-1953

The Railway Companies Bow Out

Robert Hendry

DALRYMPLE

& VERDUN◆
PUBLISHING

The Changing Face of Britain's Railways 1938-1953
The Railway Companies Bow Out
Robert Hendry

ISBN 1-905414-03-X

First published in 2006 by
Dalrymple & Verdun Publishing
33 Adelaide Street, Stamford,
Lincolnshire PE9 2EN
Tel: 0845 838 1940
info@dvpublishing.co.uk
www.dvpublishing.co.uk

Printed in England by
Ian Allan Printing Ltd
Riverdene Business Park, Molesey Road
Hersham, Surrey, KT12 4RG

Half title: As a taper boiler Patriot 4-6-0 thunders past the water softening plant at Newbold water troughs, with an Up Euston express on the Trent Valley line, a permanent way gang labours with shovels on the Down slow line. It is a broiling hot summer afternoon, and as one labourer pauses to wipe the sweat from his brow, a younger worker has shed his shirt to gain some relief from the stifling heat. The water softening plant represented modern technology brought to the service of the railway industry, but the men who built railways for George Stephenson would have been familiar with the job the p.w. gang is doing. This mixture of ancient and modern, change and permanence, gave a particular fascination to the early days of British Railways.

Facing title page: A Churchward Star class 4-6-0, No 4018, *Knight of the Grand Cross*, shedded at the prestigious GWR express passenger depot at Wolverhampton (Stafford Road), is bathed in evening sunlight as she prepares to depart from the Up platform at Leamington Spa station in 1947. For one hundred and ten years, Paddington and Swindon had directed the affairs of the Great Western Railway, but with the Transport Act 1947, the sun was setting on the proud Great Western Railway just as surely as it was setting on *Knight of the Grand Cross*. To Great Western men, such as Sir James Milne, the company's highly regarded General Manager, it was a sad end to an era of unequalled public service. Milne chose to bring his career to a close, but the railway he had guided so well continued into the new era with its great traditions of service. No 4018, which dated from April 1908, remained in traffic until 1951.

Front Cover: Robin Riddles was another long serving railway officer. Appointed as the Member of the Railway Executive responsible for motive power, Riddles was to define locomotive policy on the newly created British Railways, and a Riddles BR Standard Class 2 No 78000 is at Barmouth Junction at the head of a Dolgelly – Pwllheli class K pick up goods.

Rear Cover: A modern generation of writers have revelled in decrying the 'dreadful' compounds produced by Francis William Webb at Crewe. In a study carried out by an American engineer in the 1880s, these 'dreadful' compounds earned the LNWR second place after the GNR in running costs per train mile for express trains. Given that the GNR trains were habitually much lighter than their LNWR counterparts, it is likely that in costs per ton mile, Webb's engines took premier place. The compounds succumbed to rising train loads in the early 1900s, but other Webb engines, including the lively Webb 5ft 6 ins 2-4-2Ts, soldiered on into the post war era. The motor fitted No 6669 makes a spirited departure from the former LNWR station at Leamington Spa in 1947. Such was the diversity of the railway scene in 1947, that just a few yards separate this scene from the evocative portrait facing the title page.

CONTENTS

INTRODUCTION 6

1. THE EDGE OF THE ABYSS 16

2. WAR ON THE LINE 21

3. 'ONCE EGGS HAVE BEEN SCRAMBLED,
   I DEFY ANY COOK TO UNSCRAMBLE THEM' 28

4. HURCOMB'S EMPIRE 50

5. THE RAILWAY EXECUTIVE TAKES CHARGE 58

6. CRISIS IN ULSTER 78

7. 'BUS OR RAILBUS, THAT IS THE QUESTION?' 92

8. THE HOWDEN TOUCH 102

9. CAITHNESS TO THE BORDERS 114

10. CROESO Y CYMRU 126

11. A WEST COAST PERSPECTIVE, 1948-1953 140

12. 'A MILLION TONS OF STEAM' 152

13. SERVICES WILL BE WITHDRAWN 175

14. THE RAILWAY EXECUTIVE YEARS,
    MYTH AND FACT 182

INDEX 191

INTRODUCTION

Two significant events took place at the start of 1948. One is well known. British Railways came into being on 1st January. The second event is less well known; I was born! This momentous event was not celebrated by public holidays or grand ceremonial, though to be truthful, neither was the birth of British Rail. My parents were happy to encourage my obvious delight in railways, reasoning that it was an interest that could only be good for me, as it encouraged a knowledge of geography, history, social history, engineering, physics, mathematics and many other subjects. It provided exercise, and it is hard to imagine a more sensible or positive hobby for any youngster, whatever some of our mentally challenged psychiatrists and educational 'experts' may say to the contrary.

Apart from full sized railways, my father had a large O gauge railway that was signalled and worked in accordance with prototype practice. I was allowed to play on the railway, but before long I wanted to work trains in the proper way, like my father and his friends. We hear of the unbridgeable age gap between the generations, but on that model railway, I have seen an 80 year old and an 18 year old work as colleagues. Because of his interest in full sized and model railways, my father knew many railway officers, and visits to railway

installations that were out of bounds to the public ensued. On one occasion when I was very small, I was taken to the Rugby Locomotive Testing Station. To see a steam engine with its wheels rotating fast, but standing still, was thrilling. It was also incredibly noisy. Sometimes, senior railwaymen returned the compliment, and visited our railway. I recall one 'running' when our guests included the District Operating Superintendent, and the District Locomotive Superintendent, both of whom were put to work at appropriate jobs, one as a signalman, and one as shed master. On another occasion, there was an unexpected phone call from the Testing Station. A very high-ranking officer from Headquarters was in Rugby, and it would be appreciated if he could be shown over the layout, whilst some changes were being made at the test house. Who our unexpected guest was, I do not know, but from the deference shown by the local officers who accompanied him, it could well have been Robin Riddles himself. If so, I may have met England's last steam locomotive designer. Over the years, the process even became international, with guests including the Executive Vice President of a US Railroad. From long before my school days, railways were an integral part of my life. As a result, I have happy childhood memories of the traditional railway age when thousands of steam locomotives existed, when country stations abounded with quiet goods yards, where there were old fashioned wooden wagons to climb on, and nice friendly porters, signalmen, guards and enginemen. I can still recall my first footplate ride, and the first time a friendly ticket collector succumbed to my request, 'Please can I keep my ticket'.

My father realised that this enchanting world was about to change, and much that he had known all his life, would disappear. He decided to record it on film before it was too late. As the months rolled by, familiar engines vanished and shiny new diesels and DMUs appeared. Well, they were shiny to begin with, but not for long, as the railways were short staffed and cleaners were scarce, so the diesels became as dirty as the steam engines they were replacing, not that I cared, as I didn't like them. The steam engines were more fun. Not only were engines vanishing, but railway lines were shutting as well. A secondary route ran from Rugby to Leamington. When I was little, the push pull trains were worked by delightful Webb 2-4-2Ts with tall chimneys. They were replaced by Ivatt 2-6-2Ts in the early fifties, and it was on an Ivatt tank on the Leamington line that I had my first main line footplate ride. In due course, some evil person said the line had to be shut, and it was. In the early Sixties, the name of Dr Beeching became prominent. His mission in life appeared to be the single-handed destruction of the rail network, and he even produced a report saying what he proposed to axe. My father bought a copy, and as more and more lines closed down, it became a race to see as much as possible before it went. Stations, signal boxes, carriages and wagons were all under threat, partly due to the modern diesel trains, and partly because of closures, and in 1968, the last of the 20,000 standard gauge steam engines on British Railways drew its fire for the last time. Although shiny modern electric and diesel locomotives might pull the trains, and we did have modern air-braked wagons, power signal boxes, welded rails and other signs of a new railway age, we still had tens of thousands of 4-wheel wagons many with handbrakes alone, mechanical signalling, and operating features that had remained unchanged for a century. It was a fascinating paradox.

This was the story that I set out to tell. Visually, it makes a fascinating and compelling picture, but my father would often pose the question, 'Why'. As a GP, when he was confronted with a patient with a particular illness, it was the question he asked himself, so it was natural for him to apply it in a different

Opposite page: 'This railway system of ours is a very poor bag of assets. The permanent way is badly worn. The rolling stock is in a state of great dilapidation. The railway stations and their equipment are a disgrace to the country'. Looking at this portrait of the Leamington Spa Avenue station of the London, Midland & Scottish Railway, and seeing the shabby paintwork, the sagging canopy that has been propped with a temporary leg, and the perished roof covering, which was coincidentally taken at about the same time as Hugh Dalton, the Chancellor of the Exchequer, was using those words to castigate the railways during the 1946 sitting of Parliament, it is hard not to agree with him. However, Dalton was not a popular figure, even amongst his colleagues in the Parliamentary Labour Party. He was regarded as sharp-tongued, harsh, ruthless and unsympathetic, and once the government had decided upon Nationalisation of the Big Four railway companies, it made brutal sense to rubbish them, to justify the lowest possible price for the compulsory takeover that was coming. What it overlooked was that the railways had managed to keep their systems to a commendable level up to the outbreak of war in 1939. Then, they had put their own interests aside, and had thrown their energies into the war effort. Resources and manpower that should have been used to maintain the system were diverted to serve the needs of the nation. They had been major victims of the German bomber offensive from 1939 to 1941, and of massive overwork during the war, for which a grateful nation had never fairly recompensed them, demanding they carried war traffic, but declining to pay them for the privilege of wearing out their equipment in doing so. Finally, and most tellingly of all, to the vexation and puzzlement of most people, rationing that had been justified during the war, became even more stringent when the enemy was defeated, and the railways came low in the queue for vital resources, so that the companies' ambitious plans to restore their systems to their pre-war state were constantly frustrated. Unintentionally or deliberately, the government made sure that the railways were a very poor bag of assets, and having done so, blamed them for it. It was not fair, but it was politics, and fairness and politics have seldom gone hand-in-hand. Dalton's vicious criticisms, however unfair, contained sufficient truth to be damaging, and were to set the railways and the politicians on a course that has led us to where we are today. *H J Stretton-Ward*

LMS platform ticket printed black on thin buff card.

context. As I started to gather illustrations for a book charting the changing face of Britain's railways, I realised that interesting though the visual changes were, 'why' was even more interesting. What had led to the extraordinary changes that took place on Britain's Railways in my lifetime? A child born in 1875 would have seen remarkably few changes to the railways he had known as a youngster if he lived to be three score year and ten. The liveries might have changed, but some of the engines he would have seen in his infancy were still running. Many of the signal boxes that had been built in the 1870s and 1880s were still in use. Operating practices had changed remarkably little. It was an era of comfortable permanence, yet suddenly it started to change. In the fifty years from 1948, the railway world changed at a pace unequalled at any time in history, save for the formative years from the 1820s to the 1860s, when we went from no railways at all, to a national system.

Many enthusiasts have a specific interest in one railway or one aspect of one railway, and I encountered the ultimate expression of this when I met a gentleman who was adamant that there was only one locomotive engineer who was any use. His name was Nigel Gresley. According to my informant, only one of Gresley's designs was any good, and this was the A1/A3 Pacific. It seemed sad that the achievements of *Mallard* were consigned to the rubbish bin of history, but so be it. Seemingly, only one A1/A3 Pacific was any good out of the entire class, and it was numbered 4472. Finally, 4472 was only any good if he was firing it. This condemnation of twenty thousand plus steam engines that I had regarded as excellent just a few minutes previously, seemed excessive. My father was interested in railways, and not just locomotives. He was knowledgeable on signalling and freight stock, on tickets and timetables, and he passed that interest in the broader picture on to me. I learned to appreciate the magnificent legacy handed down to the GWR by Churchward, or the equally sound work done under Francis William Webb on re-signalling the LNWR. Bulleid's Pacifics became firm favourites, despite their quirks, and who could disregard the sleek lines of an A4, even if they were no use, as I had been told! That interest embraced not just the Big Four or British Railways, but other lines as well. I heard of azure blue 4-4-0s that handled express trains between Belfast and Dublin, of archaic wooden bodied wagons in Northern Ireland that carried wagon plates of a company that had been taken over as long ago as 1903, and other amazing survivors.

Many writers have spoken of the rivalry between the Big Four, and provided such comparisons are not to denigrate a rival, but to learn what strengths and weaknesses different companies possessed, they can be helpful. Would we appreciate the task Stanier faced on the LMS, if we did not know how far LMS motive power development had fallen behind the GWR before he took the Swindon gospel to Crewe and Derby? With Nationalisation in 1948, most writers have regarded such comparisons as impossible, but this is not so. The railways of Ireland were subjected to the same influences that shaped their English counterparts, and until partition of Ireland in 1921, the whole of Ireland was part of the United Kingdom, and Northern Ireland remains a part of the UK to this day, with its own separate railway system. Whilst politically separate for a lifetime, the railways of Eire had developed in the British mould, and although there are many divergences today, there is much in common. My earliest training was in the sciences, and scientists love a control experiment where one variable is tested at a time. In this way, the effects of each factor can be assessed. In the real world, this is seldom possible, but the tribulations of the Irish railways between 1945 and 1953 reveal how different systems fared. Over the years, I had acquired a complete set of the Annual Reports and Accounts of the British Transport Commission, and British Railways, and a wide range of Accounts and Reports of many other systems, including the LMS, LNER, GWR, Southern, the Great Northern Railway (Ireland), CIE, UTA, the Belfast & County Down, the Londonderry & Lough Swilly and the County Donegal Railways. At first, they were nice 'collector's items', but after training in accountancy, I started to look at them with a professional eye, and comparisons between the policies of one operator and another began to emerge. I had studied the financial crisis that developed on BR between 1948 and 1953, but it was only when I started work on this book, and analysed the Irish data alongside it, that I realised that if not the 'control experiment' that a scientist would prefer, it came close to it. BR went from financial viability to crisis within a few years, and generations of writers have condemned the Railway Executive, which ran BR from 1948 to 1953, for its stupidity. Having examined the finances of the Irish lines, they also moved from stability to chronic loss making within a couple of years, and the gap between viability on the archaic, under-funded and poorly managed CIE, or the highly progressive and well led GNR(I) or CDRJC was less than five years. Did an understanding of events in Belfast, Dublin or far away Donegal help answer the paradox over BR? Up to a point it does, but the BR crisis was far more curious, as I was to discover.

At first, we planned one volume covering the Transition Era from the 1940s to the 1980s, but a list of topics jotted down on the back of the proverbial envelope highlighted several hundred views. Even with superficial two line captions, which would offer no chance to ask 'why', this was beyond the confines of a single volume. The options were a superficial approach, omitting much that was worth covering, or to restrict the time frame to a more manageable period, covering later years separately. The story is so fascinating, with so many unexpected twists and turns, that the publishers agreed to this approach, with the proviso that it had to cover more than one day in the life of BR! As the project developed, it became clear that the events between 1939 and 1947 were crucial to understanding 1948, and the early years of British Railways. The Big Four railway companies devoted their energies to providing a transport service that would help win the war, but it was only when I ventured into the arcane world of Whitehall, that I realised how much time and effort had been expended by politicians and civil servants alike on costly and time consuming re-organisation plans, even though Lord Brabazon of Tara, an exceptionally forceful Minister of Transport, who was also a pioneer OO gauge modeller, was aghast at the whole idea. Although the Labour landslide election of 1945 made Nationalisation inevitable, it seems that the mandarins in Whitehall had set their hearts on having their own train set to play with, irrespective of Labour policies.

After looking at the war years and the last year of independence, we look at the transition from the Big Four to a BR image, and discover the tortuous interplay between the British Transport Commission and the Railway Executive. We visit Ireland to see how different railways were coping with similar problems, and then have a look at the other Celtic fringe countries, Scotland and Wales, which have their own parallels with Ireland. We home in on the West Coast Main Line to provide an in-depth study of how one route evolved between 1948 and 1953, and then set the birth of BR motive power and rolling stock into context. We find out how the infant BR faced the branch line crisis. The replacement of a Labour government dedicated to Nationalisation by a Conservative administration with diametrically opposite views led to a rethink. By this time, politicians, media and civil servants alike, were all obsessed with the deteriorating state of the BTC's finances, and it was clear that the division of control between the BTC and the Railway Executive had not worked. As the railway industry limped into Coronation year 1953, it became clear that another massive reorganisation was in the pipeline. Like the best TV drama, where the audience is left with a cliffhanger, we have stopped the story at that point. It makes good drama, and allows the reader to pause and put himself in the place of those who were doing the job, and ask 'Have we got it right at last?'

With hindsight, it is easy for an author to display his own wisdom, and many historians have savaged leading figures from history, be they generals, admirals or locomotive engineers. Today, it is fashionable to criticise Robin Riddles, who was in charge of motive power development on BR in the early years, just as it is customary to revile the generals on the Western Front in World War One. Sometimes the criticisms are merited. Sometimes they are unjust, and in looking at the dawn of British Railways, I have invited readers to place themselves in Riddles' position, to take into account the factors that had shaped his career and applied to the BR of 1948-1951, without the benefits of hindsight, and to ask what they would have done? Indeed, I have gone further, and suggested that it was not the incompetence of the Railway Executive, or the remoteness of the BTC, that generated a crisis on BR, but the combination of an unworkable administrative and financial structure foisted on the railway industry by politicians and civil servants, coupled with the unprecedented pace of change, that shaped the early years of BR. Another contentious issue is whether a more positive attitude to lightweight railcars and economical working might have saved some branch lines. Opinions vary from the extremes of a 'Conspiracy Theory' in which a sinister pro-road lobby sabotaged every effort to save branch lines, to an 'Infallibility Theory' in which closure must be right, as officialdom can do no wrong.

The words 'Railway Finance' persuade many readers to turn over the page quickly, but as I researched the background to this book, I discovered that I had encountered a 'Railway Whodunit', where the 'crime' was the decline of the proud and profitable railway network of pre-war days to a railway that had become the butt of music hall jokes and parliamentary invective by the late 1950s. Unlike the usual detective novel, where there is no obvious suspect on page 1, a myriad of judges had condemned the suspect before the reader had even reached page 1. Having studied how calamity befell the railways of Ireland in the late 'forties, I was not convinced by the case for the prosecution, however neatly it was presented, but with few clues to go on, it was hard to work out what really happened. One by one, the clues came together, and a picture emerged that not merely upset the glib case that has been trotted out so often in the past, but completely upset the ideas I had been moving towards. Unlike the novelist, who can control his characters, to reach the ending he requires, the characters in my story had minds of their own, and wrote an ending I had not believed possible, though some research I had done years before on a quite different topic ought to have alerted me sooner. From page one of this book, there are pointers, but the real clues come in the final chapter, which is as it should be, and where we find our what really happened to our railways between 1947 and 1953.

Unless the subject is very narrow, and the Transition Era on Britain's railways is immense, the question of what to include or exclude rears its head. The problem confronting any author is seldom what to include, but what text and what illustrations must be left out. It is a balancing act I am only too familiar with, and in one book, the reject heap contained twice as many views as the book itself, and they were rejected not for technical flaws, but because there was no room. Even after the time scale of this book was cut back, over 750 illustrations made the shortlist. In the end, an author has two choices. One is to cover many different topics, each with just one illustration. The other alternative is to cover fewer aspects in greater depth. Both are valid, as the broad-brush treatment covers more ground, yet omits the detail that is so helpful in understanding a particular event. Conversely, an 'in-depth' treatment can omit important aspects of a subject. In previous books, I have favoured an in-depth treatment, examining selected aspects, and I have followed the same principle here. If there is something you feel should have been covered and is not, please ask yourself which views would you have omitted to allow for it. Then you will begin to understand the choices I have faced.

I had the good fortune to live through the Transition Era. Both my father and I wished to explore the railway network before it changed out of all recognition, yet there were constraints on his ability to do so. My father was a doctor in general practice, from when he left the Royal Army Medical Corps in 1945, to his retirement over thirty years later. He was one of the old school of doctors, who followed in his father's footsteps, and it produced a commitment to patients that is lacking today. The notion that the GP 'knocks off' at 5.30pm, rather like a factory worker, and does not book on until the following morning, or that weekends are free time, would have been alien to him. My father, and another doctor shared 24-hour duty seven days a week, 365 days a year. Because his colleague had a young family, and my father was a kindly man, he invariably did 24-hour duty on Christmas day. The notion of handing care of patients to an anonymous out-of-hours doctor would have revolted him, but the price he, and many doctors of his generation, paid, was that half of their lives was spent 'on duty'. That curtailed the time he could spend on photographing the trains that meant so much to him, but I have no doubt what his choice would have been, if he could have had the freedom of today, or the commitment of yesterday. Whilst there was much that we could not see, due to time and distance, and because much of the data that we take for granted today, was not then available, we were able to explore a surprising amount, but I have supplemented our own views with those of some talented railway photographers. Jack Stretton-Ward was a pioneer enthusiast, whose personal friends included Sir Nigel Gresley, and it is possible that it was Stretton-Ward who talked Gresley into restoring Stirling No 1 to running order to take part in some pioneer railtours in the late 1930s. He started taking still photographs in 1911, and after a break for War service in 1914-18, and to set up in business, he resumed photography in 1927, and continued until a few weeks before his death in 1957. Ray Tustin was another lifelong enthusiast who started his photographic career just before World War 2. Ray took his camera overseas during the war, and photographed the changing face of Britain's Railways from the 1940s to the 1970s. Peter Parish was another friend whose work complemented the collections referred to. I have supplemented those photographic records with a few earlier or later views where these help illustrate a particular topic, but the majority of the views are contemporary. Taken together, they provide a remarkable portrait of a dramatic era in the evolution of no fewer than fourteen separate railways in the British Isles between the late 1930s and 1953.

My first acknowledgment goes to my father, Dr Robert Preston Hendry, (1912 – 1991), who encouraged my youthful interest in railways, and guided my first steps in photography, research and railway modelling, and who took me on countless visits to railway installations from a very early age. In this, he received the wholehearted support of my mother, Elaine Hendry (1906 – 1986), who reasoned that it was a worthwhile interest to encourage. Without the kind co-operation of many railway officers, many of the illustrations in this book could not have been taken, and one of the most rewarding aspects of this book is that in the concluding sections, where the facts and statistics are set out, I hope that I have been able to do belated justice to the officers who ran Britain's Railways in the much criticised period from 1948 to 1953. I would like to pay tribute to Clive Partridge, a friend from school days, who has risen in the railway service over the years to a management role in route modernisation, and who has brought a professional railwayman's eye to the manuscript. My Wife Elena spent her childhood in the Soviet Union, where railway enthusiasts were virtually unknown, but overcame her astonishment that anyone would want to take pictures of the railways, and has accompanied me on railway trips in recent times, becoming an accomplished photographer in her own right.

Below: After over eighty years of use, the 1850 Brunellian train shed at Banbury was in poor condition by the 1930s, and the Great Western Railway set aside £99,000 to create a smart new station, the first third to be expended in 1939. The date could hardly have been worse, and with the outbreak of war, the project was suspended 'for the duration', words we will encounter repeatedly in these pages. This view of 54xx tank, No 5404, with a one-coach auto train in the Up platform at Banbury, on 18th September 1948, shows what an easy target the railways were for Dalton's invective. Shabby paint, rotting timbers, missing glazing, and a structure that has had to be propped up, do not create a good impression, yet photos taken just a few years earlier show that although the Great Western was right to plan for its replacement, it had not been too bad until six years of minimal attention had taken a savage toll on an ageing structure. Although Dalton had painted a picture of how state ownership would transform the railways, the reality was very different. The Brunel train shed dragged on past its centenary, and was not demolished until 1953, and it was not until 1958, ten years after Nationalisation, that Banbury finally received a new station. As has so often been the case, political rhetoric and reality did not match, and it was the railwayman that had to take the blame. *R E Tustin*

GREAT WESTERN RAILWAY.
PASSENGER RATED TRAFFIC (404)

From LEIGH COURT G.W. 35
To
Route Via
Consignee
Paid £ To Pay £
Date 19 Train

No. of Box
or Truck

400,000 BM 320 3/43 S.

Above: This 3ins x 4.5ins GWR label of March 1943 is printed in black, with PASSENGER RATED TRAFFIC in red, on thin buff card stock, and is reproduced full size. Unlike the standard wagon label, it could be used for small consignments or for a complete wagon load of traffic moving by passenger train. A typical instance would be one of the celebrated GWR 'brown stock' vehicles which carried merchandise of some sort, but complied to coaching stock regulations over braking, suspension etc. Details are provided of the consignee, the amount paid and still to pay and of the train the consignment was to travel with. Leigh Court, the sending station is rubber stamped in violet ink, the numeral 35 being a GWR reference coding.

Below: Implicit in Hugh Dalton's scathing comments that the railways were 'a disgrace to the country' was the promise that when they were under proper political direction, things would be better than in the bad old days of private enterprise. Students of the Colonel Stephens lines, that amazing collection of cash strapped local railways that were run by the Colonel, were used to scenes of dereliction, and might be forgiven for believing that this is the sort of scene that was in Dalton's mind, though it is doubtful if he knew anything about the Colonel's railways. In fact, it was actually on the long Great Eastern branch that ran north from Wymondham Junction to Dereham and Wells, and is of Crossing No 35, the Hoe Street crossing, near North Elmham, and just about the mid point of the branch. The GER, serving the flat land of East Anglia, was a line where level crossings abounded, each requiring its own keeper, who was often the wife of one of the local permanent way men. In return for a small wage, a house let at a nominal rental, and a small garden in which to grow vegetables, the company was able to have its myriad of gates tended at an affordable cost, whilst providing housing in convenient locations for its staff. At Hoe Street, one former crossing keeper had a large family, but the GE had the answer. A redundant coach body arrived by rail, and was unloaded and made into additional bedrooms. As the family grew up and moved away, the need for the additional accommodation dwindled with the results we see in this view. No doubt, Mr Dalton would have called it a disgrace, but the view was actually taken on 6th April 1971, more than twenty years after the railways had passed into public ownership! To use one photo in this way is as unfair to BR as Dalton's remarks were to the Big Four, but reveals how an indisputable fact can be twisted to give whatever answer is required. The reality was that with the rising operating costs and declining traffic on many lines, deficits were soaring, and BR was in an impossible situation. Even spending money on basic maintenance pushed up the deficit, and if the coach body was no longer needed, now that the crossing keeper's family had grown up and moved away, maintaining it in pristine condition would have added even more to the deficit, and made the closure case for such lines even stronger.

Tickets sometimes provide a commentary on social conditions. The first of these two London Transport ticket provides admission to South Kensington station to shelter from the German Blitz. Tickets were necessary as trains were still running and people leaving the station needed to produce a train ticket or shelter ticket. The white star on the second ticket gives a clue to its purpose, as it is for US Army personnel on duty.

Above: When I was a child, scores of branch lines existed. They had been a part of life for as long as anyone could remember, serving villages and small towns. Except in the most rugged parts of England or Wales, there were few communities that were more than five miles from a railway station. Often, the local station was within a few minutes easy walk, and the would-be passenger could go to the station, and ask the booking clerk how to make the most complicated journey. A well-thumbed timetable that proclaimed it was issued by 'The Railway Executive', from their headquarters at 222 Marylebone Road would be found. In a few minutes, the train times, connections and fares were all jotted down. Maybe you wanted to travel from Glasgow to remote Killin in Scotland, where the railways were thin on the ground. That was no problem. Four trains a day that would make the necessary connections. Maybe you wanted to visit Hayling Island. This was not a problem. The Southern Region timetable was more than three times the size of the Scottish Region book, and had a green regional colour rather than the blue of the Scottish book, but otherwise it was similar. Until I opened my 1949 Southern Region timetable at Table 37, I had not realised that although it had been issued for station use, no one had ever turned up the Hayling Island service, as the pages were uncut! In September 1949, fourteen trains ran each weekday between Havant and Hayling Island, a distance of 4½ miles. At Havant, you left the main line train, and found a diminutive 0-6-0T with a tall chimney waiting to take you to Hayling Island. The engine looked as if it dated from the time of Queen Victoria, and appearances were not

deceptive. It was a Stroudley Terrier, fifty of which had been built from 1872 onwards for the London, Brighton & South Coast Railway. Built as London suburban engines, they had been cascaded to lightly laid country branches, where their sprightly performance belied their age. Because of a lightly built wooden viaduct at Langstone, they were so indispensable to the Hayling Island branch, that they survived until passenger services were abandoned in November 1963. LBSCR No 62, *Martello*, which was built in 1875, progressively became No 662, Southern 2662, and BR 32662, and survived until 1963, when it was sold for preservation on the closure of the Hayling branch. To the spectator, coaling at Hayling Island seemed as archaic as the engine, as coal was shovelled by hand from a wooden stage into the diminutive bunker, and the fireman then scrambled on to the toolbox to adjust the coal supply, as in this idyllic 1952 portrait. It may not have been modern, but it was enchanting.

Third class & saloon rail and sea single privilege ticket, c1951. Printed on pale green card with red CHILD overprint.

Opposite page top: Shortly after my parents were married in 1938, my father was posted to Tidworth, a large army camp in Southern Command. They lived above a grocer's shop in Station Road, near the railway station. By 1938, it was run by the GWR, but until 1923, it had been a short branch from the main line of the independent Midland & South Western Junction Railway. It was my father's introduction to the MSWJ, and left a lifelong affection for this struggling cross-country route that was run for a while by Sam Fay, before he went on to greater glory as general manager of the Great Central Railway. By the end of 1938, just three of the 29 engines that the MSWJ had handed over to the GWR survived, but they were truly remarkable machines. MSWJ No's 10-12 came from Dubs in 1894, and became GWR No's 1334 –1336. Because they were suited to the light trains on the Lambourn Valley line, they lingered on long after their more modern MSWJ stable mates had gone, and all three lasted into the BR era. 1334 and 1335 went in September 1952, but 1336 seemed to enjoy a charmed life, and by the early fifties, the infant railway enthusiast lobby had grown sufficiently active to run a variety of railtours with unusual motive power, or to explore unusual railways. On 9th May 1953, No 1336 returned to her old haunts, and to the MSWJ Swindon Town station, at the head of a Gloucestershire Railway Society special. The end for 1336 came in March 1954.

Opposite page bottom: The Great Northern main line was built in the teeth of opposition from the 'Railway King', George Hudson, and was associated from its earliest days with the great locomotive works established by the GNR at Doncaster. Known as 'The Plant', its centenary in 1953 was commemorated in spectacular style, by the return to steam of two of the most legendary locomotives ever to work out of King's Cross. After the celebrated GN locomotive engineer, Patrick Stirling died in 1895, his successor was H A Ivatt, who came from the Great Southern & Western Railway in Ireland. Ivatt discovered that increasing loads were too much for the magnificent Stirling singles, and built the first of his 'small' Atlantics in 1898. No 990, which most unusually for the GNR, was named *Henry Oakley*, ran until 1937, when it was set aside for preservation. Ivatt felt that the new engine, though a marked advance on the Stirling 4-2-2s, was not powerful enough, and in 1902 introduced his 'large' Atlantics, the prototype being No 251. They were superb machines, and when 251 was withdrawn by the LNER in 1947, the company lavished a great deal of time and effort on restoring it to its original condition. On 20th September 1953, both engines were returned to steam to work a double headed special, named 'The Plant Centenarian', from King's Cross to Doncaster. They are seen at the 'The Cross' a few minutes before departure time at 10.40am. The driver on No 251 was Bill Hoole, a well-known East Coast engineman, and early supporter of the Talyllyn Railway. To the enthusiasts of today, the pre-group liveries are a fascinating recreation of former glories, but many of the enthusiasts at 'The Cross' more than half a century ago had known the GN colours at first hand in their youth.

Above: A well-known participant on 'The Plant Centenarian' was J N Maskelyne, editor of Model Railway News, a Brighton devotee, and the author of several books. Maskelyne came from a remarkable family, which included the Astronomer Royal, Nevil Maskelyne, (1732-1811), and John Nevil Maskelyne (1839-1917) a famous magician who also invented a cash register, the first typewriter made in Britain, and played an important role in the early cinema. Another family member was the 1930's magician, Jasper Maskelyne, who was responsible for camouflage during World War 2. Sharing the same names as his grandfather, J N Maskelyne (1892 – 1960) was born at Wandsworth Common, London, and educated at St Pauls School, Hammersmith and Kings College, London. Elected to the Institute of Loco Engineers, he wrote 'Locomotives of the LBSCR', and 'Locomotives I have known', and edited MRN and Model Engineer from 1935 until his retirement in 1956. He was President of the Stephenson Locomotive Society from 1925, and on the withdrawal of Stoudley's London Brighton & South Coast Railway 'B' Class 0-4-2, No 214 *Gladstone*, he led the first locomotive preservation project by a private body in 1927. In the September 1940 MRN, he published one of the most important letters in the history of Model Railways. It came from Lt-Col. J T C Moore-Brabazon MP, soon to become Minister of Transport, 'Being … not without mechanical experience, lately with misguided confidence, I plunged into 'OO' gauge. I write this letter that others may be warned against false optimism as to the present state of the craft. All model railways to run successfully should be looked upon as mechanisms of precision. The smaller the gauge the greater must be the precision in order that they should operate'. He noted that different makers used incompatible standards, and advocated a standards committee. J N Maskelyne (Model Railway News), G H Lake (Railways), and R J Raymond (Model Railway Constructor), got together, and issued the first standards reports in 1941 whilst the British Railway Modelling Standards Bureau was set up under Maskelyne's chairmanship. Recalled as a 'charming old boy' of typically Edwardian bearing, and remembered for his pipe and rolled umbrella, his entertaining writing attracted many readers to the hobby.

1 · THE EDGE OF THE ABYSS

If you were to ask a dozen different commentators when the Golden Age of Britain's Railways was, you would get a dozen different answers. Some would say 1913, with the pre-group companies at the height of their power; others would suggest the 1890s or even the 1870s, for railway profits had been squeezed by rising costs ever since the 1870s. Some would say 1938-39. Railway profits were not as high as they had once been, but the companies were still powerful and financially stable. The standard of service they offered to passengers was higher than at any time in the past, and magnificent motive power had lifted performances far above anything possible in 1914. For the shareholder things were not as good as they had once been, but if you were a passenger or worked for the railways, they were a lot better. On the international horizon, things were a bit more unsettled. Herr Hitler was demanding a slice of Czechoslovakia, and the Czechs were unreasonable enough to say no. This intransigence looked as if it might precipitate a war in Europe. In England, my father watched as troops dug trenches on the green next to Station Road in Tidworth, where he was a newly commissioned army medical officer. The Prime Minister, Neville Chamberlain, was an early disciple of shuttle diplomacy, and entrusted his life to one of the

new airliners, and flew to Munich to meet Herr Hitler in March 1938. When he returned home, he was clutching his umbrella, and brandishing a piece of paper, declaring it meant 'Peace in Our Time'. The unreasonable Czechs had been told that they would have to hand over a large slice of their country to Herr Hitler, but that was a small price to pay for European peace, unless you happened to be a Czech, of course. Mr Chamberlain was acclaimed throughout England, though a rebellious and unpopular backbencher, whose glittering parliamentary career had come to an abrupt end years before, was ungrateful enough to stand up in the House of Commons and say, 'We have sustained a defeat without a war'. It was an ungracious comment, and he was howled down, but it was not the first time that Winston Leonard Spencer Churchill had been unpopular. At Paddington, Euston, King's Cross, and at Waterloo, senior railway officers desperately hoped that Mr Chamberlain was right, but feared he was not. For some time, they had been making plans, so that the nation's railways would operate efficiently in the event of war, but their plans were top secret, and on the surface at least, it was business as usual.

Opposite page: It is 1938, and Mr Chamberlain's visit to Munich is still fresh in everyone's mind, as a well groomed GWR 'Star', No 4058, *Princess Augusta*, makes a vigorous departure from Leamington Spa, and passes Prospect Terrace, at the start of six miles of adverse grades that will take this graceful Churchward engine to the summit near Southam Road and Harbury station. Although almost a quarter of a century had elapsed since 4058 first emerged from Swindon works in July 1914, on the eve of one world war, and she had been demoted from first line express duties by C B Collett's magnificent 'Castles' and 'Kings', she is well maintained, and despite the vicissitudes that will befall England ere long, will remain in service until April 1951. The row of ventilators on the skyline to the left locate the GWR locomotive depot at Leamington Spa, whilst the former LNWR secondary route from Leamington to Rugby runs from behind the shed and horizontally across the picture. Although demoted from premier express work, the afternoon Up stock train was traditionally a very heavy turn, with its mix of BGs, Siphons and 4-wheel 'brown stock' vans. The rear of the train is not visible, but the stock in view will gross over 350 tons. The afternoon Up stock train, which also conveyed engine parts between the various loco depots scattered along the Birmingham main line and Swindon, continued to run in the dying days of Western steam almost thirty years later, by which time it was a 'Castle' turn that I tried to photograph as often as I could. Whether under private or public ownership, such was the timeless nature of the industry for so many years. *H J Stretton-Ward*

Below: During the glorious summer months of 1938, events in far-away central Europe seemed remote, and most people's attention turned to holidays, and that meant a week or a fortnight beside the seaside. The Big Four all served a myriad of resorts. The Great Western carried tens of thousands of holidaymakers to the Cornish Riviera. The LMS took northern mill workers to Blackpool and Southport, or to Liverpool, for the four hour trip by steamer to the Isle of Man. The LNER served the Norfolk coast resorts and the busy east coast beaches at Whitby and Scarborough. The Southern Railway, which was the smallest of the Big Four, was not left out, with a string of resorts from the mouth of the Thames, all the way around the South Coast and into Devon and Cornwall. All four companies produced informative holiday brochures, which were keenly read at the time, and are now prized collectors' items. Old railway maps show a joint Southern and Great Western line diverging from the GWR just outside of Weymouth, and serving such delightful communities at Melcombe Regis and Wyke Regis, before reaching Portland, that astonishing semi-island connected to the mainland by a shingle and sand spit, called the Chesil. Rails have long vanished from Portland, but when Adams class '02' 0-4-4T No 221 was photographed leaving Portland on 16th July 1938, it would have seemed inconceivable that the busy seaside community could ever lose its trains, or that in less than two years, crowds of happy holidaymakers would be replaced by men in battledress looking out anxiously over the seas in anticipation of different visitors wearing field grey uniforms and coal scuttle helmets. *R E Tustin*

Above: Although the Southern was the smallest of the Big Four, and regarded as the least important, under the inspiring leadership of Sir Herbert Walker, it had transformed the backward companies south of the Thames into the best and busiest suburban network in the world, and its money came not from the seaside excursion traffic, useful though this was, or heavy industry, but from the crowds of commuters who flocked in and out of London every weekday. The Southern had created a thriving electrified suburban network in little more than a decade, transforming the cramped and inadequate stations it had inherited in the process. New buildings, as at Surbiton, were frequently in the so-called 'Odeon' style, on account of their alleged similarity to contemporary cinemas. They complemented the new electric train services, and provided greatly enhanced passenger facilities, that have already outlasted the Southern by twice the company's lifespan.

Below: The LMS was the largest of the Big Four, but in its first decade, was bedevilled by a deadly rivalry between its two most powerful constituents, the London & North Western and the Midland Railway. The grouping caught the North Western at an awkward moment, as many of its senior officers had either died in office or retired, and their successors lacked the authority to challenge the powerful and well-established Midland officers at Derby. The result was that Midland rule spread rapidly through the LMS, and after a brief spell when George Hughes of the LYR ruled over the motive power

department, but was constantly sabotaged by Midland intrigues, the MR writ, under Sir Henry Fowler, ran unchecked. Derby had remained wedded to small engine policies and when these were applied to larger designs, such as the Fowler 7F 0-8-0s, the results were disastrous. In 1926, a leading businessman, Sir Josiah Stamp who had spearheaded the formation of ICI, was brought in as President, to sort out the mess. Realising that Midland rule had been catastrophic, but aware that North Western rule would be equally unpopular, Stamp sidetracked diehards of both camps. His most inspired move was to bring in W A Stanier, a lifelong GWR officer, and C B Collett's principal assistant, as Chief Mechanical Engineer of the LMS in 1932. The West Coast Main line was facing a motive power crisis, with the Royal Scot 4-6-0s giving increasing trouble, and it is a measure of Stanier's drive, that his first top link express passenger design appeared in June 1933. Two prototype engines, 6200 and 6201 were built, the four cylinder layout of the front end closely following the GWR 'Kings', with which Stanier had been closely connected. To ensure adequate grate area on the longer LMS runs, a trailing truck was provided, creating the first Pacifics on the LMS. Despite the adoption of sound Swindon based practice, the first two Pacifics were disappointing to begin with, and it was not until a high degree superheat was adopted, that they showed their true

worth. 6200, *The Princess Royal*, races south through Brinklow with a 6 coach train in the mid thirties, soon after she received a Stanier curved sided tender. By 'Princess' standards, a six coach train was unusually short, so is a welcome prototype for the modeller. *H J Stretton-Ward*

Below: Valuable though passenger traffic was, the Big Four, with the exception of the Southern, earned most of their profits from moving freight. GWR No 1748, an open cab '655' class large 'Wolverhampton Pannier' blasts her way up the 1 in 105 Hatton bank between Warwick and Birmingham in the summer of 1939. Energetic though 1748 is, her efforts pale into insignificance compared to the volcanic eruptions from the banker, which is a large and energetic '51xx' class Prairie, which had come on the train at Warwick, and will drop off at the top of the bank at Hatton Junction. With the relief line available to the right, the sight of a lowly class K freight battling its way up the hill on the fast line is unusual, adding spice to an already enchanting glimpse of Britain's railways on the eve of War. No 1748 had been built at Wolverhampton in July 1892, and in the days when Northern and Southern division steam were quite distinctive, was firmly in the northern camp, though a few of her sisters migrated south in the 1920s. No 1748 survived until February 1946.
H J Stretton-Ward

Above: The London & North Eastern Railway, with 6,451 route miles in 1923, was almost as large as the LMS, with its 6,911 route miles, but traffic was much lighter, passenger receipts in 1923 being £17.5m and £26.0m respectively. Freight receipts showed a similar picture at £36.0m and £47.0m. Road competition and industrial recession hit the LNER severely, passenger traffic declining by 18% over the next fifteen years across the four companies, but by 25% on the LNER. This hit profits and dividends. LNER ordinary shares were divided into preferred ordinary and deferred ordinary, and the last dividend on the preferred ordinary stock was ¼% in 1930, whilst the hapless deferred holders fared even worse. Unlike the LMS, where Lord Stamp brought in William Stanier to modernise the locomotive fleet, the LNER had to make the best of what it had, and Nigel Gresley, its outstanding Chief Mechanical Engineer, devoted the scant resources he had to achieve the best effect. Rather than dilute its effect by piecemeal penny packet improvements, Gresley allocated his funds to projects where they would make a difference. In the 1920s, the A3 Pacifics, and in particular 4472, *Flying Scotsman*, became one of the most prestigious locomotives in the world. In 1935, Gresley produced the most memorable steam locomotive of all time, the streamlined A4 Pacific. Although there were just 35 of them, one of which was destroyed by enemy action during the war, the silver-grey livery applied to the initial engines, and the

garter blue that later became standard, captured the spirit of the age. An almost brand new 4902 *Seagull*, which was to be the penultimate A4, and had only appeared that June, is seen here at Kings Cross on the 3rd August 1938. When *Mallard* achieved her remarkable 126 mph, setting the world speed record for steam traction, the A4s received their final accolade, placing them on a pedestal from which they will never be dislodged. Despite minimal resources, Gresley's skill as an engineer, and instinct in devoting resources where it would have a disproportionate publicity impact, had scored the two greatest PR triumphs of the Interwar years, with Flying Scotsman and then the A4s. *R E Tustin*

Kings Cross to 'blank' half day excursion on salmon card stock, with green 'R' overprint. The destination would be filled in by hand.

2 · WAR ON THE LINE 1939-45

Hitler's invasion of Poland, and the resultant outbreak of War in September 1939, showed how empty Chamberlain's rhetoric had been after Munich. More importantly, it posed a grave threat to the survival of civilisation, although how great was not appreciated at the outset, with the usual 'Home for Christmas' attitude that had bedevilled the British approach to armed conflict over many generations. A string of catastrophic reverses saw the fall of Norway and most of continental Europe lost by the summer of 1940, with the expulsion of the British Expeditionary Force from France. The German bomber offensive from the summer of 1940 created ever greater damage to the infrastructure, destroying houses, factories, railways, ports, and all manner of property, and causing harrowing loss of life. For a time, British military effort was concentrated in North Africa, on the North Atlantic, in building up home defences, and in creating a bomber force capable of inflicting grievous blows on the Third Reich. All of these placed immense demands on industry and on transport. Although motor vehicles played a far more crucial role than in 1914-1918, railways still bore the brunt of the challenge, and the railway industry faithfully and loyally played a vital role in defeating the Nazi menace. Railways became a strategic service, and brandishing a camera in their vicinity was to invite arrest as a Nazi spy. As a result, few views, other than official photographs taken by the railway companies, or by government photographers for propaganda purposes, exist, and they have appeared in a host of books, including some propaganda booklets issued during hostilities. In illustrating this section, rather than use well-known official scenes, I have selected rare material shot by the late Ray Tustin at some risk of official disfavour, but who was to don uniform himself in due course.

Below: The former London and South Western Main Line between Waterloo and Basingstoke had always been busy, carrying traffic for Southampton and for Salisbury and the West of England. With the outbreak of war, holidaymakers were replaced by troops, as the area fell under the auspices of army Southern Command, and it was on Southern Command that the German invasion was expected to fall in 1940, and as the prospects of invasion receded, and the thoughts of an allied invasion developed, it was the training grounds around Salisbury, and the ports along the south coast that would be crucial to its success. Except for the grimy state of H15 4-6-0 No 474, photographed on a stopping train pulling away from Winchfield on 29th June 1941, the station is still well kept, and two years of reduced maintenance have not yet inflicted grievous harm on permanent way, structures or rolling stock.

Below: The devastating impact of total war had been dimly perceived, as the menace of Nazidom developed in the 'Thirties'. On the outbreak of hostilities, the railways were placed under the control of the government, which wisely opted for a loose rein, held by the Railway Executive Committee. The REC, which had been set up in shadow form as the clouds of war gathered in 1938, comprised the general managers of the Big Four railway companies, and of London Transport, working under the loose supervision of the Ministry of Transport (later the Ministry of War Transport). Minor undertakings, such as the Colonel Stephens lines, the Mersey Railway and the various joint lines were also controlled undertakings, though not represented on the REC itself. Initially chaired by Sir Ralph Wedgwood, the Chief General Manager of the LNER, the REC was later run by Sir Eustace Missenden, general manager of the Southern, after Wedgwood's retirement. The REC acted as a channel of communication between the government and the companies, passing on directions over levels of station lighting, carriage lighting, evacuation trains, military production requirements for the railway company workshops etc. It replicated a similar system from World War One, and worked smoothly and harmoniously. In contrast to the days of peace, when the railway companies were only too keen to encourage business, and falling traffic had been a problem, the railways were soon hard pressed to cope, and one of the key duties of the REC was to adjudicate between the priorities accorded to passenger and freight traffic and to military and civilian needs. Ray Tustin managed to grab this superb study of GWR pannier tank No 1597 on a mixed freight at Llangollen station on 8th July 1941. In most portraits of World War Two, authors have concentrated on the military side, or on the effects of the blitz, and official photographs often do this, but the reality is that day to day life continued much as it had before the war, but with new pressures superimposed on staff and management alike. Deciding on what revenue the companies should earn in time of war was a difficult issue, as it opened the companies to charges of war profiteering, and the politicians hit upon an ingenious idea whereby the companies would not actually be paid for the much heavier workload they would actually perform in time of war, but would receive a guaranteed annual net revenue of £43.5m, which was based on their peacetime earnings. The government would take any surplus earned above this figure, but by 1941 when the companies finally agreed the deal in the national interest, it was already clear that it would work out against their interests. Between 1941 and 1945, the railways would have earned £412.6m, but the Treasury was able to appropriate £195.3m. As the railways were wearing out their assets in the national interest, the calls on funding for post war renewals was bound to be massive, and the government had taken a major step on the road to bankrupting them. This predatory and oppressive attitude by civil servants and politicians of all parties, had set a terrible precedent, and the nation was to reap its reward in the years to come. *R E Tustin*

Opposite page top: Although passenger traffic remained heavy due to wartime fuel rationing, and military needs, an 'Is your journey really necessary' campaign was mounted to discourage frivolous travel. This was to clear the lines for freight traffic. Johnson 2F No 3141 heads a Down stopping goods or 'pick-up' along the Midland Peak route near Darley Dale on 25th June 1943. The train comprises loaded coal wagons, with a rake of tank wagons in wartime utility grey at the rear. Riber Castle stands out on the skyline above No 3141. The Johnson 2Fs were a Victorian design that appeared in several sub-types from 1875, and by 1902, no fewer than 865 had been built, making it one of the most numerous locomotive

types to see service in the British Isles. Many later received larger boilers, upgrading them to class 3 status, but despite the modernisation plan pursued by Lord Stamp, president of the LMS and Sir William Stanier, vast numbers of these venerable machines still survived in 1939. Although the railwaymen had loyally got down to the job of moving the nation's freight in time of war, the politicians and civil servants were less focussed on winning the war. Labour party policy had long dreamed of nationalising all significant industries, including transportation, its most recent airing being in Herbert Morrison's 1938 pamphlet, British Transport at Britain's Service. With a National government appointed for the duration of the war, which included Labour ministers, the Nationalisation voice was now more strident. It also had its echoes within the civil service, one faction producing a report that advocated a nationalised transport monopoly embracing road, rail, docks and even coastal shipping, as early as October 1940. As the REC system was working well, neither Winston Churchill, nor the then Minister of Transport, Lord Brabazon of Tara, favoured diverting time and effort from winning the war to squabbling over how transport should be reorganised, and the Coates-Robinson proposals, as they were known, were shelved. However the battle was not over, and Brabazon's successor at the Ministry of War Transport, Lord Leathers, was another pragmatist, saying bluntly that 'the war effort would be hindered and not helped' by wasting time on such matters. However, Labour members of the government remained committed to Nationalisation, whilst the chief civil servant within the MOWT, Sir Cyril Hurcomb, remained a shadowy figure, but was strongly influenced by Herbert Morrison. *R E Tustin*

Right: Although passenger traffic was discouraged, new facilities were provided where wartime demands produced new traffic flows, one example being on the Southern line to Reading, where single line working was in force on 1st October 1942, in conjunction with the construction of Longcross Halt, which lay a short distance east of Sunningdale. The train engine, No 846, is a Southern class S15 4-6-0. The S15s were Robert Urie's final 4-6-0 for the London & South Western Railway, construction of the first twenty starting in 1920. A further 25 engines to an improved design were added by Maunsell between 1927 and 1936. No 846 was the penultimate engine, coming out of Eastleigh works in November 1936, and costing £14,145. Although minor improvements, as at Longcross, did take place, the railways went over to war work, producing tanks, guns, torpedoes, shells, aircraft and the myriad of other parts required in modern warfare. Railway needs came well down the queue, with coaching stock particularly badly hit, and running at about 16% of pre-war levels between 1940 and 1945. Permanent way renewals were also deferred, and by 1945 arrears amounted to almost 2,500 miles of track. Freight stock suffered from incessant use, and overloading became commonplace, a practice that was officially sanctioned when the pre-war 12 ton coal wagon was re-rated as a 13-tonner, without any structural alterations. Similar alterations applied

across-the-board. The private owner wagon had long been a bone of contention with railwaymen, as it was not so well maintained as company stock, and often used the old style grease axle boxes. The decision to requisition the half million POWs, mostly used in the coal trade, simplified shunting, as wagons were common user, but it was bought at a terrible price. The better owners had maintained their wagons properly, and even the laggards had to do some work, or risk having their wagons banned, but with government pooling, no maintenance facility of any sort was put in place. Instead of the admittedly patchy repairs of pre-war days, no repair policy existed at all, and the companies were understandably reluctant to take on half a million wagons with no added manpower or materials. Wagons that had been in good condition rapidly deteriorated under government control, and many became unfit for service. *R E Tustin*

Opposite page top: World War II is usually seen as a 'high tech' struggle, but this WD consignment note recalls the existence of the Army Pigeon Service.

Opposite page bottom: Military needs were accorded priority, and the companies loyally supported this, although it placed severe demands on them. During the First World War, the government chose the Robinson 8K 2-8-0, better known as the O4, from its LNER designation, for mass production for the army's Railway Operating Division in France. Apart from engines built for the GCR from 1911, 521 of these versatile 2-8-0s were built for military use between 1916 and 1919, the last examples coming out after hostilities had ended. Left with many surplus engines, the government was keen to dispose of them to the mainline railways, and LNER 6312, which had been built as ROD No 1636 by Robert Stephenson & Co in July 1919, was sold to the LNER in 1923. In October 1939, the government decided to send up to 300 RODs to France, but the fall of France in 1940 ended this scheme. Hitler's attack on Soviet Russia in 1941, and the need to bolster Russia's inadequate war industries, led to the costly Murmansk convoys, in which thousands of allied seamen lost their lives, and to a less well known effort to send supplies through Persia and the Middle East. In 1941, ninety-two O4s were requisitioned to send to Persia, where the railways were operating under allied control, but plans later changed, and Stanier 8Fs were sent to Persia, and the O4s went to Egypt and Palestine, which then embraced modern Israel, Jordan, Syria and Lebanon. LNER 6312 was one of the engines selected in October 1941, although not officially withdrawn from LNER stock until 1943. She became War Department 778, later 70778, and was sent to the Haifa-Beirut-Tripoli Railway, which was then under construction. An oil-fired and spotlessly clean 70778, with WD separated by the traditional upward pointing arrow, is at the head of a typical mixed Haifa train at Saida on 20th December 1945. Local youngsters are clamouring for 'Baksheesh', or money from passengers, a feature of Middle East rail travel that both my parents remembered well, when they were serving in Middle East Forces. *R E Tustin*

Above: The supply of ROD 2-8-0s was not sufficient to meet anticipated wartime demands, and when Robin Riddles, who had been the LMS Mechanical & Electrical Engineer (Scotland), became Director of Transport Equipment at the Ministry of Supply, it was not surprising that he should select the Stanier 8F 2-8-0, as the standard war locomotive. 208 engines were built to War Department orders in 1940-42, and over fifty engines requisitioned from the LMS as well. As with the RODs, their main use in World War Two was with Middle East Forces in Egypt, Palestine, Persia and later in Turkey. Numbered between 300 and 623 (with gaps) in the WD series, engines on the Egyptian State Railways were further renumbered in the 8xx series, to avoid conflict with other ESR stock. This magnificent study of 888 at Bulaq shed on the ESR on 4th March 1945, shows the Western numbering on the left, and the Arabic numerals on the right, 888 being three inverted Vs. Except for the auxiliary water tank, which was used on some of the long runs, as for example on the Western Desert line through El Alamein, the photo could easily have been taken at an LMS shed.

Opposite page top: Robin Riddles' appointment as Director of Transport Equipment at the Ministry of Supply in 1939, was complemented by his becoming Deputy Director General of Royal Engineers Equipment in 1941. Although he selected the Stanier 2-8-0 as an interim war locomotive, he realised that the complex taper boiler and other sophisticated design features placed a heavy demand on skilled manpower and resources, and developed a simplified engine with a parallel boiler and round topped firebox. 935 were built in less than two and a half years, the last examples appearing in May 1945. All but three went overseas before the end of hostilities, but as military needs slackened, many returned to the UK. With wartime arrears of maintenance, the Big Four were short of heavy freight power, and the LNER in particular was glad to receive many on loan. As in 1918, the government was left with hundreds of engines on its hands after the end of hostilities, and in November 1946, the LNER purchased 200 at £4,500 each, which was far below the cost of building a new locomotive. They became class 07, and were numbered in the 3000 series. In December 1948, the BTC took another 533 engines that had returned to the UK, and the class was eventually numbered from 90000 upwards, and known as 'Austerities' or WDs. LNER No 3010 heads a heavy coal train south through Staverton Road on the GC London Extension in March 1948. 3010 was built by NBL in July 1943 as WD No 7339, later becoming WD 77339. It became LNER 3010 in April 1947, BR 63010 in May 1948 and BR 90010 in July 1949, and survived until 1965. After service on the GC, it went to the Western Region, seeing service at Shrewsbury, and St Philips Marsh before moving to Westhouses and Gorton. Although lacking the refinement of the Stanier 2-8-0s, these rugged machines got by with limited repair facilities, and put in over twenty years of hard slogging. They were a good buy at £4,500 each. It may well be that Riddles' success with the wartime engines he had designed for the Ministry of Supply was a key factor in his appointment as Motive Power supremo of the Railway Executive in 1947. If so, they may be the engines that shaped the future of BR motive power policy throughout the 1950s. *H J Stretton-Ward*

Opposite page bottom: America's entry into the war, following the treacherous Japanese attack on Pearl Harbor on 7th December 1941, was followed by an Anglo-American summit meeting, at which it was agreed that a massive US expeditionary force would be sent to the UK, to take part in the liberation of Europe. During the build-up period, the sheer weight of US troop movements would swamp existing motive power stocks, and once the Allied armies stormed ashore in France, the need for railways to support the supply lines would be acute. An American style 2-8-0 was shoe-horned into the more restricted British loading gauge, so that the engines could operate in the UK prior to D-day, and 2,120 locomotives were built from 1942 onwards. As I write these words, I have a copy of a 1943 drawing issued by Major S H Bingham, 'Officer in Charge Military Railways' in front of me. It shows the typical US lines of these engines, with bar frames, a wide firebox, with steel as opposed to copper inner box, boiler mounted sandboxes to keep sand warm and dry, and maximum accessibility of parts. Given the sensitivity of photography in wartime Britain, views of S160s in the UK are rare, so this view of USATC No 2134, which was Alco works No 70616 of 1943, on the LMS and GWR joint loco shed at Shrewsbury on 4th August 1944, is most welcome. A large

number of S160s were allocated to the GWR, but all were shipped to Europe after D-Day. After the war, they were widely distributed on the continent, some even running in Russia, but only one engine remained in the UK, on the Longmoor Military Railway. When this was scrapped, the class became extinct in the UK, until examples were imported in the preservation era. The heavy demands on motive power, which also saw the GWR lose a batch of elderly Dean goods 0-6-0s, brought railway freight services close to collapse, given the increased freight traffic due to military traffic, and efforts to save on road fuel and tyres. *R E Tustin*

Above: A mass of paperwork passed between the Forces and the Railway companies, some SECRET, some NON-SECRET.

3 · 'ONCE EGGS HAVE BEEN SCRAMBLED, I DEFY ANY COOK TO UNSCRAMBLE THEM'

Col Eric Gore Browne, presiding at the Southern AGM, 7 March 1946

Under the leadership of Winston Churchill, between 1940 and 1945, the British people had been inspired to defy the most formidable threat to civilisation in their history, and to emerge steadfast and triumphant. VE-Day, in May 1945 brought a sigh of relief from railwaymen, but Japan was still in the war, and hostilities would continue in the Far East until August 1945. Long before Japan had come into the war, Churchill had given a pledge that as soon as the war was over, there would be a general election. Although he could have said that the war 'being over' would now include the defeat of Japan, Churchill was punctilious, where parliamentary promises were concerned. The election duly took place, and to widespread astonishment overseas, he was swept out of office, and the Labour Party came to power. Despite the personal esteem in which Churchill was held as wartime leader, the people were tired of the politics of the past, and ready for change.

One of the fundamental beliefs of the new administration under Prime Minister Clement Atlee, was that important industries should not be left to private ownership and run for the benefit of stockholders, but should be under state ownership. Just four months after Labour took power, Herbert Morrison's long-held ambition to end the power of the railway companies came a step nearer with a government statement on 19th November 1945, that Nationalisation would take place. The companies, which had unstintingly given their all during the war, though deprived of much of their rightful revenue by government, decided to fight for their survival, marshalling a formidable range of arguments, stressing their own outstanding record in peace and war, and contrasting it with the lacklustre performance of nationalised railways in other parts of the world. Given the massive parliamentary majority enjoyed by the Labour government, and the indifference that any government with that sort of power has always shown to common sense, no argument, however well presented, stood any chance of prevailing, and the railway companies must have realised that the election results had spelled their doom, giving an especial poignancy to their desperate fight for survival. At the GWR Annual General Meeting at Paddington on 6th March 1946, Viscount Portal, the last chairman of the GWR, and after whom a 'Castle' class 4-6-0 was to be named, threw the government's own words back in their face, 'The Lord President of the Council, when broadcasting to America last August is reported to have said: 'There is only one justification for either nationalization or private enterprise – that is efficient service in the interest of the nation. If only nationalization will secure this result then we must nationalize. But if private enterprise can do it, well, then, let private enterprise remain.' If this is to be the test, neither the record of the railway companies nor the experience of nationalization of railways in other countries would justify the policy which the Government propose to adopt'.

The Southern was often seen as the mildest of the main line companies, but its chairman, Col Eric Gore Browne DSO, presiding at the Southern Railway AGM on 7th March 1946, the day after the GWR meeting, spoke proudly of the company's war record, and then let fly at the government in no uncertain terms. In an attempt to make the government's draconian Nationalisation plans seem less dictatorial to Britain's overseas allies, government ministers had voiced words of sweet reasonableness to America in 1945, and similar remarks were made in Toronto on 10th January 1946, Gore Browne pounced on such comments as 'It is the public interest that counts and the real field for argument is how best can industry be organised or managed with a view to achieving economic public advantage. It is up to the nationalisers to prove their case that there will be public advantage by Nationalisation. It is no less up to the anti-nationalisers to prove their case that the public interest can best be served by private ownership'. He retorted, 'On my own behalf and on behalf of all my colleagues, and, I venture to think, on behalf of all of you, the Shareholders, I challenge the nationalisers to prove their case. I accept the challenge to prove that public interest can best be served by private ownership of the Southern Railway. It is a principle of English justice that a man is held to be innocent until he is proved to be guilty; and is it unfair to claim the same privilege for a public utility company with our record?' Gore Browne pointed out that the slow recovery to pre-war conditions was due to damage done by war, the number

Opposite page: At the time that the GWR was circulating its shareholders to rally support, ten 'Castle' class 4-6-0s, Lot No 357, were under construction at Swindon. It is well known that the last of this batch, 7007, *Ogmore Castle*, was renamed *Great Western* to mark the demise of the GWR in 1948, but few enthusiasts realise that another two engines in this lot carried commemorative names as well. No 7000, which entered traffic in May 1946, was named *Viscount Portal*, after the company's last chairman, whilst 7001 was named *Sir James Milne*, after its last general manager. I photographed No 7000, *Viscount Portal*, departing from Moreton-in-Marsh with the 5.10pm Worcester (Shrub Hill) to Paddington express on 28th July 1963, with the silhouette of her chimney and smokebox etched on the brickwork of the signal box. Advancing dieselisation meant that she was withdrawn that December, but for a few months, it was still possible to see a GWR engine hauling GWR stock past a GWR signal box. The WR summer timetable, from 17th June to 8th September 1963, revealed the writing was on the wall for Western independence. Ever since 1948, the WR had retained a GWR look to its passenger timetables, with a 'chocolate and cream' cover. In reality, the cream was just the shade of paper used for the WR timetable, but that is splitting hairs! The 1963 timetable was very different, with a Dragon Red and white cover, heralded inside as 'a new look'.

Below: The motor industry was an important part of the post war economic recovery plan, and traffic from the Morris car plant at Cowley, near Oxford called for a supply of 4" x 5" GWR wagon labels printed on thin buff card. The print date 5/47 appears at the foot of the label.

of government trains that still ran, and that only 25 % of their skilled staff who had been called up, had been released from the forces. He threw down the gauntlet,

'May I make it abundantly clear: that your Board accepts the challenge to prove the case for private ownership of your Company before any impartial committee or commission which His Majesty's Government may think well to appoint and charge with the duty to examine the efficiency of the Southern Railway; and that your Board challenges His Majesty's Government to prove that by Nationalisation of surface transport, a better or cheaper service will be given to the public, or that the salaried and wages staff will be better off.'

Gore Browne had called the government's bluff, but he must have known that there was no conceivable way that the cabinet would hazard the Nationalisation bill before an impartial review. Pointing out that only 29% of the world's State owned railways were self-supporting, he reminded listeners that during World War One, the US Railroads were under tight government control, and required a subsidy of $2m a day. In World War Two, the railways were left to run their own affairs. They moved prodigious quantities of equipment and troops, met public needs, and contributed around $4m a day to the National exchequer. Gore Browne looked to the future, 'is it in the public interest, or yours that this great public utility company, the Southern Railway, should be sacrificed at the altar of a political theory, the practical results of which are to say the least of it, obscure, and may be disastrous? And once eggs are scrambled, I defy any cook to unscramble them'.

The government did not take up Gore Browne's suggestion of an impartial enquiry, and it was just a matter of parliamentary priorities that the Transport Act was not passed until 1947. It established a publicly owned British Transport Commission, which was to be the parent body of an organisation that would direct virtually every aspect of inland public transport by road, rail, and water in mainland Britain. Through subsidiary 'Executives', it would take over not merely the existing 'Big Four' railway companies, the Great Western, Southern, London, Midland & Scottish and London & North Eastern Railways, but the remaining private lines such as the Colonel Stephens group of companies, London Transport, the Canals, the road haulage companies, the railway interests in the Provincial and Scottish Bus Groups, railway-owned ships serving the Scottish Isles, Ireland, the Continent and the Channel Isles, the Hotels executive, British Transport Police, the world famous travel agents, Thomas Cook, the Dundalk, Newry & Greenore Railway, which was located partly in Northern Ireland and partly in the Republic of Ireland, the LMS Northern Counties Committee railway in Northern Ireland, a half share in the three foot

gauge County Donegal Railways Joint Committee, an interest in British & Foreign Aviation Ltd, and a couple of continental ventures, one entitled the Societe Anonyme de Navigation Angleterre, Lorraine Alsace! The legislative programme had been so full ever since 1945, that the Transport bill did not receive the care that such an important piece of legislation merited, but with a massive majority in the Commons, the government had no problems in forcing it through, irrespective of its defects. The Transport Act received the Royal Assent on 6th August 1947.

The full time members of the new British Transport Commission were appointed on 8th September 1947, although a government decision on the salaries they would receive was not forthcoming for another six weeks! The BTC did not have the luxury of sitting back for that length of time, as they had to get the entire organisation up and running by 1st January 1948. It was a ridiculous timescale, but to their credit, they managed it. Who were the people who were appointed to run the BTC? In more than a century since the railway industry had come into being, a fund of experience and knowledge about running large transport organisations had grown up. Companies such as the London & North Western Railway or its successor the London, Midland & Scottish Railway had a full time chairman who had come to the organisation as a result of a successful career in industry or commerce. In the 19th century, the LNWR had been led by Sir Richard Moon, an austere but successful chairman. In the early 20th century, Sir Gilbert Claughton proved to be an equally talented chairman. The LMS had been torn by strife between the North Western and Midland factions at first, but the appointment of Josiah Stamp, an outsider, as President, created a new and forward looking structure.

The railway boards of 1947 contained many directors with years of experience and skill in supervising large organisations, but such was the level of mistrust between the Labour government and the 'City', that Labour politicians could not bear to entrust their new baby to the old, and, in their eyes, discredited servants of capital. The Minister of Transport, Alfred Barnes, had little understanding of transport, but was a stolid party man. Rather than take informed advice on who might best handle the task of co-ordinating public transport, he selected the Permanent Secretary to the Ministry, Sir Cyril Hurcomb, GCB, KBE, to chair the BTC. Hurcomb was a life-long civil servant, steeped in the ways of Whitehall, and had also been a past president of the Institute of Transport, so unlike his political boss, brought considerable knowledge to the role. More importantly, he had worked with Herbert Morrison, who was the Labour guru on Nationalisation and public transport, and was himself a devotee of central direction of transport. Whether a civil service mentality would be ideal in running a massive transport organisation was open to doubt, but Hurcomb had the right views and was safe, unlike more colourful characters who knew something about running a railway, such as Viscount Portal, chairman of the Great Western Railway, or the combative Col Eric Gore Browne, the chairman of the Southern Railway. Hurcomb's deputy was the Rt Hon Lord Ashfield, who lived at Sunningdale in Berkshire. Ashfield was chairman of the London Passenger Transport Board, and another past president of the Institute of Transport. Unlike Hurcomb, there could be no doubts as to his experience, drive, or knowledge of transport and business. Born near Derby in 1874, and emigrating to the United States with his parents a few years later, Albert Henry Stanley started life as an odd job man with the Detroit Street Railway, becoming its general superintendent by the time he was 28. Moving to the east coast, he was appointed as general manager of the Public Service Corporation of New Jersey at the age of 32 in 1907, but US commercial backers dominated the evolution of London's electric underground lines at this time, and a few months later Stanley was sent across the Atlantic to become general manager of Underground Electric Railways Ltd, welding the Underground into a formidable and brilliantly led transport undertaking. He was to serve as President of the Board of Trade from 1916 to 1919, for which he received his peerage, as first Baron Ashfield of Southwell. Returning to the Underground, he became the first chairman of London Transport on its formation in 1933.

Given the Labour party's political roots, it was inevitable that union representation was seen as a priority on the new BTC, so John Benstead, C B E, the former general secretary of the National Union of Railwaymen, was appointed to the BTC. The Co-operative movement also had long standing links with the Labour party and the Rt Hon Lord Rusholme, the former general secretary of the Co-operative Union Limited and President of the International Co-operative Alliance, joined the BTC. The remaining full time member, and the only one with main line railway experience was Sir William Valentine Wood, K B E, President of the Executive of the LMS after Lord Stamp's death, and another past president of the Institute of Transport. The combination of Ashfield and Wood, might suggest that experienced railwaymen were well represented in the highest reaches of the BTC, but events were to show that although Hurcomb shrank from issuing clear directives, leaving his colleagues on the BTC and the Railway Executive to flounder in a morass of confusion, he overshadowed the other members of the BTC, who became little more than a rubber stamp, approving his

vague theorising. Lord Ashfield was undoubtedly brilliant, but was in his seventies, and slowing down, so was no longer the man to challenge Hurcomb. Sir William Wood, the other professional railwayman, had worked in the accountant's office of the Belfast & Northern Counties Railway, later the Midland Railway, Northern Counties Committee, from 1898 to 1916, and was seconded to the Ministry of Transport from 1919 to 1924, before becoming Controller of Costs & Statistics on the LMS. Closely associated with Stamp, he co-authored a textbook, 'Railways' with Stamp, which was first published in 1928. The title was misleading, as it concentrated on railway economics and statistics. Appointed a Vice President of the LMS in 1929, and knighted in 1937, Wood's career was closely linked with Stamp, and on the latter's death during the Blitz in 1941, he became President of the Executive of the LMS. An analyst, rather than an 'ideas man', Wood was a talented administrator, but not an imaginative leader in the same mould as Stamp. The remaining members of the BTC lacked experience of transport management, but on 1st January 1948, these weaknesses were not apparent. The BTC would be a massive undertaking, and its assets would come to a staggering £1,573,042,111 on 1st January 1948. Even today, after more than half a century of inflation, an organisation with assets in excess of £1.5 Billion is regarded as big business. Average family income is put at around £400 per week today (2005); contrast that with a time when a worker was well paid if he earned £6 a week, and the size of these figures becomes apparent.

Control of the different forms of transport would be delegated to subsidiary 'Executives', and within four days of their appointment on 8th September 1947, the BTC had considered who should be appointed to their most important subsidiary body, the Railway Executive. This was crucial, as the BTC was to be a strategic policy making body, laying down broad principles, but the daily operation and conduct of its different activities was to be left in the hands of the Executives. Officially, the BTC had acted extraordinarily quickly, suggesting suitable members for the RE to the Minister of Transport, who approved the composition of The Railway Executive on 12th September, but how real that process was is open to doubt. Given that Alfred Barnes had selected the members of the BTC by himself, rather than seeking outside advice, one wonders whether the names submitted to him were candidates favoured by the BTC, or the names that Barnes wished the BTC to favour. As the appointments to the executives were actually made by the Minister, rather than the BTC, this reduced BTC control over its subordinates to a shadow. Whatever the real story, the ministry dragged its feet, not making the formal appointments to the RE until 21st November. These dates, which seldom appear in accounts of the birth of British Railways, are important, as they show the time pressure the politicians had generated.

Although the title and functions of the RE might be new, its members had a lifetime of experience. The chairman was Sir Eustace Missenden, OBE, former General Manager of the Southern Railway, and a highly respected railwayman. Missenden had been born into a railway family, his father having risen to station master. Missenden had joined the SECR in 1899, becoming London District Traffic Superintendent in 1920. A series of operating roles followed, culminating in the post of SR Traffic Manager in 1937. When the SR manager, Gilbert Szlumper, who had succeeded Sir Herbert Walker in 1937, was appointed Director of Transportation at the War Office in September 1939, Missenden took over as general manager. It was a difficult time, with heavy wartime traffic to cope with, and Missenden was awarded the US Freedom Medal with Gold Palm, with a citation which paid a glowing tribute to his war work, 'Sir Eustace Missenden for exceptionally meritorious conduct in the performance of outstanding services as General Manager, Southern Railway Company of Great Britain, from April 1942 to September 15th, 1945. Sir Eustace was responsible for supervising the vast amount of US military traffic moving over his railway system on a rigidly adjusted schedule. The success of operation OVERLORD depended in no small measure on the ability of Southern Railway to move troops and equipment. The intelligent supervision, co-ordination and personal interest of Sir Eustace proved of enormous value to the US Forces'. Missenden was at his happiest when he was out amongst the 'Southern Railway family' he had worked with all his life, and was painstaking in his attendance at railway events such as retirements, flower shows, sports events and ambulance meetings, the latter being especially dear to his heart. His acceptance speech, when awarded the US Freedom Medal was characteristic, 'This is an honour for the whole of the Southern's staff. I am exceedingly proud of them and of this award'.

V M Barrington Ward, CBE, DSO, an operator with a reputation for toughness, and for not suffering fools gladly, had been a Divisional General Manager of the Southern Area of the LNER, whilst David Blee had briefly been the Chief Goods manager of the GWR. Blee's selection was due to the perceived need for each of the Big Four to have 'its man' on the RE, and the fact that many of Blee's GWR colleagues were so disgusted at Nationalisation, that they retired from the railway service, or elected to stay with the new Western Region, rather than to move to an alien executive. R A Riddles, CBE, who was to be placed in charge of mechanical engineering, was a highly respected locomotive engineer, with a wartime reputation for getting things done, and had served as wartime Director of Transport Equipment at the Ministry of Supply. Although he had become a Vice President of the Executive of the LMS, Riddles' elevation over the heads of the existing chief mechanical engineers of the Big Four to be their chief in the new hierarchy was a potential source of friction and resentment, but the BTC seems to have blithely ignored this. J C L Train, MC, M Inst C E, had been the Chief Civil Engineer of the LNER.

The General Secretary of the National Union of Railwaymen had been appointed to the BTC, whilst W P 'Bill' Allen, CBE, the General Secretary of the footplate men's union, the Associated Society of Locomotive Engineers and Firemen, was appointed to the RE, ensuring that the two principal rail unions were represented in the new structure. These appointments, which neatly balanced the union power base, were actually a token measure, taken by Alfred Barnes to sooth the feelings of the rail unions, who were demanding Workers' Control over the industry, now that private enterprise had ended. Barnes, though having little knowledge of transport, would have been well aware of the effects of such a move in early post-revolutionary Russia, where major industries were initially run by workers' councils, a situation that threatened the survival of Bolshevik rule, as productivity and discipline disintegrated. Faced with a threat to their own survival, Lenin and Stalin moved rapidly to end workers' control, and impose their own aparatchiks. Barnes was desperate to avoid that mistake, and by ensuring that ex-union men were in a minority, had acknowledged the union demands for worker-control, without handing real power to the NUR and ASLEF. In what at first sight appeared to be a neat move, as Bill Allen would understand the men's viewpoint, he was put in charge of labour relations and negotiations. Allen, who had been a moderate and responsible union leader, was now faced with the reality of running a railway, and the knowledge that funding was not limitless. Cast in the role of a 'poacher turned gamekeeper', and reviled by his former colleagues as a turncoat, when he failed to meet their demands, Bill Allen was undoubtedly distressed to find that his new role had become a poisoned chalice. It would have been better had labour relations been entrusted to another member of the RE, with Allen acting as an advisor. In that way, the RE could have benefited from his knowledge of the men, whilst his former colleagues would not have seen him as a traitor. Sadly, this was just one of the many ways in which the individual talents of the members of the RE were frittered away, due to the hurried and chaotic way in which it had been set up.

Unlike the company era, where senior officers reported to the general manager, and through him to the board, so a clear hierarchy existed, the members of the RE had not been appointed by Missenden, or even by the BTC, but by the Minister. Missenden realised that he had to lead by consent, rather than by command, but this negation of the traditional role of the chairman or chief executive was a serious flaw, and it says much for Missenden's abilities that he was able to do so. In the early months of the RE, he was undoubtedly helped by the presence of General Sir William Slim on the RE. The only permanent member who was not a professional railwayman, Slim was a distinguished soldier, with a knack for earthy diplomacy and getting to the bottom of a problem. Whatever reservations one might have over the BTC, the undoubted pool of talent within the RE would suggest a winning formula, but both bodies were to become embroiled in petty squabbles, that reflected little credit on either side. Lord Ashfield, the most experienced and only member of the BTC to have the wholehearted respect of transport professionals, passed away on 4th November 1948. He was in his mid seventies, and although he gave freely of his time in advising the BTC on how to set up the new organisation, he was grappling with a new form of creature, and was no longer possessed of the vigour of youth. The Railway Executive had suffered a serious blow a few days earlier. Bill Slim, although not a railwayman, had impressed his colleagues with his commonsense approach, and he and Ashfield might have pulled things together, but he was appointed Chief of the General Staff, and submitted his resignation as a member of the RE on 28th October 1948.

In its wisdom, the government had rushed the Transport Act on to the statute book, but the Act left the relationship between the BTC and RE obscure. In principle, the BTC was the policy making body; the RE managed and co-ordinated the rail system, and the regions carried out day-to-day tasks. Quite where policy ended and central management began, or where central management ended and day-to-day tasks began, no one really knew. A clear chain of command that had been taxed to the limit in running an organisation as large as the LMS, had been replaced by a three tier system that had to run something more than twice the size of the LMS, where the responsibilities of each tier remained obscure, and where a proportion of the people concerned had no experience of running any business, let alone a transport service. With the greatest goodwill on all sides, it was a leap into the unknown, with conflict built in to the system from top to bottom.

Below: It is sometimes said that the compensation paid to shareholders was excessive, and the BTC claimed this was so some years later to justify its own financial embarrassment, and subsequent writers have been happy to repeat such claims parrot fashion. The facts reveals differently. By 1946, almost £170m had been raised in share capital and debentures to create the Great Western Railway, and the net revenue had exceeded £6.6m every year for the past decade, save for 1938, when it dropped to £5m, due to a short lived fall in revenue. Although the GWR board prudently cut the dividend to ordinary shareholders to ½% that year, and restricted it to 3½% in 1939, in every other year it was 4% or above, making the GWR the most successful financially of the Big Four. A measure of the spiteful nature of the 1947 act was given by a GWR computation submitted to shareholders in March 1947. Under the proposals in the Transport Act, holders of GW debentures and shares would not receive cash compensation, but government stock bearing 2½% interest. For debenture holders, the loss in income would vary between 4.5% and 30.2%, whilst the holder of the GWR Consolidated Ordinary Stock fared worse, as he would lose 70.5% of his income. As many holdings had been built up by the elderly as a nest egg for their retirement, the government had stolen two thirds of their income, causing genuine hardship to many prudent and thrifty people. Not surprisingly, the GWR directors pressed for compensation to be set by an independent tribunal, but had to accept a stock yielding 3%, rather than the 2½ % originally proposed. The thief, in his kindness, had agreed to steal a bit less. *H J Stretton-Ward*

IMPORTANT.

Post Card stating we are in favour of all possible steps being taken by the Board of the G. W. Rly to oppose Nationalisation as affecting the Gt. Western Rly.

GREAT WESTERN RAILWAY.

PADDINGTON STATION,
LONDON, W.2.   *returned* 26/7/46

June, 1946

To THE STOCKHOLDERS.

STATE OWNERSHIP AND CONTROL OF TRANSPORT.

The Stockholders will be aware that in November last the Government announced that it was their intention " to introduce during the life of the present Parliament measures designed to bring transport services, essential to the economic well-being of the nation, under public ownership and control."

In view of the probability of the Government introducing into Parliament in the early stages of next session a Bill for the Nationalization of the railways and long distance road haulage services, your Board consider it essential to obtain, at once, the views of the Stockholders.

The many tributes which have been paid to the efficiency with which the railways have met the needs of the community under both peace and wartime conditions make it obvious that the present railway administration has built up an organization which can deal efficiently with the problems of the future, and there is no evidence that Nationalization will give better service to the community. A fundamental change of this character will, in the opinion of your Board, inevitably have a disturbing effect on trade and industry throughout the country and on the economic life of the community in general.

At the conclusion of the formal business of the Annual Meeting of the Proprietors held on the 6th March last a resolution in the following terms was moved by a

Above: This June 1946 circular to stockholders was just part of the GWR campaign, but has added interest on account of the manuscript annotation. Stockholders were not always individuals, and this circular was sent to the Isle of Man Railway Co, which had a holding of GWR shares. A M Sheard, a railway manager himself, and a staunch opponent of nationalisation, initialled his own response, 'Post Card stating we are in favour of all possible steps being taken by the Board of the G W Rly to oppose Nationalisation as affecting the Gt Western Rly returned'. Interestingly, similar ideas had been floated in the Isle of Man, and resolutely condemned by Sheard in a campaign that left his railway free of state control, and allowed him to save it in his own forceful and extraordinary way, which we will look at in a later volume.

Above: Hugh Dalton had described the railways as a 'disgrace to the country'. What did the Railway Executive inherit? The Great Western Railway was the most individual of the Big Four, for it was not a new company set up as a result of the Grouping in 1923, but a continuation of the old GWR of Brunel and Gooch, enlarged to include other smaller companies, mostly serving the South Wales valleys. Even before the grouping, the GWR had a strong identity and a tradition of doing things its way, and often, it was a much better way than its rivals. The GWR pioneered the use of Automatic Train Control, with a warning device in the cab to tell drivers when they were passing a distant signal at Caution. The GWR vacuum brake worked to a higher vacuum than other companies. The performance of its locomotives prompted Gresley to improve an already good design after the GWR 'Castle' class 4-6-0s soundly defeated the Gresley Pacifics on exchange trials in 1925. When W A Stanier took over as CME of the LMS, he moved from Swindon, and exported the gospel of GWR excellence to the heathens in Derby. The other three companies each had to forge a new identity, a process that was especially painful for the LMS, but the GWR continued on its way, confident that Paddington and Swindon knew best. In 1935 the company celebrated its centenary, and in the traumatic post war years, when the threat of nationalisation threatened to extinguish the Great Western flame forever, Paddington strove resolutely against political dogma, but lost. The GWR entered the nationalised fold reluctantly, worried that its vision of the future was to be entrusted to less able hands. Two 'Kings' and a 'Hall' make ready to depart under Bishop's Road bridge at Paddington in this early post-war scene. The centre locomotive, 6005 *King George II*, is from Stafford Road, the big GWR express passenger depot at Wolverhampton, and carries the 985 reporting code of an afternoon Down Wolverhampton express.

Women played an important role during the war, taking over many jobs that had previously been the preserve of men, and this had its impact on post war humour, as with this cartoon which appeared in the July 1947 issue of the LMS staff magazine 'CARRY ON'.

"She used to be a railway porter."
Drawn by Louis Ollier, M.P.D., Crewe.

Opposite page top: Although prestige passenger classes such as 'Kings' attracted the most attention, they were massively outnumbered by the legions of 0-6-0Ts used on humble shunting duties. In the days when wagonload and less-than-wagon-load freight predominated, this necessitated a vast amount of shunting, and the GWR used over 1,000 saddle and pannier tanks for decades. The majority were to standard designs, such as the 57xx 0-6-0PT, but the GWR was economical, and rather than squandering engines absorbed in 1923, many were 'Swindonised' and served into the BR era. BPGV No 4, later GWR No 2194, was one of a batch of 0-6-0STs built for the Burry Port & Gwendraeth Valley Railway Co at the start of the twentieth century. It was Avonside Engine Co No 1463 of 1903, and was named *Kidwelly* on the independent BP&GV, retaining its name after it was absorbed into the GWR in 1923. Along with sister engine No 5 (later GWR 2195), it was transferred to Weymouth Quay in 1926. 2194 later went to Cardiff Cathays, and then to Taunton shed. She is shunting the yard at Bridgwater on 12th June 1952, and was withdrawn the following February. The leading wagon in this evocative scene is a GWR shunter's truck, whilst the freight stock includes four cattle vans, a wooden bodied general merchandise high and some wooden bodied former private owner coal wagons. This combination, with a mixture of stock being shunted by an elderly tank loco at a busy yard at a small market town, typifies the railway industry at the dawn of the BR era. Because it had no need to forge a new identity after 1923, the GWR held a unique place in the affections of many of its staff, and its manager, Sir James Milne was highly regarded within the railway industry. Milne was horrified that the mantle that had come down from Brunel, Gooch, Saunders and the other great men who had built up the GWR, would pass to civil servants and politicians, and rather than serve the new order, preferred to retire. Even the offer of chairmanship of the new Railway Executive, failed to move him, as his stand was one of principle, so the country prematurely lost the services of one of its most outstanding railway managers. Several of his officers felt equally strongly, and retired or refused to leave the Western Region for the higher reaches of the BTC or RE, determined instead to defend Great Western traditions to the best of their ability. Other railway officers felt that the railway industry and the nation needed skilled hands to guide it, as life did not end on 31st December 1947, so opted to serve on. *R E Tustin*

Opposite page bottom: The Big Four were not just 'Train Operating Companies' to use a modern phrase. They were integrated transport concerns, with interests in connecting road passenger and freight, sea and air services. Of the Big Four, the Great Western had the smallest shipping fleet, but even so, it included numerous fine vessels. The main routes were from West Wales to the South of Ireland, and from Weymouth to the Channel Isles. The *St Julien*, seen leaving Weymouth in September 1949, was one of a pair of vessels built by John Brown of Clydebank in 1925, the other being the *St Helier*. Of 1885 gross register tons, and powered by single reduction geared turbines, they had a top speed of 18 knots,

making them slower than contemporary vessels being built for the other companies. When new, they were provided with two funnels, the rear funnel being a dummy for appearance sake, but the effect on a ship that was just 282 feet long, and of modest tonnage was awkward, and the dummy was removed in 1927-28. This left one narrow funnel and a replacement funnel was provided a decade later. The other main line companies used buff funnels with a black top, but the GWR applied a narrow black band to the top of a red funnel after this second rebuild, an idea applied to a few other steamers at the time. It was, however unsightly, and by 1949 *St Julien* had received the BR buff funnel with a normal black top. She made her last sailing from Guernsey on 27th September 1960, and was sold for scrap the following year. At the close of 1945, the GW fleet comprised eight steamers which had been built between 1925 and 1934, and which varied from 307 to 1,116 net registered tons, their largest ship, the *St Andrew* still being requisitioned, plus three smaller ferries which together were of 391 net registered tons.

Below: Millions of handbills were produced to advertise special events, this one being printed in dark blue on pale cream paper. The use of the much-derided 'shirt button' emblem in the post war period is interesting, as it was no longer favoured on rolling stock by this time.

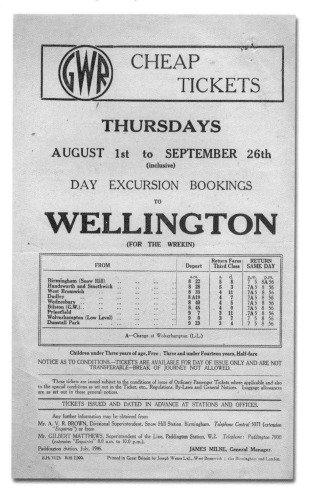

A MESSAGE FROM THE LMS ACTING PRESIDENT

YOU will have heard with pleasure of the appointment to the British Transport Commission of our President, Sir William V. Wood, K.B.E.

I have been appointed to act as President of the LMS, and I want to take this opportunity of sending my good wishes to you all.

To-day, in common with other industries, we face great difficulties because of world shortages of the essential things we need to replace the ravages of war, but I am encouraged by the knowledge that, in the past, you have overcome difficulties which seemed insurmountable, with the gratifying result that we did not fail the nation at any time.

At the end of this year the LMS with other Railways will pass into National ownership, and from my long association with you, I feel I shall not ask in vain for your help in maintaining the highest possible standard of efficiency and public service, so that when the LMS becomes part of the Nationalised transport system we may take justifiable pride in our achievements.

G. L. Darbyshire

Opposite page top: H G Ivatt, son of H A Ivatt of the GNR, was the last CME of the LMS. He was a progressive engineer, advocating roller bearings, self-cleaning smokeboxes, rocking grates, Caprotti valve gear, and maximum accessibility for servicing, all features he felt would be vital in the post-war era. He had followed diesel traction developments in the USA, which had gained a significant lead over Europe in the 1930s, and consolidated that in 1939-1941. The LMS was already replacing steam shunters in marshalling yards with 350hp diesel shunters, so it was logical to consider an experimental main line diesel locomotive, and Ivatt found a keen collaborator in Sir George Nelson, the head of English Electric, who hoped for export possibilities, provided US firms did not get too great a lead over British companies. Preliminary negotiations were concluded in May 1946 with the deadline of completing the prototype before the LMS fell victim to nationalisation. Working to this tight time scale, English Electric and Derby completed the locomotive on 8th December 1947. The LMS provided the mechanical components, whilst English Electric supplied the traction motors, the main generator and the 16SVT Mk 1 diesel engine to power this 1600 hp locomotive. The project was spread amongst several English Electric works, the main engine crankshaft being designed at the EE plant in Rugby. Marcus Bramham, a friend of my father, who was living in retirement in his 90s as this book went to press designed the crankshaft, and is probably the last surviving member of the design team. I spoke to Marcus, who confirmed the time pressure, but said that at drawing office level, no one was told the reason for the hurry. Cast iron had replaced steel for many engineering jobs during the war, and Marcus revealed that the crankshaft was of a special hematite cast iron, one of the design problems being lubrication on such a large engine. Efforts were concentrated on finishing 10000, and delivery of the second prototype, 10001, did not take place for another six months. Operating alone, they were equal to a Black Five, but working in multiple, they could tackle the heaviest expresses. 10000 was finished in glossy black with its numerals, LMS lettering, and a waist band in raised polished castings to ensure their survival for as long as possible. The plan worked as 10000 displayed its ancestry long after most LMS engines had lost their titling. It was tested on the West Coast and Midland Main Lines, and on the Southern Region. 10000 is at St Pancras on 25th August 1948. *R E Tustin*

Opposite page bottom: This September 1947 portrait of Clifton Mill station on the Rugby-Market Harborough-Peterborough route shows an LMS station in typical post-war condition. Although the ornamental valance on the right hand building is damaged, the structure is sound, without the subsidence seen at Leamington (see introduction). Unlike the other companies, where a standard colour scheme evolved, the LMS gave autonomy to its district engineers, and on the Stamford line, Lilbourne, which was the next station, was finished in warm milk chocolate brown and light stone. From this view it is likely that Clifton Mill was similar, though the paintwork is weathered, and flaking from the window frames.

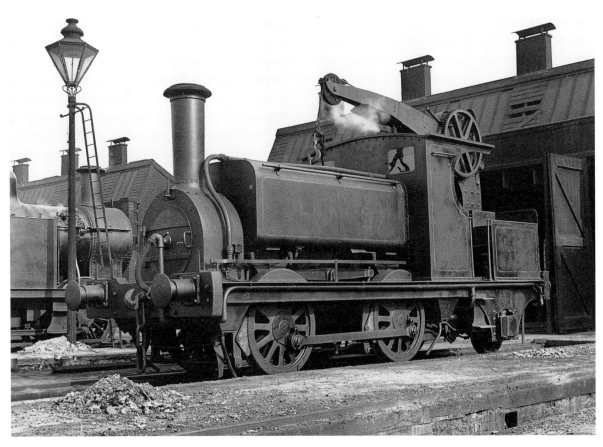

Above: The LMS contributed the most modern engine to the RE, but also had the oldest engine on the Big Four on 31st December 1947. The unique North London Railway crane tank dated from 1858, and had been NLR No 29A. It became LNWR 2896, LMS 7217, and then 27217. Unlike LMS engines with 4 figure or 10xxx numbers, which received a straight 40,000 addition to their numbers, the few survivors in the 2xxxx series were individually renumbered, to leave the 6xxxx range available for ex LNER classes. The crane tank, which was used at Bow, became BR 58865, and was withdrawn in 1951. This view, which has been attributed to other photographers, was taken by Jack Stretton-Ward, at the NLR shed at Bow in 1931. After withdrawal, preservation was mooted, but the scrapman won the day. The LMS was not as profitable as the GWR, but usually paid about 1.5% on its ordinary stock in the 1930s, rising to 2.5 % between 1942 and 1944. Its final dividend of over 4% in 1947 was some compensation to shareholders who would lose their holdings and receive British Transport 3% stock. The government was as malicious to LMS shareholders as to GW shareholders, £100 of LMS ordinary stock being replaced by £29 10s of BTC 3% stock. In the last decade of its life, the average ordinary dividend was 2.4%, or £2.40 on £100 stock. The BTC stock would yield 0.87p, or a little over a third of the average figure over the previous decade. *H J Stretton-Ward*

Opposite page top: Whilst country stations have a special place in the railway folklore, it was the main lines that carried the nation's traffic. The West Coast Main Line had long been one of the busiest routes in the world, and had evolved over decades. Under the chairmanship of Sir Richard Moon, the LNWR was accused of parsimony, but the shape of the modern WCML was created in Moon's time, including the 1880s rebuilding of Rugby Station. Under the leadership of Lord Stamp in the 1930s, new signal boxes were provided at several locations including Rugby and Crewe. At Crewe, power frames were provided, but at Rugby No 7, a new mechanical box replaced an older LNWR box that was suffering from subsidence. Although the LMS favoured colour light signals, some of which are visible in the distance, costs dictated a mix of colour lights and semaphores. At junctions, the civil engineer wants a gentle divergence to permit the highest speed, but beyond a certain angle, there is a risk of derailment on a diamond crossing, so a conflict arises at any multi track junction. The solution was a 'switch diamond'. Unlike a fixed diamond, the rails in a switch diamond move in the same way that the blades of a point move, and the signalman must set the route accordingly. We are looking towards Rugby station from the 'Down Trent', with the switch diamonds set for the 'Up Birmingham'. Switch diamond became increasingly common in the 1930s at large junctions, but this installation dated from the introduction of the celebrated LNWR '2-Hour' Birmingham expresses before World War One. Today, diamond crossings are out of favour, with a ladder junction, which consists of a series of shallow high-speed crossovers, being preferred.

Right: Lacking the financial strength of the LMS, the LNER was more frugal, and away from the main lines, the pre-grouping era lived on, save for a different coat of paint, and new lettering. This time warp was most obvious in the north of Scotland, where the former Great North of Scotland Railway provided an enclave of LNER territory reached only by running powers over the LMS. Locomotives for GNS section came from Kittybrewster shed, a picturesque roundhouse north of Aberdeen station, served by an open air turntable. No 6852, *Glen Grant*, which was built by NBL in 1920 as GNSR No 52, is on Kittybrewster turntable, and is a Heywood superheated class F 4-4-0, though the design is a development of William Pickergill's unsuperheated 4-4-0s of 1899. Uniquely, amongst the main line railway companies of Britain, the GNSR never owned a single 0-6-0 goods locomotive, entrusting everything from expresses to wayside freight trains to its ubiquitous 4-4-0s. Despite the appearance of a few ex NBR 4-4-0s and some Holden B12 4-6-0s specially built for Scotland, the D40s, as they became under the LNER, remained on first line work, even double heading Royal trains on the Ballater branch. The standard of cleanliness on the GNS section was always high, and the superheated D40s, which were allocated to specific crews, were kept in especial-ly fine condition. Although a pre-war view, this 1930s portrait on Kittybrewster turntable, of 6852, which became 2279 under the Thompson renumbering scheme, epitomises the timelessness of the LNER.

Below: Due to the shortages of cash, Gresley had to concentrate his funds on a few prestige engines, so pre-grouping classes remained in first line service far longer than on the LMS. Fortunately the GCR, GER. GNR, NBR and NER had all enjoyed competent locomotive superintendents, and their designs, though not as efficient as the most modern types, were sound. Twenty-eight of the Robinson 9Q class 4-6-0s had been built in 1921-22 for the Great Central, and a further ten were added under the LNER, as Gresley was happy to add to an existing design from another engineer. They were a 5 ft 8 ins mixed traffic design, and were capable of a good turn of speed, although short travel valve gear meant that they were heavy on coal, being known as 'Black Pigs'. Primarily used on fast fitted freights and summer Saturday excursions in their heyday, these pre-group engines and their counterparts from the other absorbed companies, were more typical of LNER express services, than the spectacular A4s, but were less commonly photographed. Based at the principal GC sheds, they traversed much of the GC system, and travelled far afield on excursions. One of their regular turns was on the Marylebone – Immingham boat trains. 5465 had been built as GCR 465 at Gorton works in 1921, and became 1373 in September 1946 under the Thompson renumbering scheme. Her appearance at Staverton Road on the GC London Extension, thundering north at the head of a rake of Great Western stock, which she will have taken over at Banbury, on a through south west to north east working, recalls the importance of the Banbury connection to the GCR, and the heyday of the B7s on excursion work. The growing number of Thompson B1 4-6-0s at the close of the LNER era meant that although all 38 B7s entered BR ownership, the last four went in 1950. Although the other three companies saw significant improvements in their income during the war, LNER finances remained fragile. The last year that an ordinary dividend was paid was in 1930, and by 1931, the company could not pay a full dividend on its lowest ranking preference shares, of which there were five categories. By 1943-44, it was only the top two categories that received payment in full, the holders of the 4% Second Preference stock receiving 2¾% only. The post war period, with government control still in force, meant that wage settlements had to be accepted so as not to harm the export drive, whilst rates and fares were kept down for political reasons, driving the LNER ever closer to collapse. Although the LMS, Great Western and Southern could have survived without assistance for some years, and with a more commercially effective policy, might have avoided the problems of the early BR years, it is doubtful if the LNER could have continued unaided for long.
H J Stretton-Ward

Above: Most of the Southern traffic was concentrated on the dense network of commuter lines stretching out for some 50 miles south and west of London. Sir Herbert Ashcombe Walker, who had managed its largest constituent, the London & South Western Railway, with conspicuous success for a decade, became general manager of the new company, and realised that none of its constituents were highly esteemed, nor was the service they offered on a par with the northern companies, or the Great Western. Walker's advocacy of electrification of the inner suburban services of the LSWR had already paid dividends, and the Southern invested heavily in third rail electrification from the start. Soon it was not just commuter services that Walker was considering, and the third rail reached Brighton and the south coast by the end of 1932. Southern officers joked that they might not have the biggest railway in the world, but they had the biggest electric tramway in existence. Set 4338, seen at Waterloo as the leading unit in a two set formation on 23rd August 1947, had started life as a 3-car 1496 class unit built for an early Southern electrification project. Dating from 1926, they were intended for the former South Eastern & Chatham section. They had steel panelled bodies on teak framing, and the motor coaches had slightly rounded driving ends, setting a long-standing tradition on the Southern. The success of the SR electrification attracted more and more passengers, and by the early months of the war, criticism of overcrowding was rife. From 1942, the Southern began strengthening its 3 car electric sets to 4 vehicles. The 1496 class were converted in 1945-46, acquiring a new 10 compartment trailer in the process, and could now accommodate 370 seated passengers, but in peak conditions, would often carry many more. They were coded 4-SUB, to indicate a 4 car suburban set, and renumbered 4326-4354. *R E Tustin*

Below: The Big Four moved some departments into the country due to the risk of air raid damage, this 1938 pre-printed card from the Audit Accountant's Office showing he had moved from London Bridge to Dorking North station as early as May 1940.

Opposite page top: R E L Maunsell, the chief mechanical engineer of the Southern Railway, provided a limited number of capable 4-6-0s for main line express work and 2-6-0s for mixed traffic duties and for the West Country, but with funds concentrated on the London suburban network, an already over-age steam fleet had to soldier on as best it could. Walker and Maunsell cannot be blamed for this policy, as it made sense to direct resources to where the best returns were to be expected, but its long-term effect was to see the age of the steam fleet rise inexorably. Drummond class K10 4-4-0 No 343, and the empty Devon Belle Pullman stock, is the centre of animated discussions between a uniformed member of staff and two bowler-hatted officials at Clapham Junction on 23rd August 1947. The Devon Belle had been introduced on 20th June 1947, with the strong backing of the SR manager, Sir Eustace Missenden in an attempt to replicate the success that prestige services such as the Golden Arrow, Brighton Belle and Southern Belle had created on the Eastern and Central sections of the SR. No 343 had entered service in December 1901, fitted with an experimental water tube boiler that economised on fuel, but was so troublesome that it was replaced by a conventional boiler in 1906. Except for 343, which was wisely kept close to Nine Elms works, the class made their home in the West of England on mixed traffic duties, but gradually became widespread, some even being loaned to the LMS to assist the War effort. Even major accident damage was repaired on the K10s up to 1946, but withdrawals began in 1947, the last of the 40 engines going in 1951. No 343 was an early casualty, being withdrawn in January 1948. The nearest coach is one of the two Pullman observation cars, No's 13 and 14 built for the Devon Belle. They required to be turned after each trip, and shunted to the rear of the train for the next working. Both had been built by the LNWR as ambulance coaches in 1918, rebuilt as Pullman kitchen cars in 1921, and rebuild yet again in 1947. *R E Tustin*

Opposite page bottom: Oliver Bulleid is a controversial figure, with partisans extolling his genius, and critics condemning his failures. After serving as Gresley's assistant on the LNER, he became CME of the Southern in 1937 at the age of 54. Bulleid realised that the lack of new steam, though understandable, threatened a crisis, with many engines at the end of their lives. Whilst further electrification was planned, new steam was urgently needed on the non-electrified sections, and Bulleid obtained approval for a new express type shortly before the start of World War Two. Passenger locomotive construction was largely halted during the war, but due to the special conditions of the Southern, which needed powerful engines for military traffic, but would have little need for heavy freight power in peacetime, work continued on the 'Merchant Navy' Pacifics as a mixed traffic design. Bulleid had many revolutionary ideas, but instead of trying them out gradually, as is sound engineering practice, had to cram them into the new engines at the design stage. This, and a redesign of the motion, in which a geared system in an oil bath was replaced by chain drive, created significant prob-

lems. The new engines, with their air smoothed casings, were visually and mechanically unlike anything that had gone before, and with a major rebuild in the 1950s, handled the heaviest Southern Region express services until the demise of steam in 1967. There was also a need for a smaller design for the lightly laid lines in the West Country. After starting out as a 2-6-0, it grew via a 2-6-2, into a smaller version of the 'Merchant Navies'. Once again, Bulleid used the peculiar circumstances of the Southern to develop a passenger design in wartime. In numbering these new engines, he adopted the continental system of including the locomotive axle arrangement in the number, but instead of the continental practice of calling it a 2C1 or 231, he designated it 21C. As the first hundred numbers were left for the big Pacifics, the first 'West Country' to be completed in June 1945 was 21C101 *Exeter*. Appropriately shedded at Exmouth Junction mpd, the depot serving Exeter, 21C101 is prepared for the all-Pullman summer-only Devon Belle, which was inaugurated on 20th June 1947, with Plymouth and Ilfracombe portions. A dramatic red and white headboard and side flashes created an eye-catching effect, but traffic never reached expectations, and the service was discontinued after the 1954 season. 21C101, was withdrawn as BR 34001 in July 1967, and was one of just three 'West Countries' to amass over 1m miles in service.

Below: With the busy channel services and the commuter and holiday routes to the Isle of Wight, the Southern was a major shipping line, as well as a railway operator, and when consideration was given to names for the new heavy Pacifics, British wartime victories were first considered, but there had not been enough of them in 1941, so other ideas were scouted. Union Castle line had been a long time user of the Southern's premier port of Southampton, and their chairman suggested the Merchant Navy theme. 21C2, later 35002, duly became *Union Castle*, but 21C1 was understandably reserved for the Southern's own maritime arm, Channel Packet, the plate bearing the house flag of the relevant shipping company in the centre of the roundel. The SR flag comprised a red cross edged in white superimposed on a dark blue ground with white letters SR. The plates were left or right handed, so that the flag flew from the front – or possibly the bows – of the locomotive, so this is the right hand plate for *Channel Packet*.

Above: Apart from the cross channel services, the Southern served the Isle of Wight. The oldest route was between Portsmouth and Ryde, the railway link beginning in 1847. The PS *Ryde* was launched by Denny of Dumbarton on the Clyde on 23rd April 1937, but had hardly settled into her routine of carrying summer trippers to the Isle of Wight, before the Admiralty requisitioned her for war service as a minesweeper. She was the first SR paddle steamer to be returned to the company in 1945, going back into service almost immediately. 220 feet long, and of 602 gross register tons, the *Ryde* was a sister ship to the 1934 PS *Sandown*. Driven by a triple expansion 3-cyl steam engine developing 133hp, she could make the journey between Portsmouth and Ryde in 22 minutes. *Ryde* was the last paddle steamer on the IOW section, and was preserved as *Ryde Queen* at the Wight Marina after being withdrawn, but suffered fire damage in the 1970s. She is at the IOW berth adjoining Portsmouth Harbour Station in 1953. For the harried commuter of today, anxious to travel between Ryde and the mainland as quickly as possible, the modern fast craft on the Portsmouth-Ryde service may be a blessing, but they lack the charm and grace of yesteryear. Fast craft were not to appear until the 1980s, though a Southern officer, writing as long ago as 1939, speculated that diesel driven semi-hydroplane craft might be built in the future.

Below: The PS *Ryde* carried a Southern badge on her paddle box. Such decoration began in the early days of steamer construction, and remained popular up to the demise of the paddle steamer. PS *Ryde* was a worthy member of an illustrious family, and spent her last years running from Clarence Pier in Southsea to Ryde Pier Head. Apart from the canard about excessive compensation being paid to shareholders, another 'story' is that the directors and management lost interest after 1945. Given the way they had been treated, this would be understandable, but what really happened? Eric Gore

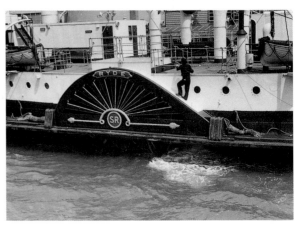

Browne's list of work in hand in 1946 show how seriously the companies took refurbishment, although government restrictions on steel allocations played havoc with progress. The draft Transport Bill, which was published on 27th November 1946, was another blow. Clause 15 was entitled 'Disclaimer of agreements', and permitted the BTC to renounce any agreement that had been made after 19th November 1945, if they felt it was unnecessary or imprudent. Was a GWR order for a ship, or an LNER order for 25 diesel locomotives, necessary or prudent? No one could be sure, and the companies had to face this added difficulty. Small capital items could be justified, but was a five-story cold store at Southampton docks 'necessary', however wise it was for a prudent business to build such facilities, as the SR could probably have managed without it. Was the SR involvement in peripheral activities permissible? In April 1947, Missenden had attended the SR Ambulance Movement competition. Before the war, there had been over 4,000 members, but with wartime problems this had dropped to 2,000. Missenden said 'Let us do our very best to see that we on the Southern Railway have an Ambulance Movement of 5,000 trained men'. On 22nd September 1947, 'Missenden House', the first Southern Railway home for old people, was opened at Woking by Eric Gore Browne, who said it was 'a dream come true'. Despite such discouragement, the other companies did the same, Cammell Laird, for example, launching the *St David* at Birkenhead for the GWR in 1947. She was the 14th and last ship built at Cammell Laird for the GWR.

Below: The government had a few more tricks to play. Labour shortages, high absenteeism and strikes crippled coal production after the war. To avoid a collapse of services, the government pressed the Big Four to adopt oil firing, and provide fuelling facilities at selected depots. Government funding was offered, and the companies set to work in 1947, the Southern planning to adapt 110 locomotives. Early in 1948, the government realised that buying the fuel oil for the hundreds of engines that were to be converted, would place a heavy drain on the exchequer, as this was before the discovery of Britain's North Sea oil reserves, so the policy was abandoned! By the time the government had worked out that oil did not grow on trees, and that the measure would not go down well in the coal fields, which was one of Labour's traditional bastions, the Southern had adapted 33 locomotives, all of which would need reconversion, if they were to be of any use. That much of the cost fell on the government was poetic justice, though hard luck on the hapless taxpayer who footed the bill. However, irreplaceable works capacity and materials had been squandered in this farce. Out of fifteen T9 class 4-4-0s scheduled for conversion, nine were converted in September 1947, including No 731. The conversion included an oil tank in the coal space, additional steps on the tender, oil hoses connecting the engine and tender, the oil burning equipment and alterations to the firebox. With the government about-face in 1948, most of the converted T9s were stored by October 1948, as re-conversion to coal burning was not worthwhile with elderly locomotives with a short life expectancy. Although some of their unconverted sisters remained in traffic until the sixties, the oil burners had all gone by 1951, after lying idle for two and a half years.

Above: Despite media hysteria that has endured from the dawn of the railway age, and becomes more unbalanced rather than less, a British passenger train has always been an exceptionally safe way to travel. Those in the popular media who have condemned rail travel as dangerous for no better reason than it helps sell newspapers, and may have encouraged ill-informed travellers to desert rail for less safe means of transport, deserve contempt, rather than any appreciation for their efforts. No matter how careful railwaymen are, and the standard is exceptional, accidents do occasionally happen, and it is ironic that 1947, the last year of the company era should have seen a fine record marred by several accidents. A total of 121 fatalities were sustained in 1947, the only higher figure that had been recorded being in 1915, as a result of the dreadful Quintinshill collision on the Caledonian Railway, where 224 persons lost their lives. The year started badly with 7 fatalities at Gidea Park on the LNER on 2nd January. The Polesworth derailment on the LMS in July 1947, accidents at Doncaster and Burton Agnes on the LNER, and two collisions in October 1947, at South Croydon on the SR, and Goswick in Northumberland, pushed the death toll beyond 100, and another four accidents in November and December, with between 1 and 4 casualties each, completed a sad year. By comparison, a collision at Chertsey, which involved Urie class S15 4-6-0 No 508, resulted in no fatalities, though there was some damage to the front end of No 508, which was built at Eastleigh in 1920, and ran until November 1963. She is seen at Feltham on 9th July 1947, whilst awaiting works attention.

Unlike the other companies, which drew 34 to 43 percent of their income from passenger traffic before the war, the Southern received 73 to 77 per cent of its income from pas-

sengers, and whilst passenger receipts on some rural routes declined, its busy electric services recouped the losses, and in 1937 Southern passenger revenue still stood at 99% of its 1923 levels. Unlike the LNER, the Southern came through the war in good condition, paying all its preference shareholders, and even distributing 2% on the deferred ordinary stocks, which, as the name implies, came at the bottom of the queue. Despite wartime restrictions, 108 new passenger carriages were turned out in 1945, whilst new Merchant Navy and West Country Pacifics were transforming the steam fleet as well. Refurbishment of the Southern owned Southampton Docks began, and despite losing 12 out of the pre-war fleet of 42 ships, some routes were in operation by the end of 1945 and three new vessels were on order in 1946. Col Eric Gore Browne revealed more plans at the Annual general meeting that year. They included more electrification, additional new ships, more station renewals, and closer collaboration with road hauliers, if the government would provide a fairer framework for the railways to work under. The Southern ended the war run-down, due to wartime conditions, but with an ambitious programme to refurbish track, stations and stock, and confidence that it could work with road haulage constructively. Gore Browne was emphatic, 'It is not the capital position about which your Board is anxious, but a Sword of Damocles hanging over our heads is not an incentive to enterprise… If they could only be sure of the future they could proceed with confidence, thereby stimulating industry and doing their bit towards pulling the country out of its present financial difficulties at a time when the need is so great'. The government had ensured that the two and a half years between the end of the war and the demise of the Big Four were largely wasted.

A MESSAGE FROM THE CHAIRMAN

Parliament has passed the Transport Act, 1947 and, on New Year's Day, 1948, the ownership of the Southern Railway and of all its interests passes to the State.

Colonel Eric Gore Browne,
D.S.O., O.B.E., A.D.C.

I send this message to all Southern Railway men and women from myself and from all my colleagues on the Board.

We thank you for the service which you have given to the Company throughout its existence, magnificent in its loyalty and in its efficiency. It is a proud reflection that owing to your efforts and to the courage and vision of those who created, developed and financed our Company, the Southern Railway has attained pre-eminence amongst the railways not only of this country, but throughout the world.

For myself it has been a real privilege to be closely associated with you for over seventeen years, and, during the war just ended, to have seen at close quarters something of the contribution which you have made to final victory. And I have made many friendships which I hold most dear and which I shall always cherish.

Now, "the old order changeth giving place to new". In sending to all of you our best wishes for the future, it is the earnest hope of my colleagues and of myself that you will take with you into the service of the Railway Executive the Southern family spirit which has contributed so much to our success. If you will carry this spirit with you into the wider sphere which lies ahead, giving your loyal service to all who direct and manage our national transport system, then we and all your country-men may look forward with confidence to success in this great adventure.

Goodbye! Good Luck!

CHAIRMAN'S ROOM,
    WATERLOO STATION, S.E.1.

December, 1947.

Above: We will invite Lt-Col Eric Gore Browne to say 'Farewell' to the company era. In his final message he spoke of the Southern family spirit, and asked that railwaymen should give their loyalty to the new Railway Executive. Privately, he was apprehensive. Knowing the magnitude of the task facing the Southern, Gore Browne felt it would take ten years to refurbish the railways after the devastation of war, and that the massive changes proposed by the 1947 Act would take a similar period to assimilate. He felt that a needless re-organisation would divert effort from rebuilding work, and that subjecting the railways to close political control, and the vagaries of party politics, when long term planning was vital, could only harm the industry and the country. In the succeeding sections, we will see whether his forebodings were justified.

SR Cheap Day Excursion printed in black, with red CD overprint on buff card stock.

4 · HURCOMB'S EMPIRE

In 1948, New Year's Day fell on a Thursday. It was a dull morning, which is not uncommon in London in January, and though the weather was inauspicious, it heralded the biggest shake-up in British transport in history, for it was not only the railways that were affected, but London Transport, the canals, a large number of docks, and many shipping services, buses, lorries and hotels as well. Although Scotland has celebrated New Year with a public holiday for many years, this was not the case in England in 1948, and as Sir Cyril Hurcomb walked through St James' Park to take up his new post at the BTC, instead of going to the Ministry of Transport, he must have pondered at the change from being a senior civil servant to being the ruler of one of the largest business undertakings in the world, and what the future would hold. Before looking at the birth of BR itself, we will briefly explore some of the other aspects of the BTC.

Above: After the Railway Executive, the London Transport Executive was the next most important element in the BTC, with its immense fleet of Underground trains, trams, trolleybuses and buses, all operating under the guidance of Lord Ashfield, who had come to England in 1907, and had served the travelling public of London with distinction for more than 40 years. Unlike Glasgow or Liverpool, where electric trams took to the streets early, and were taken to the heart of both cities, the electric car did not venture on to the streets of London until 1901, and the fragmented nature of London's urban transport with a myriad of companies and local councils precluded a properly integrated service, until the formation of London Transport in 1933 merged no fewer than 92 separate transport undertakings into one. Despite these disparate origins, its 328 route miles and 2,630 cars meant it was the biggest tramway in Britain, and one of the largest in the world. The LT fleet included some imposing equipment, including the sophisticated Feltham cars that had appeared shortly prior to the formation of LT. One hundred 'Felthams', to be built by the Union Constructions & Finance Co of Feltham, were ordered by London United Tramways, and Metropolitan Electric Tramways, and had power operated doors, enclosed cabs for the driver, and clean streamlined ends. Feltham car 2164 is seen at Tooting Broadway on 14th May 1950. However, the robust nature of the tramcar meant that thousands of pre-1914 cars soldiered on into the Thirties, by which time, they looked outmoded compared to the sleek new buses and trolleybuses. By 1933, most tramways were run by town or city councils, and public opinion had turned against the tramcar. It was no longer politically expedient to back the tramcar against the more modern bus option, and as one system after another closed, the anti-tram bias became unstoppable. In its first two years, LT decided to abandon almost half its tramway mileage in favour of trolleybuses, and that was only the beginning. By 1936, LT had decided on abandonment of the entire tramway system, but the outbreak of war in 1939 halted conversion, and the last trams were to survive until 5/6th July 1952. *R E Tustin*

Below: The former London County Council metal bodied class E3 cars, of which No 187 is an example, were a more traditional design, with open platforms, but performed effectively, and looked smart in the LT colours of bright red with lining around the edge of the metal dash. The last stronghold of trams in London was on the routes south of the Thames. Routes 33, 48 and 78 served West Norwood, the 33s running via Westminster Bridge, the Embankment, the celebrated Kingsway tram subway, Bloomsbury, the Angel, and Essex Road to Finsbury Park (Manor House station). In 1938, the full journey took about 68 minutes, with cars running at 5-10 minute headways. The lack of motor vehicles, save for a solitary lorry, is the most striking feature in this portrait of the tram terminal at West Norwood in 1950. Petrol was still rationed, and cars a luxury item for the affluent. In this view, and the previous illustration, cyclists also appear, as the pushbike was a convenient and cheap way to get around. Trams, or to give them their modern name, Light Rapid Tran-

sit – LRT – are now fashionable again, so their abandonment by LT may seem strange to younger readers, but from the 1920s to the 1960s, the tramcar was seen as unfashionable, and its removal from the streets was heralded as progress. In eliminating trams, LT was following and reinforcing contemporary attitudes, but one has to wonder whether a more positive attitude with new stock, the closure of older routes, where traffic flows had dried up, and the opening of new routes, as happened in Liverpool and Glasgow for some time, might have been preferable. Had LT modernised its tramway system, it is possible that the old fashioned image that did so much to kill the tramcar would not have become quite so strong.

Above: The decline in the London tram fleet between 1933 and 1948 had been matched by a rise in trolleybuses to 1,746 vehicles by 1st January 1948. The oldest vehicles were the original sixty buses in the A1 and A2 classes built for London United Tramways Ltd in 1931. They were 56 seaters with AEC 663T chassis, 56 seat UCC bodies, which were similar in many respects to the Feltham tramcars, and English Electric or BTH electrical equipment. A1 No 24, at Hampton Court on 30th June 1939, was fitted with English Electric equipment. They had been introduced from 16th

May 1931, when LUT began converted tram routes in the Teddington and Twickenham area to trolleybuses, with 17.26 route miles converted by the end of the year. Nick-named 'Diddlers', they had one central headlight, as in tramway practice, and a motorbus bonnet, rather than the full fronted cab of later designs. Trolleybus routes were num-bered from 601, often taking the number of the tram route they replaced with 600 added to the old route number. Route 604, on which No 24 is employed, ran from Hampton Court to Wimbledon, via Hampton Wick, Kingston Bridge, and New Malden. By 1938, the trolleybus network had spread in West London from Surbiton to Twickenham, Chiswick, Acton, Cricklewood and North Finchley, with a route running south from Hammersmith across Putney Bridge to Clapham, Croy-don, Sutton and Crystal Palace. In East London, a separate group of routes served Walthamstow, Stratford, Barking and Canning Town, whilst further routes south of the Thames served Woolwich, Erith and Dartford. *R E Tustin*

Opposite page bottom: Prior to the take-over by LT in 1933, LUT acquired one more trolleybus. This was the solitary class X1 vehicle, No 61 of 1933, which was fitted with a unique AEC 691T chassis, No 691T001, and a 74-seat centre entrance UCC body, with a modern full fronted design, and conventional twin headlights. No 64 is depicted at Hampton Court on 14th August 1939. Immediately after its formation in 1933, London Transport decided that the trolleybus was

the way forward, and by the end of the war, over 250 route miles were in operation, 224 miles being former tram routes, but in 1946, LT announced that the remaining tram routes would go over to bus operation. Although 77 trolleybuses were on order, this suggested that the trolleybus system might be out of favour, and the first route to be converted from trolleybus to bus came four years later. In 1954, LT announced that the trolleybus system would be replaced by the new Routemaster double deck bus, the entire system going between 1959 and 1962, ten years after the last of the tramcars had gone. No 61 is also on the 604 route, and displays adverts for Picture Post, and Crosse & Blackwell's Branston Pickle. *R E Tustin*

Below: The first RT double decker motorbus appeared from AEC in 1939, and production continued for London Transport until 1953, when they were superseded by the new Routemaster. When they first appeared, it is doubtful if any-one anticipated that they would be a part of LT stock until 7th April 1979, a period of forty years! No fewer than 4,675 AEC RTs were built after the war, including RT2327, KGU 356, seen crossing Westminster Bridge with County Hall in the background. A further 2,131 Leyland chassis were provided to produce the RTL, as not even the four thousand plus AEC chassis satisfied London's demand for new buses in the early post war period.

Opposite page top: Until the formation of LT in 1933, the Metropolitan and Metropolitan District Railways were separate companies, although sharing the Circle line. The District, which was a part of the Underground group, came under the sway of Albert Stanley, later Lord Ashfield, and the 1914 'E' stock cars, although built by Gloucester Railway Carriage & Wagon Co, had definite American outlines. An E-stock driving motor car is the rear vehicle on this formation, taken at Kew Gardens on 24th April 1948. The elliptical roofed E stock was able to operate with the earlier monitor roofed C and D stock, which make up the rest of this 6-car set. In front line service up to 1949, but whittled down to a dozen cars by 1954, the surviving C, D and E cars eked out their last days on the Earls Court & Olympia services that ran on exhibition days only, where I can just recall them. Although the District owned, or part-owned, just 26¾ route miles, District trains operated over 58 miles of track, when running powers and leased lines were taken into account. The District, along with the London Electric Railway, the City & South London Railway, the Central London Railway, and the London General Omnibus Co, formed 'The Common Fund Companies', sharing revenue and profits in agreed ratios, and with over 1,800m passengers carried by group companies each year prior to the fusion into LT, District shareholders earned a steady 4% to 5% dividend. The creation of LT in 1933 added the Metropolitan Railway, the tramway companies and municipal tramways and the independent bus operators to the fold. Apart from close working within the Common Fund companies, the group also worked closely with the main line railway companies, as this view recalls, as Kew Gardens station is on the Southern (ex LSWR) branch between Acton, Turnham Green, and Richmond. London Transport entered the BTC fold in 1948 with 18 electric locomotives, 2,206 electric power cars, 1,655 trailer cars, 7,032 buses, 1,746 trolleybuses, 864 trams and a variety of service stock, including 13 steam locomotives.

Opposite page bottom: The explanatory memorandum to the Transport Bill proclaimed, 'The general duty of the Commission is so to exercise their powers as to provide, secure or promote the provision of an efficient, adequate, economical and properly integrated system of public inland transport', and this paragraph was repeated verbatim in the first Annual Report of the BTC. With the take over of the Tilling Group, the BTC controlled many of the leading provincial bus companies, and many people expected this would mean closer co-operation between rail and bus services, but to Hurcomb's neat civil service mind, the juxtaposition of BTC buses and trains suggested undesirable competition between state owned services. Rather than co-ordination, Hurcomb favoured closing lightly used railways in areas where the BTC already controlled the bus services, and the first annual report made ominous reading, 'The Commission interpret this to mean that for efficiency the system must be reliable, speedy and safe; for adequacy it must eventually provide in some form (but not necessarily in every form) in every place sufficient means of conveyance...' Hurcomb pressed the

Railway Executive to set up a Branchline committee to facilitate such closures. Few writers have explored the crossplay between the road and rail sides of the BTC, but if we are to understand the complex events from 1948 to 1953 on the railways, this is essential. The reason the BTC inherited many but not all bus companies was largely historical. In the early days of motorbus operation, the railway companies had run their own bus services, but these interests had been largely transferred to bus companies in which the railways had a substantial shareholding in the 1930s. Many of these were a part of a national bus group, Thomas Tilling Ltd. The chairman of Tillings, Sir Frederick Heaton, was in favour of merging the Tilling Group interests into the BTC, and in November 1948, Tillings sold their road haulage and omnibus interests to the BTC for £24.8m, the sale being backdated to the start of the year. The Scottish Motor Traction Group had also expressed a willingness to dispose of its bus operations to the BTC, although the third major group, British Electric Traction Ltd, was strongly opposed to a BTC take-over, and indicated it would fight nationalisation. Given the Commission's wide powers, its long term objective was acquisition of all bus undertakings, but unlike the railways where there were only a few companies, making absorption a simple matter, compulsory acquisition of the entire industry would be complex, and the BTC decided to satisfy itself with the Tilling Group and SMT to begin with. The Tilling Group included sixteen major bus operators, covering areas as far apart as the Isle of Wight and the Caledonian Omnibus Co in Scotland. Apart from the operators, the Tilling interests embraced the Bristol Tramways & Carriage Co's chassis manufacturing plant at Brislington near Bristol, and a body building plant, Eastern Coach Works, at Lowestoft. They had built most vehicles required by the Tilling Group, and also made outside sales before they became BTC owned, but one peculiar effect of the 1947 act was that whilst BTC-owned concerns could build stock for their own use, or sell second hand equipment, they were prohibited from manufacturing for general sales. This was a legacy of a 19th century injunction obtained by the UK locomotive builders to prevent the LNWR manufacturing locomotives at its Crewe works for sale to the LYR. As a result, the Bristol-ECW combination were only able to build for BTC undertakings, and within a few years, a glance at a bus would reveal if the undertaking was BTC controlled or not. Hants & Dorset was one of the Tilling companies. These two Hants & Dorset buses, taken at the Palmerston statue in the centre of Romsey, recall two classic Bristol-ECW products. Double-decker No 1268, KEL711, is a Bristol KS6B with an ECW L27/28R body and dates from 1950. The K series was in production from 1937 to 1957, this particular chassis being 27 feet in length with a 7ft 6ins wide body. The body was a Lowbridge type, with the upper gangway offset to one side, to permit a reduction in overall vehicle height. The single decker. No 807, UEL731, is an LS5G with an ECW 43-seat bus body. The LS, or 'Light Saloon' was an early underfloor-engined single decker, produced from 1951 to 1958, and was powered by a 5 cylinder Gardner diesel engine.

Above: The lowbridge body, with its offset gangway was one solution to routes where double deckers had to negotiate tight bridges, but it was inconvenient for passengers, and in 1949, Bristol developed an experimental cranked chassis which permitted a lowheight body with a conventional centre gangway. The first production models were delivered in 1953. One area with low bridges was the Isle of Wight, where bus operations were run by Southern Vectis. The company began in 1921, and became jointly owned by the Southern Railway and the Tilling group a few years later. Southern Vectis No 518, KDL 414 is an early LD6G 56 seat Lodekka dating from 1954, and is negotiating the reverse bends in Shanklin Old Village on the busy Ryde-Ventnor route. The Isle of Wight was a prime candidate for the rationalisation Hurcomb had in mind. Although the railways were busy in summer, limited winter traffic and the lightly used lines in West and Central Wight meant that receipts generated on the Island did not cover expenses. The branchline committee proposed closure of the entire network, but opponents pointed out that at least 50% of passenger journeys originated on the mainland, and on summer Saturdays, it would take 62 bus departures an hour from Ryde to replace the trains. The plans were dropped, but between 1952 and 1966, the entire system save for the stump from Ryde to Shanklin was closed as Hurcomb had wanted, and travellers to and from Ventnor no longer had the choice of bus or rail.

Opposite page top: Acquisition of the railways was easy. Other than the Big Four and LT, the remaining railways were either subsidiaries of the Big Four, or minor independents such as the Colonel Stephens lines. On the bus side, it was more complex, with three big bus groups, two of which were willing to co-operate, scores of municipals, and thousands of independents, varying from large fleets to some with a single bus or coach. Typical of the vehicles run by the smaller independent was this Bedford OB single decker which is on a connecting service between Okehampton station and the town centre. The design had appeared in 1939, and was multiplied after the war, until it became the archetypal vehicle in the smaller fleet, remaining in use into the 1970s. As any immediate attempt to take control of the fragmented bus industry in 1948 would have caused severe administrative indigestion, due to the number of operators concerned, Hurcomb left the independents alone, but the first BTC Annual Report revealed that this was temporary, as the BTC had powers under the 1947 Act to prepare area schemes. The report commented ruefully 'The requirements of the Act in relation to area passenger road transport schemes contained in Sections 63 and 64 and the Eighth Schedule to the Act are detailed and complicated, and no scheme can be drafted without full knowledge of all road passenger undertakings, whether municipally or privately owned in any given area, and of their statutory obligations and working arrangements'.

Right: Although the railways dominated the BTC portfolio, they were not the the oldest element. That honour went to the canal network. Even if the Transport Act 1947 had not vested the independent canals, such as the Grand Union Canal Co in the BTC, the Commission would have been a major owner of inland waterways, as hundreds of miles of canals had been acquired by the railway companies in the 19th century, to buy off the opposition of the canal proprietors, or to avoid competition. The independent canals came under the immediate jurisdiction of the Docks & Inland Waterways Executive, but the railway-owned canals were briefly vested in the Railway Executive, until the necessary legal formalities could be carried out to transfer them to the D&IWE. The process was not as simple as one might think, as different wages and employment structures had grown up, and employees of the former railway canals were not keen on giving up any benefits they had enjoyed as railway employees, even though their careers might have been spent far from the tracks. Unlike the railways, which provided the infrastructure and the train services, until the chaotic privatisation of the 1990s, the canals provided the route, but 'carrying companies' which might be a company with hundreds of boats, or a single family, performed the haulage work. No immediate attempt was made to take over the independent carriers, but some of the canals also had their own carrying companies. At the end of 1948, the BTC owned 1,149 carry-

ing craft, which was about 15% of the total working boats, but the number rose at the start of 1949, with the acquisition of the most celebrated carrying company of all, Fellows, Morton & Clayton Ltd. They added 107 motor boats, 65 butties, two properties in Birmingham, and a number of motor vehicles. Originally hauled by horses, internal combustion engines had made an early appearance, but it was quite feasible for one powered boat to haul a second unpowered butty. A pair of Fellows Morton & Clayton boats are unloading at the timber wharf at Pasture Lane, Leicester, in 1949.

MESSAGE FROM THE RAILWAY EXECUTIVE TO ALL RAILWAY MEN AND WOMEN

ON the first day of 1948 the Railway of Great Britain become the property of the British Nation. From that day on, every one of us railway men and women is working in the direct service of our country. And all that Britain means and can mean to us and to the world is something worth working for.

In restoring, maintaining and increasing the prosperity of Britain, British Railways have a vital part to play—a part that nothing else *can* play.

We have to weld the great Railway Undertakings of the past into a still greater whole, into one organisation that will give the people and the commerce of Britain the best, the safest and the most efficient railway service in the World. In these days of difficulties and shortages, that will not be easy.

You have accomplished wonders under the most difficult conditions of working and living. We shall do all we can to improve those conditions as resources are allotted to us, but it will need from all of us a lot of hard work, a lot of patience and a lot of good humour. But to this great task those of you who have been long in the Service bring unsurpassed practical experience ; those of you who are younger can bring enthusiasm, energy and freshness. And we have our great traditions, traditions of service, of skill, of difficulties overcome, and of courage. Those traditions go on unbroken.

Let every railway man and woman remember that, whatever his or her part in this vast organisation, it is important. That it counts in the comfort, courtesy, punctuality, economy, and safety of the service. That how it is done really matters. Our task is a great one and a difficult one, but we *can* do it—and we *will*.

EUSTACE MISSENDEN, Chairman for the Railway Executive.

5 · THE RAILWAY EXECUTIVE TAKES CHARGE

Opposite page: The Railway Executive have been criticised for the attention they paid to establishing a new British Railways livery in the early weeks of 1948, as if this was unimportant. In fact, they were quite right to do so. The politicians had demanded a new beginning, with co-ordination as the theme. Had the Railway Executive been indifferent to establishing a 'Corporate Image', they would have attracted vehement criticism from those who had regarded the railway management as dyed-in-the-wool servants of capitalism, and left to their own devices, the six new regions of BR would have been even less likely to pull together. Unlike some modern makeovers, where a fortune is wasted on over-priced consultants, and a hurried re-branding, the RE was more economical. Until new British Railways liveries could be established, locomotives continued to appear in pre-nationalisation colours, but with company lettering replaced by BRITISH RAILWAYS. Rebranding was quite slow, and engines were still to be found in pre-nationalisation liveries in the mid fifties. To my astonishment, I even discovered one engine

with Great Western lettering on the tender in 1964 just a few months before the demise of Western Region steam! Although the Eastern and London Midland Regions both adopted the clear and highly readable Gill Sans lettering, the Western Region retained the graceful Egyptian serifed lettering it had used for decades. Traditionally, the GWR had used gold lettering, shaded in black and red, but with the gold leaf used in making transfers in short supply during the war, transfer manufacturers were obliged to use chrome yellow, with or without their customer's approval. I have seen unused 1940s transfers in both styles. When unused, they are virtually indistinguishable, and after a few weeks in service, I doubt if anyone could tell them apart, and few people at the time or since, realised that many post war gold transfers were actually chrome yellow. 5022, *Wigmore Castle*, displays her new ownership, as she pulls away from Leamington Spa General station with an Up express in March 1948. Many numbers were duplicated and some were repeated three or even four fold, as with the 1000 series where there were the GWR

'Counties', a mixture of SR Stirling designs from the SECR, Midland Compounds on the LMS, and the Thompson B1s on the LNER. Until a renumbering scheme was devised, instructions went out to add a regional letter to the number. The WR reluctantly placed a small White W below the polished brass number plate on a handful of locomotives including 5022. It was one of about 17 'Castle' class 4-6-0s so treated, and as soon as the Western Region had successfully lobbied to retain its cherished number plates, the suffixes were quickly over-painted. The grimy state of the platform starting signal is indicative of how run down the railways had become.
H J Stretton-Ward

Right: Although the Western Region had to use the British Railways totem on this 1951 letter from the Commercial Superintendent's office at Paddington, rather than emblazon Great Western Railway across the top of the sheet, as had been the case for 110 years, the letter head was printed in chocolate brown, and the paper itself was a very pale cream, rather than white. The GWR might be dead in theory, but had no intention of lying down tamely!

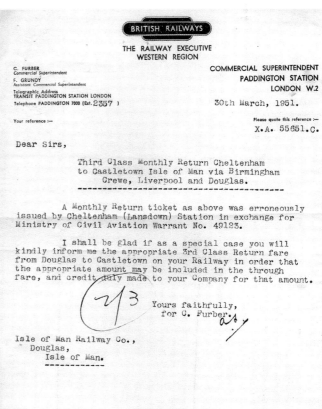

Above: The driver of this former South Eastern & Chatham Railway class L 4-4-0, No 31775, leans against the cab cut out to keep an eye open for the road in 1952. At the end of the war, the GWR had returned to its traditional image as soon as possible, but on the Southern, Missenden and Bulleid wanted a lively and more modern image than the pre-war Olive green. The SR began repainting a wide range of classes into Malachite green in 1946, No 1775 receiving the striking Bulleid green with yellow and black lining, together with the SOUTHERN title in 'Sunshine' lettering on the ten-

der. It is sometimes stated that 31775 went into BR transitional livery in April 1948, but the Southern inscription on the tender shows she did not receive a full repaint, but patch painting, with the SR number on the engine and on the tender being replaced by the new 30xxx BR number in sunshine lettering, with the SOUTHERN lettering untouched on the tender sides. The L class 4-4-0s were on the drawing board as Wainwright's career was coming to a close. Board dissatisfaction with the state of the locomotive department, Wainwright's 'laid back' approach to work, and board irritation with

his addiction to un-superheated engines with slide valves, brought matters to a head. Even Wainwright's placid acceptance of superheating could not save him, and he was retired on health grounds in November 1913, his design staff updating the design prior to R E L Maunsell taking over on 1st January 1914. Because of the urgent need for motive power, Maunsell accepted the design, and twelve engines, No's 760-771, were ordered from Beyer Peacock. Such was the crisis that another ten, No's 772-781, were ordered from Borsig & Co of Berlin, one of the few occasions that Continental engines had been ordered by a British railway company. Amazingly, the first Borsig engines arrived in May 1914, with the rest by the middle of June. It was a close run thing, as the First World War broke out seven weeks later! Renumbered 1760-1781 by the Southern, they became 31760-31781 in BR days. 31775, a Borsig engine, fell victim to the Kent Coast electrification during the summer of 1959. The class became extinct in December 1961.

Opposite page bottom: The T9 'Greyhounds' were Dugald Drummond's most successful and best-loved engines on the LSWR, and were built between 1899 and 1901. After the grouping, some, including No 119, were transferred to the Eastern (ex SE&CR) Section, where the capuchon on the front of her stovepipe chimney was shortened. Many engines later lost these vestigial capuchons, but No 119 retained it to the end of her life. Rostered for Royal train and VIP work, she was given a deluxe livery at Eastleigh in 1935. During the war, the T9s were painted in austerity black, with the exception of No 119, which retained her pre-war finery. She was repainted in Malachite green with black and white lining in May 1946, and again repainted in May 1948 when she received her BR number and BRITISH RAILWAYS title in SR

'Sunshine' lettering. She is seen at Dorchester on 20th September 1952, but sadly was withdrawn the following December. *R E Tustin*

Below: Johnson 2F 58308, a long-term Rugby engine, which still displays a grimy LMS on the tender, began life as MR No 2709, and was a late member of the '1873' class, first introduced in 1885. Construction continued until the early 1900s, 2709 being out shopped in 1902. Under the 1907 MR renumbering scheme, she became 3738. Many of her sisters were rebuilt with larger boilers, to become Johnson/Deeley Class 3 goods, but 3738 received a Belpaire class 2 boiler and a Deeley cab. By 1948, the multiplication of the Ivatt 2-6-0s in power class 4, required the freeing of numbers in the 3000 series, so BR opted to separate the class 2 and class 3 engines, the class 3s receiving numbers in the 432xx range, and the class 2s from 58251 upwards. Official records state that 3738 was renumbered 58308 in September 1950, making her the last but one engine to receive her 58xxx number. Although displaying a BR number, it is in 10 inch LMS serif lettering, and is doubtful if LMS serif lettering would have been used at this late date. Sadly the photo is undated, but from other views, was probably taken in 1948/49. It is possible that 3738 was renumbered using LMS serif lettering soon after the renumbering scheme was drawn up, but before BR Gill Sans transfers were available, and that the records were not updated. Another photograph taken by my father in 1950 shows 58308 with Gill Sans lettering. It seems likely that when the engine was repainted with Gill Sans lettering, no one knew when the number had actually been changed, and rather than report this to HQ, it was easier to log the change as 1950.

Above: 40182, a Stanier class 3 taper boiler 2-6-2T, based at Leicester (Midland) shed, 15C, pulls forward out of the Ashby bay at the north end of Nuneaton (Trent Valley) station to the Up slow platform with a local passenger train for its home station. The former LNWR South Leicestershire branch diverges from the Trent Valley main line just south of Nuneaton station, and joins the Midland main line at Wigston, just south of Leicester. 40182 has received her new BR number and BRITISH RAILWAYS Gill Sans lettering on the tank sides, but does not carry standard BR lining out on the tanks or bunker, so is in a hybrid livery. When new, these Class 3 tanks, which were the least satisfactory of Stanier's locomotives, received LMS black livery, lined out in red, but wartime repaints were in unlined black. It is probable that 40182 is in unlined LMS black, and has been patch painted with its BR number and title, but faded 1930s LMS red lining would be invisible, if there was much grime on the tank sides, so we cannot be sure.

Opposite page bottom: The LMS Garratts are popularly linked with slow moving coal drags on the Midland main line, and many enthusiasts refuse to believe that they got on to the West Coast Main Line, but here is the proof, with 47988 by Rugby No 5 signal box about 1949. The Garratt is in an unusual variant of the Gill Sans livery, with BRITISH on the front tank, the numeral on the cabside, and RAILWAYS on the coal bunker. The leading wagon is a 7-plank LMS mineral wagon with a wooden chassis and side and end doors, and carries the small 1930s LMS lettering to the left of the door. The second wagon is a former Glasshoughton Collieries open, No 1697, and bears a Castleford inscription as its home station, but with the pooling of coal wagons on the outbreak of war, more than a decade has passed since Glasshoughton Colliery determined its movements, and the wagon is now a part of BR stock. The top plank has been replaced, but has been left unpainted, giving the wagon an untidy appearance. Beyond the signal box, which is still in LMS colours, probably light and dark stone, with a black and white nameboard, an Up Euston express is heading towards Rugby station, which is visible in the left distance. Most of the stock is of Stanier design, and is still in LMS crimson lake livery. Beyond the rear coach, the cattle dock sidings are crammed to capacity, and a mix of stock occupies the rest of the yard. This busy scene, with motive power, stock and structures in a variety of liveries, typified the early BR period, whilst the dingy state of the paintwork on the signal box and wagons reveals how run down the railway system was at this time.

Above: Gresley A4 No 60028, *Walter K Whigham*, which is starting away from the south end of Peterborough station with an Up express on 8th July 1949, had received a repaint from wartime black to LNER blue in October 1947, but was one of four A4 Pacifics to receive BR purple livery in June/July 1948. Given the widespread hostility to this unattractive colour scheme, an early decision was taken to switch to blue for further repaints, although existing engines remained unaffected for some time. 60028 retained purple livery until October 1950, when she was repainted into standard BR 'first line' blue, but this livery was also doomed to early extinction, and she received lined green in February 1952, her fourth colour scheme in less than five years. The A4 Pacifics, with their modernistic styling, were well suited to the functional Gill Sans lettering, which had been devised by the artist Eric Gill for the LNER, but the purple was no more pleasant than the modern GNER livery on the East Coast Main Line. Uniquely, the purple engines were the only A4s to carry BRITISH RAILWAYS titling and lining out on the tender and fine lining on the edge of the running plate as well. The lining and lettering were not in the familiar pale cream, but in silver-white which helps explain the high contrast between the lettering and paintwork. In contrast to the grimy state of many LM Region engines, Kings Cross 'Top Shed' made sure that their express passenger engines were immaculately turned out, as the condition of 60028 reveals.

Above: If a BR image was to be created, a new livery was needed, and on 30th January 1948, Robin Riddles arranged a livery parade at Kensington (Addison Road) for the Railway Executive members. Arguing that Midland/LMS crimson lake would be unpopular on the other regions, where green had predominated, Riddles arranged that three Stanier 'Black Fives' were lined up in LNER apple green, GWR Brunswick green and SR malachite green, but no final decision was taken. Riddles had secretly arranged with Crewe for another Black Five to receive the old LNWR livery of black, lined out with a fine red line and a broader cream/grey line. Delighted at the thought of putting one across the Midland, Crewe gave

'their' engine an exhibition finish. Asked if he had anything more to show the Railway Executive, Riddles' reincarnation of the Crewe spirit hove into sight. RE members were impressed, and it is said that General Sir Bill Slim, who must have known more about railways than he is credited with, or was a quick learner, realised what Riddles was up to, and turned to him, saying 'You Bastard, Riddles'. Although the RE might have backed Riddles' personal preference, the BTC wanted a more colourful finish, so fourteen engines were turned out in various shades, and unleashed on the railway network later in 1948. LNER apple green, when lined out in black and white, looked dramatic, but former LMS 'Patriot'

4-6-0 No 45531, *Sir Frederick Harrison*, received an ultra light shade of apple green, and was lined out in North Western fashion. The result was insipid, yet garish. One reason Riddles favoured black was the difficulty in recruiting sufficient cleaning staff, and this portrait of a grimy 45531 at the south end of Crewe station in 1949, reveals how disreputable even a first link express locomotive could become. Eighteen Patriots were rebuilt with a Stanier double-chimney taper boiler, transforming their looks and performance. The Palethorpes sausage advert to the right of 45531 was a familiar sight on railway stations at this time.

Opposite page bottom: For first line express duties, a variety of liveries, from light blue through deep ultramarine, to an almost purple shade, were tried out. My father said that some were repellent, but mercifully, the RE opted for an azure blue, similar to the Caledonian Railway 'Perth' blue, with black and white lining, rather than LNWR style lining, which did not look happy on green or blue engines. The livery was only applied to a handful of classes, including first line LNER, LMS and Southern Pacifics, and the magnificent GWR '60xx' King class 4-6-0s. I must have seen Stanier Pacifics in blue, but the only engines I can clearly recall in blue were the 'Kings'. No 6004, *King George III*, blows off at Leamington Spa General station with an Up Paddington express during the summer of 1952. Built between 1927 and 1930, the entire class remained on top link duties until 1962, when all thirty engines went in a matter of just eleven months. Apart from the blue livery, this view depicts the bicycling lion emblem adopted at Sir Cyril Hurcomb's behest. As well as setting the style for Great Western steam for the rest of the company's existence, George Jackson Churchward had a dramatic effect on coaching stock design as well, and his adoption of 70 foot long bodies placed the GWR in the forefront of coaching stock design. The Diagram D43 brake 3rds

of 1906, with their profusion of recessed doors, which earned them their 'Concertina' nickname, were still to be found on prestige services in the early years of BR. With the locomotive in a vivid blue, and set off to perfection by the black and white lining, and stock adorned in the lively carmine and cream livery, it was a colourful period.
H J Stretton-Ward

Below: Only a few classes carried the blue livery, and this delightful scene at Bournemouth Central shed on 19th July 1951, recalls the liveries applied to engines lower down the 'pecking order', and the atmosphere of a busy station in steam days. A Drummond T9 4-4-0, a Maunsell 'Lord Nelson', and a Urie H15 manoeuvre on shed, whilst another Maunsell 4-6-0 is waiting for them to clear. The days when the T9s were premier passenger engines have long gone, but they were useful on stopping passenger and freight turns, so lined black mixed traffic livery was appropriate, with a small emblem on the tender. The H15, No 30473, another mixed traffic design, is also in BR lined black livery, but the Lord Nelson, No 30857, *Lord Howe*, is far more important. Built between 1926 and 1929, the sixteen Lord Nelson 4-6-0s had been designed by Maunsell to handle 500 ton continental boat expresses on the Eastern section of the SR to and from Dover, but also did valuable work on the Western section to Southampton and Bournemouth. Until the arrival of the Bulleid 'Merchant Navies' they were the premier SR passenger engines, but were not regarded as eligible for the elite blue livery in 1948. For the second tier of express passenger types, the Railway Executive adopted GWR 'Brunswick' green lined out in black and orange, as in Great Western days. It was a choice that must have gone down well in Swindon, though it was not so popular on the LM region, or on the Eastern region. No 30757, *Lord Howe*, received BR 'standard' green in December 1949, and was withdrawn 1962.

Opposite page top: Locomotive livery is very personal, and can generate more heat than light amongst enthusiasts. Often we have a particular regard for the liveries of our childhood. To my youthful mind, the most eye-catching train was the Golden Arrow, with a gleaming Bulleid Pacific in green, lined out in black and orange, and carrying a gigantic golden arrow on the smokebox door. Medical duties sometimes took my father up to London, and occasionally, we made it a family outing, which could include a trip on the Thames, a visit to one of the London termini, a signal box, or even a loco depot, though this was rare, as his workload as a doctor seldom permitted such indulgence. Stewarts Lane, with 170 engines at its peak, was responsible for prestige services on the former Brighton and South Eastern & Chatham sections of the Southern Region. It was one of the most exciting London sheds, with 'King Arthurs', 'Lord Nelsons', 'Merchant Navy', and 'West Country/Battle of Britain' Pacifics for top link passenger turns such as the Golden Arrow or the Night Ferry boat trains. It was a compact site, with a 16 road shed, flanked by two railway viaducts to the west, one of which crossed over the other less than fifty yards from the shed building, whilst a third viaduct straddled the shed approach at the east of the shed. A number of 'Battle of Britain' and 'West Country' Pacifics, including 34083, *605 Squadron*, were kept for the Golden Arrow, and when ready for duty, looked stunning. The British and French flags on the front of the engine gave the finishing touch.

Opposite page bottom: Riddles realised that whilst a few engines had to be in bright colours to satisfy the BTC, the shortage of cleaners meant that black was the only possible livery for most engines. Although freight engines would be unlined, secondary classes would look more attractive if they were lined out. The LMS and LNER used a single red line, but this was not very striking, so was hardly worth the effort. As a North Western man, Riddles recalled LNWR black lined out in red, grey and cream, and I have already recounted the story of the Addison Road display. Given that most North Western men recalled the tactless way in which Midland crimson lake had been applied to North Western engines, Riddles must have gained pleasure in arranging for its return. Rugby mpd's No 45020 is depicted shunting stock for a Peterborough train at the south end of Rugby station on 21st June 1951.

Above: It is said that revenge is sweet, and Riddles enjoyed it in full. The Midland faction on the LMS had not only applied crimson lake to North Western engines, but insisted that the Midland 4P Compound became a Group standard. Many were built, and although adequate for the short trains on the Midland division of the LMS, were too weak for the heavier North Western trains, and were universally detested. With the adoption of LNWR style livery, the wheel turned full circle, as Midland Compounds were garbed in North Western colours! A Rugby compound, No 41105, has arrived in platform 8, with a local service from Peterborough. The 1880s train shed roof at Rugby survived until demolition by Railtrack.

Above: Riddles' re-incarnation of the glories of Crewe spread further than Derby's crimson lake had reached, even in its heyday, as it could soon be seen from Cornwall to the north of Scotland, and from West Wales to East Anglia. 67361, an Ivatt class C12 4-4-2T, which was allocated to Peterborough New England shed, received the Riddles treatment, prior to being photographed as station pilot at Peterborough in 1951. One wonders how Henry Alfred Ivatt would have responded had he seen his engines in North Western livery, but he had been dead for a quarter of a century. His reaction would probably have been to give a quiet chuckle, for Ivatt had joined the North Western as a premium apprentice at the age of 17, and had risen to take charge of Holyhead shed, before moving to the Chester district. In 1877, he joined the Great Southern & Western Railway, serving under his life long friend J A F Aspinall for some years, before becoming Loco Engineer at Inchicore in 1886. In 1895, he moved to the GNR at Doncaster, retiring in 1911. Ivatt's son H G Ivatt became the last CME of the LMSR, whilst his daughter Marjorie married a young locomotive engineer called Oliver Bulleid! Although there were rivalries in the locomotive world, there were close personal friendships, and ties of kith and kin, or of marriage.

Left: The crew of Edge Hill based Stanier 'Jubilee' 45567 *South Australia* pose with their steed to provide an excellent view of the latest fashions for footplate crews with the new totem BR cap badges at the start of the 1950s. Seen as the aristocrats of the railway work force, the path to becoming a top link driver was long and arduous. It started as a humble cleaner, picking up knowledge from day to day contact with engines and enginemen, and attending voluntary classes. The next step was to become a passed cleaner, who would take occasional minor firing turns. After some years experience, promotion to fireman was the next hurdle, working through the links from bottom to top, before promotion to passed fireman. The most humble driving turns were then open. Once again, the driver worked his way through the links, and the top duties might only come to a man in his fifties. Because promotion to the senior driving links required years of experience, footplate men had an immense pride in their calling, and I regard myself as privileged to have met some of these fine men. From a very early age, I was taken to the station in my pram by a retired top link driver, who had been a patient of my father and his father before him, in order that I might be properly 'trained. Alas, I did not think to write down his name, so that is lost, but I am sure that being introduced to steam engines at such an early age was helpful. I understand that my mentor, who had stayed on after retirement age until the end of the war, and was well known to the drivers on the West Coast Main Line, would indicate to his younger colleagues that a friendly whistle would not be out of place. Forty years after steam was banished from Rugby, I still love to hear the sound of a Stanier hooter.

Below: Although steam dominated British Railways in 1948, there was one area where it had been under challenge for more than quarter of a century. Because it was without equal in size and intensity of operation, the Southern electric network continued on its way scarcely altered by 1948. There was no suggestion of interchange trials, nor was there much technology transfer at first, as the Southern had more experience of electric train operation than the other five regions put together. Given the preponderance of SR stock in the electric multiple units taken over by BR, once the decision had been taken to adopt a separate livery for electric stock, it made sense to adopt Bulleid Southern green as the BR standard, so former LMS Merseyside cars and LNER Tyneside stock came to resemble their more numerous cousins south of the Thames. For once, the tail wagged the rest of the dog, to the delight of Southern men, who were used to coming last. As 4-SUB set No 4228 glides over Sheen Lane level crossing at Mortlake on 14th May 1950, there is little to reveal that the Southern Railway is no more than a name. This set had commenced life in LSWR days, when third rail electric services were introduced in 1915-16 under the leadership of Sir Herbert Walker, the general manager of the London & South Western Railway. 84 three car sets passed into Southern ownership in 1923, being numbered 1201-1284 by the SR. They were intended in run as single sets on lightly loaded services, as two sets in multiple giving 6 cars, or with an intervening trailer coach, to provide a 7-car formation. With ever increasing traffic, the SR decided to convert its 3-car sets to 4-car units, commencing with the 1201 series in 1942. There were two types, compartment and saloon stock, saloon sets gaining an ex-LSWR 11 compartment trailer, and being renumbered 4195-4234. The O route code with a horizontal line above it denoted the balloon shaped route from Waterloo, via Richmond and Hounslow, to Waterloo. Services proceeding round the loop in the other direction, calling at Hounslow first, carried a plain O without a bar. For railwaymen and regular travellers, it was an excellent system, conveying destination data instantly and simply. The crossing box is of LSWR origin, and once the line had been electrified, this scene would have scarcely altered for many years. *R E Tustin*

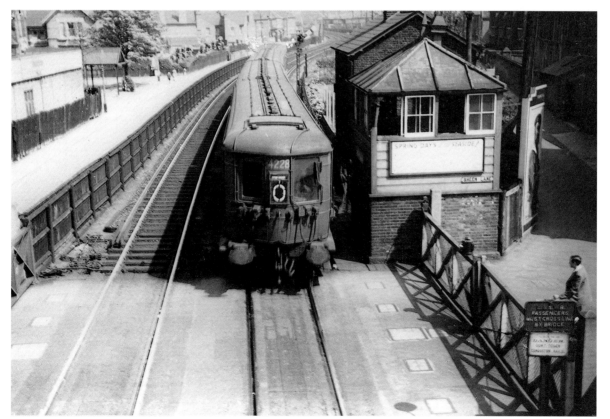

Below: Rambling was encouraged by the railway companies in the 1930s, but during the war, frivolous travel was discouraged. In 1950, the Southern Region published WINTER WALKS IN SURREY AND KENT by S P B Mais, to promote weekend traffic in winter. Mais was a popular writer with an easy and chatty style, and opened the Southern guide in characteristic form, 'WINTER is by far the best time of year for walking if you are patient enough to wait for the right sort of day. In the summer there is so much else to do, tennis, cricket, bowls, swimming or just lying in a hammock. On hot August days no one can take much pleasure in walking'. This time, his job was to promote winter leisure. He did so with aplomb, recommending the Rambler leave London not later than 9.30am, 'because the winter sun quickly loses its power after two o'clock'. In winter, he recommended short walks, 'It is all very well in summer to take a packed luncheon and lie on some sunkissed down with the scent of wild thyme all round you, but in winter you cannot enjoy eating out of doors. You need a hot meal if possible'. Needless to say, he was always well shod on his rambles, but Mrs Mais was apparently less so, 'I have seen my wife lose both her shoes in a wet meadow and have to walk thereafter stockingless and chilled'.

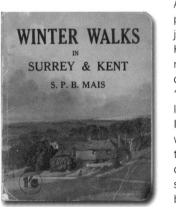

Top: Seaford is a pleasant resort on the south coast near Newhaven, and is the terminus of the former London, Brighton & South Coast Railway Newhaven branch. Unit 1823, at Seaford on 14th May 1951, is a 2-NOL unit, and carries the Central Section 28 reporting code of a Victoria and Portsmouth Harbour, Brighton and Seaford service. Under Walker's management, the Southern was progressive, with its widespread electrification, but was also frugal, and many 2-car sets were converted from ex-LSWR steam stock in 1934-36. They comprised a motor coach with driving compartment, a luggage/guard's section and passenger accommodation and a driving trailer with a motorman's section and 9 compartments, three being first class. The leading vehicle is a driving trailer, and the second car is a motor coach, identified by a side lookout, or ducket in the guard's section. It is coupled to another 2-NOL set, the motor coach being the leading vehicle on that set. *R E Tustin*

opposite page top: O V S Bulleid, who became CME of the SR in 1937, is remembered for his steam classes, but also contributed electric stock. The panelled finish of the Maunsell era was out, as were curved driving ends and the Olive Green livery that had characterised Southern stock since 1923. Ideas for flush-sided stock were in draft form by 1939, but the first unit did not appear until 1941, and even then retained domed ends. The decisive break came with 4-SUB sets 4111-4120, which emerged in 1946. The body curved inwards from waist, and made a smooth transition to the roof panels, which were painted body colour. The prototype, 4111, at Clapham Junction on 23rd August 1947, carries SOUTHERN across the front , and set the style for new electric stock for many years, not just on the Southern Region, but elsewhere on BR, where Southern influence became significant. The route code indicates it is a Central Section service from Victoria to Beckenham Junction, calling at Clapham Junction, Streatham Hill, and Crystal Palace. *R E Tustin*

Below: Although most suburban passenger services in the London area had been electrified by 1947, expresses were steam hauled, as was freight, necessitating steam servicing facilities. Operating steam and electric traction was costly, and Bulleid realised that by electrifying freight and long distance passenger services, steam traction could eventually be abolished in the London area and the whole of the south east, with resultant savings. Two prototype Co-Co electric locomotives, CC1 and CC2 were built in 1941 and 1945, becoming 20001 and 20002 under BR. A third improved engine, 20003, appeared in 1948. Their tractive effort, of 45,000 lbs, was exceptional. Because third rail electrification is dangerous in goods yards, a pantograph was fitted, so that the engines could draw power from an overhead supply when this was installed. CC2, with BRITISH RAILWAYS lettering on the body, is running through Hersham on 23rd April 1948. They were tried on the Victoria to Newhaven boat expresses, but their main work was on freights from the yards at New Cross Gate and Norwood, to Polegate or Portsmouth. All three were broken up in 1969. *R E Tustin*

Above: Apart from new liveries for motive power in 1948, the RE had to select colour schemes for the remainder of its rolling stock, as unification and a nationwide image was a key goal set by Sir Cyril Hurcomb. After a number of trials, three main liveries were selected, carmine and cream for express passenger stock, all-over carmine for suburban stock, and Southern malachite green for electric multiple units. As there were only a handful of diesel railcars in passenger service on BR, no official decision seems to have been taken, an omission that the Western region was happy to pounce on. Although the WR would have preferred GWR chocolate and cream, if that was ruled out, carmine and cream was the next best thing, and as some of the GWR cars were used on long distance fast services, the WR decreed that they merited express livery. As the GWR had more diesel railcars than the rest of BR, and Riddles was acutely aware of the need to treat

Paddington with kid gloves, the RE seems to have accepted Swindon's decision without demur. The first GWR diesel rail-car had appeared in February 1934. It was not the first diesel car to operate in the British Isles, for the LMS had tried out an experimental unit as early as 1928, but with little success, and the first company to operate diesel railcars in regular passenger service was the County Donegal Railways Joint Committee in 1931, with the Great Northern Railway (Ireland) following suit in 1932. However, the GWR, with its greater resources, had progressed from one car in 1934, to 38 cars by 1942, and with their stylish streamlined looks, had captured public imagination in the way none of its contemporaries managed. The first large batch of railcars, No's 8 to 17, came in 1936, No 12 being one of three cars fitted with lavatories for long distance services. Costing £5,164, they enabled the GWR to increase frequencies on some routes and develop traffic, or to reduce costs on branch lines. W12W, which is depicted at Birmingham (Snow Hill), moved around quite a bit in early BR days, being based at Oxford in July 1949, transferring to Reading in December 1949, and back to Oxford in 1950, before a spell at Llanelly, with a final return to Oxford.

Opposite page bottom: On non-corridor and secondary stock, the sides were painted carmine red. The ends, underframe, and bogies were black, and the roof was light grey. In theory, the lettering was unshaded golden-yellow, but in reality, it was a pale straw. Lettering on cast iron data plates on the ends was usually white. To avoid duplication of numbers, until a renumbering scheme had been worked out, locomotives had been allotted a regional prefix. With coaching stock, where so many more vehicles were involved, the prefix became permanent. At first, just a prefix was applied W for the GWR; S for the Southern, M for the LMS and E for the LNER, but the RE wanted the coach number to indicate its

regional allocation, of which there were six. From 1951, a suffix was added, indicating the region concerned. A recently overhauled M14984M, seen at Rugby Midland station c1952, is a wooden bodied non-corridor 3rd, and displays the black end, solebar and buffing gear, light grey roof and 1951 pattern number, which reveals that it is a former LMS vehicle and is allocated to the LM region. Had this coach been allocated to the Scottish Region, it would have been lettered M14984SC, whilst North Eastern region vehicles carried an NE suffix.

Above: Even though former LMS men dominated the mechanical engineering side of the Railway Executive, the RE adopted the sensible LNER system of painting wagons according to whether they were fitted or unfitted, as it simplified shunting. Fitted stock was bauxite, whilst unfitted stock would be grey. As BR grey was much lighter than the LNER or GWR shade, it would be difficult to make out the numbers in bad light, or when the wagon was dirty so numbering and other lettering was painted on a rectangular black ground. Although tens of thousands of wagons had been turned out by the LMS each year from 1923, the sheer volume of pre-grouping stock meant that many pre-1923 wagons were still in traffic in 1948. Former Caledonian Railway goods brake No 288 had been numbered 353288 by the LMS after 1923. Under BR, freight stock received a regional coding, W for ex GWR stock, S for Southern, M for LMS and E for LNER, whilst BR designs were accorded a B prefix. The black patch for the number and tare figures on the left is conspicuous, as is the black background to the NOT IN COMMON USE branding, which was applied to brake vans used on special duties. The cracked and decaying wooden framework is noticeable, as are the cracking in the headstocks and solebars.

Above: Apart from motive power and rolling stock, there was the daunting task of maintaining thousands of structures spread the length and breadth of the land. Given the number of stations, each with several buildings, the thousands of bridges, and myriad of notices, maintaining the infrastructure had been costly before World War One, and with road competition and the Great Depression in the Twenties eating into funds, maintenance had been slashed to a minimum by the Thirties. A lean decade, followed by six years of total war, when station repainting and repairs all but ceased, left the railways in a drab state by 1945. Staff shortages, rationing of vital materials and the uncertainty engendered by the looming threat of nationalisation meant that little was achieved in the remaining couple of years. The GWR goods shed at Chip-

ping Campden, in the Cotswolds, seen on 19th September 1948, is indicative of how dire the situation was. The paintwork is grimy and peeling, planks are missing, dislodged or cracked in many places, and the new wood that is in evidence has not received a coat of paint. Slates are missing from the roof of the lean-to, and from the main roof itself. Some stations that closed in early BR days were never to carry the new regional colours that were adopted after 1948, and my father and I visited a few country stations that still carried LMS colours in the mid-Sixties. I know of at least one station that was not repainted in over thirty years, but that is by no means the limit with the lead paints that were then in use, which were far superior to modern paints that peel off after a few years. I had a graphic demonstration of this in 1998. I had been meaning to repaint a window that was obstructed by a rose bush. Eventually the bush went, and attached to the window frame, where it had been hidden for many years, was the remains of a World War 2 blackout screen. It showed no traces of over-painting, indicating that the window had not been repainted in sixty years, yet in places the lead paint was still sound. *R E Tustin*

Opposite page bottom: In the early months of the Railway Executive, it was hard to believe that the companies were no more. Banbury is a thriving market town roughly midway between Oxford and Leamington on the busy Great Western route from Paddington to Birmingham. For over a century, it was also the terminus of a straggling cross country route of the erstwhile London & North Western Railway, and the end point of an even more obscure line, the Northampton & Banbury Junction Railway, which left the LNWR at Cockley Brake Junction a few miles out of Banbury and ran across the grain of the country to Towcester and Blisworth. It later became part of the Stratford-upon-Avon & Midland Junction Railway. It is the afternoon of 18th September 1948, and the sun shines down on a busy moment at Banbury (Merton Street) station. British Railways is less than nine months old, and there is little to show that the London Midland & Scottish Railway is no more. Stanier 2-6-4T No 2591 still carries her LMS number, as does Johnson 3F goods No 3544. The Stanier tank is on the 3.45pm from Merton Street to Bletchley, whilst the Johnson 0-6-0 is on the 4.45pm from Merton Street to Towcester and Blisworth. The train shed roof, which is less than 120 feet in length, so can barely hold two modern bogie carriages under cover, dates from the opening of the station on 1st May 1850, and is a relic of the early days of covered train sheds at minor termini. The Merton Street sign in the foreground is more modern, for it is an LMS Hawkseye sign, to a design that was first introduced in 1934. The lettering is in black, the background being covered in highly reflective yellow glass spheres or beads, to improve visibility at night. In a retrograde move, BR will soon chop away all the beads, in order to apply standard London Midland Region house colours of red with white lettering. Cattle wagons are seen on the right, for Banbury cattle market was one of the most important cattle markets in the area, and a 300 foot long cattle dock flanked the station. Passenger traffic had

B.R. 87215

(*Form referred to in Rules 175 clause (c), 183, clauses (f) and (g), 184 and 203*).

THE RAILWAY EXECUTIVE.

.... REGION.
(A supply of these Forms must be kept in each signal box.)

WRONG LINE ORDER FORM D.
SIGNALMAN TO DRIVER.

To Driver of Engine No.:..*working*

....*train.*

I authorise you to travel with your train on the*...line in the wrong direction to this signal box.

Catch points, spring or unworked trailing points exist at..

Signed...*Signalman.*

at..signal box.

Date.........................19......... Time issued......................m.

† Countersigned...

Signalman.
at.. signal box.

* Insert name of line, for example, Up or Down Main, Fast, Slow or Goods.
† If necessary.

never been heavy, with around five trains each way on the line to Buckingham and Bletchley, and a couple of trips each way on the Blisworth route, but numbers were falling off, and the Blisworth service ended on 2nd July 1951, the Buckingham and Bletchley services ending ten years later. Cattle traffic was also in decline, and by the mid sixties, the station lay silent, the platform projecting out like a forgotten pier into a sea of encroaching weeds. *R E Tustin*

Above: Although BRITISH RAILWAYS was used as the public face of the new era, internal operating forms, such as this WRONG LINE ORDER FORM D, bore the new title, THE RAILWAY EXECUTIVE, with space left for the region. The only reference to BR on the forms was in the re-order code, BR 87215. Wrong direction movements on running lines pose a risk of collision if they are not rigidly controlled and everyone knows what is happening. The Wrong Line order form, of which four varieties existed, was issued to the driver to sanction a wrong direction movement. It was needed in the event of a train breaking down and requiring an assisting engine to proceed wrong direction to retrieve it, a train becoming divided, so that the engine could set back to collect the rear portion, or a train being withdrawn in the wrong direction from a section, due to some obstruction ahead of it.

The Common Seal of the Railway Executive was hereunto affixed in the presence of }

Member

Secretary

The Common Seal of the London Transport Executive was hereunto affixed in the presence of }

Member

Secretary

The Common Seal of the Isle of Man Railway Company was hereunto affixed in the presence of }

Director

Secretary

The Common Seal of the Ulster Transport Authority was hereunto affixed in the presence of }

Member

Secretary

9

Sealed with the Common Seal of the Sligo Leitrim and Northern Counties Railway Company in the presence of }

Director

Director

Secretary

Sealed with the Common Seal of the Londonderry and Lough Swilly Railway Company in the presence of }

Director

Director

Secretary

Sealed with the Common Seal of Coras Iompair Eireann in the presence of }

Director

Director

Secretary

Sealed with the Common Seal of the Great Northern Railway Company (Ireland) in the presence of }

Director

Director

Secretary

11

Sealed with the Common Seal of the County Donegal Railways Joint Committee in the presence of }

Director

Director

Secretary

Signed Sealed and Delivered by the Secretary of the Irish Railway Clearing House in the presence of }

Signed Sealed and Delivered on behalf of the Postmaster General by
DUDLEY OWEN LUMLEY
(an officer of the Post Office duly authorised in that behalf by or under Section 12 of the Post Office (Amendment) Act, 1935), in the presence of }

Private Secretary
General Post Office

On behalf of Her Majesty's Postmaster General.

Left and above: From the dawn of the railway age, important contracts were completed by the use of the company seal. This was a skilfully engraved two-part metal die that was mounted in a press tool, and embossed a heraldic image onto a document which was placed between the jaws of the press. Great formality surrounded 'the sealing' of any document, as the seal could only be affixed in the presence of one or more directors. From well over 100 major railway companies and a host of smaller lines at the time of the grouping in 1923, just nine railway administrations survived in the British Isles to provide all-year passenger services by 1953. The youngest, but the biggest was The Railway Executive of the British Transport Commission, which had been set up under the Transport Act 1947. The oldest, and the smallest by 1953 was the Londonderry & Lough Swilly Railway Company, which dated back to 1853. In April 1953, all nine surviving railway administrations put their signatures to an agreement over parcels post with the British Postmaster-General and the Irish Minister of Posts. It was the last time that several of them would do so. Within a few weeks, the Lough Swilly was to operate its last train, and the Railway Executive, which had overseen British Railways ever since nationalisation, was to be consigned to the dustbin of history by ministerial dictat. Few readers will have ever seen 'The Common Seal' of the Railway Executive, let alone of all nine railways, so it seems appropriate to recall this moment in history.

In most cases, the embossed seals were pressed without ink, but the Railway Executive and LT used a thin waxed paper wafer, whilst the Ulster transport Authority used a wafer with the UTA heraldic device in red and white. Each seal had to be affixed in the presence of the company secretary and at least one director, or member in the case of the statutory authorities such as the RE or UTA. This made the process very slow, but the signatories give especial interest to the document. Four of the officers who signed in their capacity as company secretary were also the general managers, and collectively put in over 130 years service in that demanding position, a record that would now be impossible to match. Signing at the head of the page on behalf of the Railway Executive was General Sir Daril Watson, GCB, CBE, MC, former Quartermaster-General of the Army, and appointed to the RE on the resignation of General Sir William Slim. E G Marsden, secretary to the RE, had come by way of the LNER and the wartime Railway Executive Committee. The LT signatories included A Herbert Grainger, a long term member of the LT and deputy chairman, and R M Robbins, who was secretary from 1950 to 1960, and a distinguished railway author as well. Third in the pecking order came the Isle of Man Railway, one of the signatories being R Q Hampton. As a young shareholder, Hampton had suggested extending the 2½ mile Foxdale branch to the summit of South Barrule as far back as 1912, He became chairman in 1937, dying in 1953. A M Sheard,

the manager and secrctary had joined the company in 1909, becoming manager when bus competition threatened its survival in 1927 and ran the railway until 1965, having broken the spirit of the bus competition in the process. J Sydney Rogers and T B Andison signed for the Ulster Transport Authority, the latter having been secretary of the Belfast & County Down Railway for many years. S C Little had been manager of the Sligo, Leitrim & Northern Counties ever since 1916 and was to remain in office until 1956, an amazing forty years, or about half the company's lifespan. Sir Basil McFarland, chairman of the Londonderry & Lough Swilly Railway had joined the LLSR board in 1921, maintaining a family association that stretched back to the 1880s, whilst James J W Whyte had joined the Swilly in 1910, and served as manager from 1931 to 1967, replacing trains with buses and lorries in 1953. Other notable signatories included R Stanley Stokes, who signed as a director of the GNR(I) and for the County Donegal Railways Joint Committee, whilst Capt. Sir Ian Bolton signed on behalf of the BTC, the other owning partner in the Donegal. Bolton was a member of the BTC from 1947 to 1959. Bernard Curran took over as CDRJC manager when Henry Forbes died in 1941, holding office at the end of rail operations in 1959.

Below: By 1953, the Sligo, Leitrim & Northern Counties Railway had the longest serving railway manager in the British Isles. The line was unusual in never numbering any of its engines, preferring to use names instead. Beyer Peacock 0-6-4T *Sir Henry* is seen at Manorhamilton, the company headquarters on 18th June 1948.

6 · CRISIS IN ULSTER

The bicentenary of Richard Trevithick's pioneer Penydarren locomotive of 1804, and the birth of railways, coincided with work on this book. For over half of that period, Ireland was an integral part of the United Kingdom, and its railways a part of the wider British railway scene. Senior officers moved back and forth across the Irish Sea and J A F Aspinall, H A Ivatt, R E L Maunsell, and J G Robinson, rose to high office in Ireland before moving to greater fame in England. After the demise of the Southern Railway, Oliver Bulleid made the reverse journey, to take up the reins at Inchicore, the headquarters of the locomotive department of the Eire's CIE. James Crawford Park, Locomotive Superintendent of the Great Northern Railway (Ireland) from 1881, had been head of the drawing office at Doncaster when the Stirling 'look' first evolved. How much of that look was due to Stirling, and how much to Park, is open to conjecture, but when Park moved to the GNR(I), the same look appeared on the Irish line. The Midland Railway bought an important Irish Railway company in 1903, regularly moving Midland officers back and forth. The LNWR had its own Irish satellite, whilst the GWR was part owner of

an Irish railway. The links were deep and enduring, but English railway writers seldom touch on Irish railway matters, and Irish writers have been similarly selective.

In writing of railways before 1948, an author can ask how the LMS solved one problem, and what the Southern or the GWR did? The same answer might not suit all, but such contrasts can be revealing. After the creation of BR in 1948, no such comparison is possible, as the autonomy left to the regions did not permit radically different solutions, so at a time when the railway industry faced unprecedented change, a useful analytical tool vanished, or did it? The railways of Northern Ireland, which is still part of the United Kingdom, and of the Independent Eire, faced similar troubles, and their tribulations offers light on what happened on BR, as well as being of absorbing interest themselves. The sheer size of BR meant that even BR officers found it hard 'to see the wood for the trees'. The smaller size of the Irish lines means that issues stand out clearly, offering a pointer to events on BR. I first became aware of the Irish railways sometime in the 1950s. Sadly much of Ireland's rail heritage vanished before I was old enough to photograph it, but I saw a variety of Irish motive power, and had the pleasure of meeting J H Houston, one or Ireland's legendary railway officers and a delightful character as well. I was given a full set of accounts of CIE and UTA, and material relating to the celebrated Great Northern Railway (Ireland). My father and I were given a UTA pass that permitted us to photograph at any UTA rail installation, the only exception being York Road works, an exception that hardly mattered, as Mr Houston himself took us on a conducted tour!

The broad outlines of English railway history are familiar to many readers, but some may be puzzled by the background to Ireland's railways, so a summary may help. Ireland's railways were built to two standard gauges, neither of which was common in England. The main lines were built to the Irish 5ft 3ins broad gauge, whilst some secondary lines were built to 3ft 0ins gauge. Until the start of the 1920s, Ireland was a part of the United Kingdom, but the Home Rule movement led to independence for the 26 Southern counties, six counties in Northern Ireland electing to remain a part of the UK. As a result of partition, the railways operating across the border between Northern Ireland and the South became International lines. In 1925, the southern government merged the lines operating exclusively in the south into Great Southern Railways, and in 1945, merged GSR with Dublin United Transport to form Coras Iompair Eireann. The International lines remained independent. Two lines operated exclusively in the north, the Belfast & County Down Railway, and the 'Northern Counties'.

Opposite page: The principal railway operating solely in Northern Ireland was the LMS Northern Counties Committee, which had been acquired from the Midland Railway at the Grouping in 1923. They in turn had purchased the hitherto independent Belfast & Northern Counties Railway, whose title summed up exactly where it went. Its lines ran north from Belfast, one route serving the Larne-Stranraer ferry route, whilst its main line ran up the Antrim coast, and eventually to Londonderry, giving off various short branches en route. Because of its LMS heritage, the 'Northern Counties' was the most English of Ireland's railways. Its motive power fleet in 1903 comprised some engines dating back to 1856, and they were still running in 1923, as the Midland, although willing to sanction new freight stock, seemed disinclined to invest in new motive power. When the LMS took over in 1923, they found that many engines were over 40 years old, and to tide the NCC over, placed an order with NBL to build the first of the U2 class 4-4-0s. They looked like a scaled down version of the standard MR/LMS 2P, of which many hundreds were turned out by Derby, and that is exactly what they were. The driving wheel diameter was reduced from 6 ft

9 ins to 6 ft; the cylinders fell from 19 x 26 ins to 19 x 24 ins, and boiler pressure was dropped from 180 to 170 lbs. The weight fell by about 3 tons, but the tractive effort was almost identical, as the smaller cylinders and lower pressure were matched by the smaller wheels. The Midland had left the NCC alone when it came to locomotive liveries and the old dark green of the BNCR persisted, but the LMS decreed that standard LMS crimson lake should prevail. Between 1929 and 1933, many of these Irish 2Ps received handsome brass nameplates with a 'Castle' theme. The newly named No 83 *Carra Castle*, is seen at Belfast (York Road) in 1932. She was built by NBL in 1925 and ran until 1956.
H J Stretton-Ward

Below: The LMS NCC was nearing the end of its life when this Consignment note from Portstewart to Dungannon on the GNR(I) was issued in August 1946. Even a brief study of the text reveals the complexity of operating a common carrier rail system, taking everything from carriages to poultry by train.

Above: In the early 1930s, the NCC required a mixed traffic design, capable of handling expresses or a pick up goods. A broad gauge version of the Stanier taper boilered 2-6-0 might have seemed logical, but William Stanier, the newly appointed CME of the parent LMS, was happy to leave the design work for the new NCC engines to Derby. This was politically wise, as it enabled Stanier to concentrate on modernising the parent LMS loco fleet, whilst keeping the Derby Drawing office happy, after a period when its star had been in the wane. Derby wanted nothing to do with Stanier or Hughes engines, creating a tender version of the Fowler 2-6-4Ts, with the same 19 x 26 ins inclined cylinders and 200lb boiler pressure, but the driving wheel diameter was increased by 3 ins to a round 6ft 0ins. Unusually for locomotives designed during the Fowler era on the LMS, the 2-6-4Ts had been given long lap valve gear, instead of the usual outdated Midland design, making them lively and economical performers. The NCC Class W 'Moguls' as they became known, benefited from this close kinship, and were lively and effective locomotives, and a marked improvement on older NCC power. Their heyday was probably between 1934 and 1939, with the crack 'North Atlantic Express' between Belfast and Portrush. In 1938-39, the morning working, the 8.10am ex Portrush was given an 'even time' booking of 31 minutes for the 31 miles between Ballymena and Belfast, an amazing achievement considering the route. Several were named after rivers in NCC territory, and No 92 *The Bann*, built at Derby in 1933, is seen shunting at Ballymoney on 12th June 1948. They were the sort of engine that the Midland Railway might well have built for itself had the grouping not come along in 1923, so represent a fascinating missing link in MR locomotive evolution. *R E Tustin*

Opposite page bottom: In January 1931, Major Malcolm Speir, then Assistant General Superintendent of the LMS in Scotland, was appointed manager of the NCC. Speir had worked for the MR and Caledonian railways before 1914, and had a distinguished war record with three mentions in despatches and an MC. It was a timely move, as the NCC had suffered a 104% operating ratio in 1930, its first loss, other than in the general strike year of 1926, since the Midland take-over back in 1903. Speir closed some chronic loss making routes, instituted many economies in staffing and operation, and realised that traditional methods of operating lightly used services with steam trains were no longer viable. In 1931, long before the first GWR diesel railcars were running, he recommended that a pair of bogie railcars be built for services on the lightly used Derry Central section of the NCC. They entered traffic in 1933 and 1934. Two more sophisticated cars, No's 3 and 4 followed in 1935 and 1938. They were powered by a pair of Leyland 125hp diesel engines, driving via Lysholm-Smith hydraulic torque converters. NCC railcar No 1 could haul a lightweight trailer, but with no remote control capability, had to run round the car at the end of the journey. Malcolm Speir realised that with an elevated driving position, the railcar could be the central unit in a three coach train, propelling one trailer and hauling the other, so 2, 3 and 4 were provided with high level turrets at each end for the driver. The system worked well until the day that the train met a cow that had resolved to test out George Stephenson's dictum about the effect of a collision between a cow and a train. As Stephenson prophesied, it was 'too bad for the coo', but the bovine might count it a moral victory, as the lightweight trailer finished up thoroughly derailed. The idea of propelling trailers at up to 70 mph lost its appeal thereafter. Railcar No 3 is seen at Belfast (York Road) on 11th June 1948. Despite a 10% decline in passenger traffic, and a 30% drop in freight traffic, between 1929 and 1939, Speir was able to return the NCC to profitability in 1939, for the first time in a decade. Speir's economies, including wage cuts, made him some enemies, but I recall NCC men speaking warmly of 'the Major', and his dedication to the NCC long after he had left Northern Ireland. *R E Tustin*

Below: Apart from the broad gauge, the NCC still operated two separate 3 ft 0 ins narrow gauge sections in the 1940s. The Ballymena lines had developed piecemeal from the 1870s, and comprised the Ballymena, Cushendall & Red Bay Railway, which opened in 1875-76, to serve the iron mines in the hills above Ballymena, and was acquired by the Belfast & Northern Counties Railway in 1884, and the Ballymena & Larne of 1877, which was taken over in 1889. Totalling 55 route miles at its peak, the first closures came in 1930, and following a lengthy strike on the Irish railways in 1933, all passenger services ceased. The heterogeneous mixture of engines acquired from its constituents did not impress the BNCR, so in 1891 work began on a new class of compound 2-4-2Ts. Six Class S locomotives appeared between 1892 and 1920. Generally an excellent design, their only defect was an inadequate coal supply, and on two engines, the main frames were extended behind the cab, the rear radial truck was lengthened, and a coal bunker placed on the extension behind the cab backsheet. The recently rebuilt No 102, which had been built as a class S in 1908, and rebuilt with an extended bunker to class S1 in 1930, is seen at Ballymena in 1931 on the six-wheeled locomotive transporter wagon No 3045. This wagon was specially designed to move NG section locomotives between the NG lines and the main NCC works at Belfast York Road. To avoid conflict with the broad gauge Moguls that were numbered from 90 upwards, NG section No 102 was renumbered 42, shortly before a new Mogul was delivered with that number in 1940. After the closure of the narrow gauge, No 42 was stored for a while, and broken up in 1954. *H J Stretton-Ward*

Above: After the 1933 passenger closures, freight ran over most of the narrow gauge until 1940, when all but twelve miles between Larne and some paper mills at Ballyclare was closed. For the last mile between Larne Town and Larne Harbour stations, the broad and narrow gauge systems ran side by side, and a complex network of mixed gauge tracks existed at Larne Harbour. Although found in many countries where different gauges existed, mixed gauge was rare in the British Isles after the demise of the GWR broad gauge in 1892, so this view of Larne Harbour station, looking towards the quays from Olderfleet Road, is welcome. From left to right, we see one broad gauge and five narrow gauge tracks that provide access to the quays at the far end. Next is the signal box with its characteristic NCC overhung hipped roof.

CRISIS IN ULSTER 83

To the right are more mixed gauge sidings, with the funnel of an LMS steamer on the skyline. The broad gauge platforms are to the right of the steamer. When the Ballyclare paper mill closed in 1950, the Ulster Transport Authority, which had taken over from the NCC, quickly disposed of it. Official closure took place on 3rd July 1950, although the last train had run several weeks previously, as there was no longer any work for it to do. *R E Tustin*

Opposite page bottom: The other narrow gauge line to enter the UTA was the Ballycastle Railway. This 16 mile line joined the NCC main line at Ballymoney with the seaside resort of Ballycastle. It had been independent until March 1924 when rising costs forced it into liquidation. It was purchased by the LMS NCC for £12,500 and reopened. Unlike the Ballymena lines, where passenger services ended after 1933, the Ballycastle line continued to convey passengers, but by 1948, its future was in doubt. Frantic road competition arose in the Twenties, and a government sponsored road transport monopoly, the Northern Ireland Road Transport Board, which had been set up in 1935 to co-ordinating transport in the province, had become a rival, rather than a partner, and had exacerbated the problem. Class S tank No 43 is coaling at Ballymoney on 12th June 1948. Broad gauge wagons are shunted to the right of the coaling stage, and the contents emptied by hand into wicker hampers, which are stacked on the coal platform and later tipped on to the cab floor, over the tanks, or even carried on the front running plate. The UTA closed the Ballycastle section on 3rd July 1950. With the demise of the Ballycastle section, NCC narrow gauge operations had come to an end. *R E Tustin*

Above: On the broad gauge, ten class WT 2-6-4Ts, No's 1 to 10, had been delivered in 1946-47, just prior to the demise of the NCC. They were a tank version of the pre-war Moguls, and ideal for NCC needs. A further eight engines came early in 1949-50. No 4, one of the 1947 engines, and the only 'Jeep', as they became known, to be preserved, is on the turntable at York Road, Belfast. The shed was one of many improvements effected by Malcolm Speir before he returned to Scotland in 1941. Speir's successor was a former LNWR man, Major Frank Pope. After two years on the NCC, Pope was appointed Chief Commercial Manager of the LMS, becoming a Vice President of the LMS Executive in 1946. His successor R H W Bruce, took over discussions Pope had initiated with the Northern Ireland Road Transport Board, and also brought in the GNR(I) general manager, George Howden. Everyone agreed that the 1935 road rail co-ordination plan needed revision, but other events intervened. Because of its LMS parentage, the NCC became a part of the RE on 1st January 1948, and briefly, paperwork and even wagon repair plates were lettered RE NCC. The RE had no wish to run the railways of Northern Ireland, and the Ulster government had passed its own Transport Act, setting up the Ulster Transport Authority, which commenced operations on 1st October 1948. Its remit was to co-ordinate road and rail passenger and freight services throughout the province, and it took over the Belfast & County Down Railway, the Northern Ireland Road Transport Board, and the NCC, which by agreement with the BTC, was retrospectively transferred to the UTA from 1st January 1948. The NCC was legally vested in the UTA on 1st April 1949.

Opposite page top: Because of his experience in Ulster, Frank Pope became chairman of the UTA in 1948. Goaded by government demands to achieve profitability, Pope was ruthless. As well as the 28 miles of narrow gauge line closed in July 1950, 82 miles of the NCC broad gauge were axed in July and August 1950, with expected savings of £250,000. Combined with 64 miles of ex Belfast & County Down metals closed earlier that year, the UTA had closed 174 route miles in nine months, leaving it with just 200 route miles, of which only 152 miles carried passenger services. Pope's other strategy was to adopt diesel railcars. In 1951, two NCC passenger coaches were rebuilt into railcars using standard bus engines. They retained pre-war beading and panelling, but later cars were more extensively treated. Known as the MED or Multi-Engined Diesel Trains, they were formed into three car sets with two driving power cars and an intermediate trailer. The first MED car, No 8, had been coach 206, and was converted in March 1952, and is at Belfast York Road on 23rd August 1968. It was withdrawn in February 1976. Earlier multiple unit cars had been wired on a north/south basis, and if a south-facing car was removed from a set, it could not be replaced by turning a north-facing car. If a set worked round a triangle, so that it was facing the 'wrong' way, it could not be connected to a set facing the right way, and the entire train function correctly. At Pope's behest, UTA engineers developed a spiral wiring system that permitted cars to face either way, yet respond correctly to the control desk in the leading unit. By 1951, the BTC was concerned about the deficit on BR, and felt that the RE was not pruning enough branch lines, or introducing diesel railcars. Given Frank Pope's action on the UTA, halving the passenger mileage in a few months, and his expertise on DMUs, Lord Hurcomb, the chairman of the BTC, wanted him to take over as chairman of the RE, but when this was rejected, Hurcomb arranged for Pope to join the BTC instead. In May 1951, Pope was appointed to the BTC, resigning as UTA chairman to do so. He remained a member of the BTC until his retirement in 1958, yet his role in pushing the development of the DMU, and in the pre-Beeching cuts, is little known today.

Opposite page bottom: The first Annual Report of the UTA noted, 'The workshops on the railway side, and still more so on the road side, were inadequate. Had the separate undertakings continued, new accommodation would have had to be provided for both the road and rail. It became imperative, therefore, to provide new combined workshops. Fortunately a suitable site was found on property belonging to the Northern Counties Committee at Duncrue Street'. Although locomotive repairs stayed at the NCC York Road works, the new Duncrue Street works handled railway passenger and freight stock, and building and repairs to the bus and lorry fleet. Agreement had been reached as early as August 1948, before the NCC was part of the UTA, and construction proceeded rapidly. The Ulster Minister of Commerce formally opened the 15 acre site in October 1950, although parts had been in use for a year. Apart from this joint road and rail vehicle works, the UTA was unusual in building bodies on chas-

sis supplied by the bus manufacturers, most operators buying from one of the body builders. The vehicle on the right, A8503, is a Leyland PSI Tiger single decker of 1947, with a Northern Ireland Road Transport Board B34R body, which survived until 1964. The near vehicle is a 1962 Leyland PD3/4 chassis, which is receiving a full fronted double deck body with a sliding door front entrance. Sadly, government directives to break even put pressure on the infant UTA, which fragmented, the ex NIRTB men dominating UTA thinking, to the detriment of the rail side.

Below: The LNWR was absorbed into the LMS in 1923, and its black locomotives, and coaches in purple lake and white, soon gained LMS colours, but in Ireland, black 0-6-0STs continued to haul purple lake and white coaches. This time-capsule was called the Dundalk, Newry & Greenore Railway. It was 26¾ miles long, and shaped like a V on its side, with the two arms linking up with the Great Northern Railway (Ireland) at Dundalk and Newry. The point of the V was at the port of Greenore, and the reason this line resembled the LNWR was that it had been financed by the company from its inception in the 1860s. Its creation was due to railway politics in the Irish Sea, and was to give the LNWR an additional foothold in the lucrative Irish Sea business. The DNGR opened in two sections in the 1870s, and was supplied with five 0-6-0STs, which were clones of the LNWR Ramsbottom 'Special Tanks'. When a sixth engine was needed in 1898, Crewe took LNWR No 900, a Ramsbottom DX 0-6-0 goods engine, fitted 5 ft 3 ins gauge axles to it, added a saddle tank and renumbered it as DNGR No 6. Each engine was named, No 6 becoming *Holyhead*, commemorating the mainland destination of the steamers. After the partition of Ireland, the DNGR escaped merger into Great Southern Railways and later CIE, as a small part of its mileage was in Northern Ireland, and in 1948, it was excluded from the UTA, as most of its trackage was in the south. Unlike the NCC, which was transferred from the BTC to the UTA, the international nature of the DNGR precluded this, so it remained vested in the BTC. The Greenore ships had lost money for years, and with a £50,000 loss on the railway in 1950, the BTC decided to end its subsidy, but so protracted were negotiations with all concerned, that it was not until the evening of 31st December 1951 that the line finally closed, to the accompaniment of a fierce blizzard.

Above: The cost of maintaining a small railway separated from its parent company by the Irish Sea was disproportionate, so the LMS asked the DNGR's neighbour, the GNR(I) to work and maintain the line from 1933, and although the DNGR engines survived, train services were often handled by GN 2-4-2Ts or even some of their ubiquitous 4-w railbuses. GNR(I) class JT 2-4-2T No 93 is at Dundalk (Bridge St) station on 7th June 1948. The leading coach is a replacement 6-wheeler for the original 1870s stock, which had been provided by the LNWR between 1899 and 1908. DNGR coach livery followed LNWR practice, and this continued after the grouping, and when the GNR(I) took over maintenance, they continued the old colours. With the loss of many NCC coaches due to an air raid in May 1941, several DNGR vehicles were transferred to the NCC. At peak periods, the GN would loan some of their own 6-wheelers, the second vehicle being in GN varnished mahogany. No 93 hauled the last train on the evening of 31st December 1951, conveying the train crew, 400 passengers, the Newry Town Band, and a goat, the latter travelling first class. The DNGR was one of the most improbable outposts of the mighty LNWR. In a land that had more than its share of improbable railways, it was one of the most remarkable, so a First Class goat seems a fitting finale. Although there is no evidence that the goat was preserved, the engine certainly was, going to the Belfast Transport Museum, and later to the magnificent collection at Cultra.
R E Tustin

1948-1951 DN&GR Cheap Day ticket printed black on pale green card with red D.

Opposite page: The Belfast & County Down Railway, or 'Co Down', as it was known, was incorporated in 1846, and grew into an 80 mile system, serving the area east and south of Belfast. Its busiest line was a 12 mile double track route running along the shores of Belfast Lough to Bangor. A predominantly single track main line stretched 38 miles into South Down, the system being completed by five branches. It was worked by 30 locomotives and operated just over 200 passenger carriages and around 700 wagons, including service stock. By the 1880s, the Co Down was notorious for its antiquated rolling stock, as money had been begrudged for renewals for many years, and a 34-year old Englishman, Joseph Tatlow, who came from a Midland Railway family, but was working for the Glasgow & South Western Railway, was appointed manager in May 1885. Soon after he arrived, Tatlow and the new Locomotive superintendent examined all the coaching stock, and their report was devastating, calling for complete replacement as a matter of urgency. Large new orders were placed and in a short time, the Co Down had replaced its venerable 4-wheelers with modern 6-wheelers. In December 1890, Tatlow became manager of the Midland Great Western Railway of Ireland. His departure was a severe blow to the Co Down, although this was not immediately apparent, as his successor, James Pinion, who later became general manager of the Cheshire Lines Committee, was hard working and capable, but the Co Down became inward looking, and failed to keep abreast of the times after 1900. This was unfortunate, as the Co Down had been successful, paying dividends until 1925, and had the financial resources to modernise, but had still been building 6-wheelers as late as 1923. The general strike in 1926, and road competition, hit the BCDR hard, with net income dropping from over £50,000 a year to between £8,000 and £16,000, and W F Minnis, who became manager in 1926 found himself in a similar position to Tatlow, but it was no longer economically possible to upgrade the railway. In the 1940s, out of a fleet of some 200 carriages, there were just 18 bogie vehicles, of which only two were modern, whilst some of the coaches Tatlow had ordered 50 years earlier were still in use. BCDR carriage No 63, seen at Belfast Queens Quay station on 9th June 1948, is to all intents a classic Victorian 6-wheeler, but was one of the diagram 23 six-compartment all 2nds, which were built between 1905 and 1921, No 63 dating from 1915. *R E Tustin*

Above: The motive power situation was better, as the BCDR had modernised its loco fleet in the early 1900s, and just one engine dated from Tatlow's time. Over a third of the fleet were lively and efficient 4-4-2Ts built by Beyer Peacock between 1901 and 1921. Able to shunt or head an express, these class 1 tanks were the mainstay of the BCDR for half a century. Class 1 tank No 30 is at Bangor on a rake of typical 6-wheelers, into which one bogie coach has found its way, on 10th June 1948. Compared to the profitable years up to 1924, when annual receipts stood at £343,516, and good dividends were paid, the decline was rapid and painful, with income falling by over a third, to £224,945 by 1927, and profits were insufficient to pay more than a fraction of preference dividends, let alone give anything to the ordinary shareholders. This remained the case into the Thirties, and far from modernising the railway, Billy Minnis was desperately seeking economies. No new steam locomotives were purchased between 1924 and 1939, and only two bogie carriages added to stock. The Co Down, which had been archaic when Minnis took over, because of the unimaginative policies pursued for many years, became more of an anachronism with each passing year. Without adequate funds for modernisation, and at the mercy of omnibus competition that was made more potent due to government policy in the mid-thirties, it is hard to see what else Minnis could have done. An 'Irish' story, told to me with great zest by an Irish enthusiast, sums up the Co Down situation. An Irishman was asked directions by a motorist, and replied 'If I were you, I wouldn't have started from here'. It is possible that Billy Minnis shared those sentiments. *R E Tustin*

Opposite page top: From the day she entered service, to her last day in steam, a period of fifty-six years, one County Down engine possessed a special magic. No 6 came from the Gorton works of Beyer Peacock in 1894, as did every BCDR steam locomotive built after 1890. What was special about her? On a line worked largely by tank engines, with just a few 0-6-0 goods engines, she was the solitary passenger tender engine, and her 6 ft 0 ins driving wheels showed she had been built to run expresses. For much of her life, No 6 was employed on the Queens Quay – Newcastle expresses, but as her boiler aged, No 6 was demoted to the less demanding Ballynahinch – Ballynahinch Junction services, which left from the platform face on the left. After a Harland & Wolff diesel arrived in 1933, she saw limited use, mainly as spare engine when the diesel needed attention, and by 1941, was out of use with a bad boiler. It seemed that the end had come for the glamourous high stepping No 6, but with burgeoning wartime traffic, every engine was needed, and in March 1943, No 6 emerged from Queens Quay works with a new Belpaire boiler, new cylinders and a thorough overhaul. Within days, she was hauling Newcastle expresses once again, taking just under an hour for the tortuous 38 mile route, with its numerous slacks to exchange single line tokens. She is seen on a Newcastle train at Ballynahinch Junction on 10th June 1948. It was a Thursday, so this is not the legendary Saturday midday 'Golfers' express, but it is nice to see the old engine on important duties after more than half a century. She ran the last ever 'Golfers' in January 1950, and then retired to slumber in Queens Quay shed until the breakers' men came for her six years later.

Right: On a single line, there is a risk of trains from opposite directions colliding, unless some safeguard exists. The simplest safeguard was the train staff, which was a wooden or steel baton, suitably inscribed for the section it related to. This was handed to the driver of a train that was about to enter the section. As there was only one staff for each section, the driver knew that no train could come in the opposite direction. Once the staff reached the far end of the section, it could be handed to a train to make the return journey. The strength of this system was its absolute security. If the staff was not at the station, no train could leave. Its weakness was that trains had to proceed alternately in opposite directions, and two trains could not follow one another in the same direction. To overcome this weakness, the TRAIN TICKET was introduced. This was a cardboard ticket printed with the name of the section it related to. This ticket is for DOWN trains from Ballynahinch Junction to Ballynahinch. The staff had to be shown to the engine driver, but he was given a ticket, which was worded as follows 'You are authorised to proceed to BALLYNAHINCH STATION. The Train Staff to follow'. The staff would be handed to the driver of a later train, and after it left the junction, no more single line train tickets could be issued or trains dispatched, until the staff returned. Tickets also existed for the Up direction. Provided the rules were adhered to, the system was foolproof, and it was used on the Ballynahinch branch for many years. Berkeley D Wise became resident engineer to the County Down in 1877, leaving for the more prosperous Northern Counties in 1888. During his time on the BCDR, he invented Wise's Divisible Train Staff. The staff consisted of a central portion, into which

detachable brass tickets or 'permits', as they were called, were fitted. The complete staff was handed to the driver, unless two or more trains were to follow in the same direction, in which case, he was shown the staff, but given a permit. When this arrived at the far end, it was kept safely until the train staff itself arrived, when they were re-united. As a further precaution, permits were uni-directional, with Up permits at one end and Down permits at the other end of the staff, and a driver was not allowed to proceed unless the staff had the full number of permits from the opposite direction attached to it. Wise's divisible train staff was adopted on the Ballynahinch branch some years after he left the Co Down.

BELFAST AND COUNTY DOWN RAILWAY.
Train Ticket No.   **1789**   **DOWN.**
SHAPE OF STAFF ☐ **B.HINCH JUNC. TO BALLYNAHINCH** SQUARE.
To_____
Engineman of_____ *m.* Train. You are authorised to proceed to BALLYNAHINCH STATION. The Train Staff to follow.
Signature,_____
B.HINCH JUNC. STATION,_____o'clock,_____ M. _____day of_____190____   [OVER]

Below: The Co Down, though outdated, due to the policies pursued from 1900 to the 1920s, might have been more innovative under Minnis, but after 1926, there was never enough money to do so. For many years, the Harland & Wolff shipyard on the banks of Belfast Lough was a familiar sight to anyone arriving in Belfast by sea. To most people, the yard is best known as the builders of the ill-fated *Titanic*, but it was a great company with a fine reputation. It was also innovative, supplying some of the first diesel shunters to the LMS. In 1933, the Co Down obtained a 270hp 2-4-0 diesel loco from Harland & Wolff. Although this looked similar to diesel shunters Harlands had built, D1 was intended for train duties on the Ballynahinch branch. It is paradoxical that a railway with the most archaic coaching fleet in the British Isles led the way with diesel haulage of trains. Although D1, which was intended for train duties, predated Britain's first main line diesel, LMS No 10000, by 14 years, it was a diesel shunter adapted for train use, so was hardly a rival, but was joined by a second engine in 1937. Briefly known as D2, but quickly renumbered 28, this looked like a Bo-Bo, but was a 1A-A1, with the outer axle on each bogie un-powered. It was a diesel electric, its 8-cylinder 500hp diesel driving two traction motors, and providing a tractive effort of 10,000lbs. No 28 was designed to haul a 100 ton train on a 1 in 50 gradient, and cost £7,975. Compared to simple diesel shunters running elsewhere, its pre-war running costs were relatively high, at 12.504d per mile. It was returned to Harlands' in 1945 for £5,544, working on the Northern Counties until 1952, after which it was hired to the Great Northern, and after 1958, to the UTA, giving it the unusual distinction of being allocated to all three of the principal broad gauge systems in the province.

Opposite page: 1938 was a bad year for the BCDR, as receipts failed to cover expenses. The loss was only £1,351, but fixed charges had to be met, and the company could ill afford the drain. 1939 was better, with net receipts of £7,000, but apparent salvation came from an unlikely 'benefactor'. Although he was a railway enthusiast, with an extensive model railway, it is unlikely that Herman Goering had ever heard of the BCDR, but the damage wrought by his bombers in repeated air raids on Belfast prompted many people to lodge in the country, to escape the night-time bomber raids, commuting into the city each morning. Military needs also boosted traffic, and short spurs served an ordnance depot and a fuel depot on the Bangor line. BCDR gross receipts, which had fallen to £171,972 in 1938, had reached £440,433 by 1941. Carrying this extra traffic was costly, but BCDR net revenue changed from a loss of £1,351 in 1938, to a profit of £126,628 three years later. By 1943, receipts were near the half million mark, but expenses were rising even faster, and the surplus had fallen to £55,861. Fuelled by wartime inflation, expenses continued upwards, but in 1944, the Co Down still achieved a surplus of £67,505. W F Minnis, who had worked for the Co Down for 60 years, the last 18 of them as general manager, retired, and from 1st August 1944, George B Howden, added control of the Co Down to his existing job as general manager of the GNR(I). The two companies had close links, and although remaining separate, closer working offered economies, and the GN diagrammed one of its diesel railcars to work some services. The BCDR was confident enough to order a new 4-4-2T from Beyer Peacock, at a cost of £10,824 for delivery during 1945, the first new steam locomotive for over twenty years, but instead of being a new dawn, 1945

heralded the beginning of the end. Within a fortnight, the Co Down suffered the first of the blows that were to destroy it. The BCDR had a good safety record, but a collision at Bally-macarrett Junction that left 23 people dead, cost the company heavily in compensation. Net receipts dropped to £29,550, as wartime evacuees returned to the city. Military camps were run down, and by 1946, passenger receipts had fallen by almost a third. Freight receipts almost halved, but wages and other costs were rising. With petrol rationing easing, the number of private cars was increasing, whilst the Northern Ireland Road Transport Board, which had been set up in the 1930s to end the cut-throat competition that had harmed public transport, was now a major competitor. Despite stringent economies, and slashing repairs and renewals by £26,000, the Co Down recorded a loss of £50,242 in 1946. With a system that was archaic before the war, and had endured six years of hard usage and inadequate maintenance, refurbishment was vital, but the reverse was taking place. The government of Northern Ireland issued a White Paper on public transport on 8th January 1946, which recommended merging the NIRTB, LMS NCC, BCDR, and the portions of the GNR(I) in Northern Ireland. Eventually, the Ulster government followed the Southern lead, by leaving the international lines, such as the GNR(I) out of the amalgamation. Faced with increasing losses, the BCDR board did not fight nationalisation, as in England, but welcomed it, commenting in January 1947 'in the interest of the public and the shareholders, they urge upon the Government the paramount need for having this long-standing and most important question settled without further delay'. The railway's book value stood at 1.6m pounds, but when it passed into UTA control on 1st October 1948, it was paid £485,990 for the entire undertaking.

George Howden, a talented railwayman, had tried to save the BCDR from 1944 to 1948 and failed. Frank Pope, the new chairman of the UTA, was in no doubt as to the chronic state of the BCDR, whilst the highest reaches of the UTA were strongly influenced by bus men from the former NIRTB. Within days of taking over, Pope appointed a team to prepare a closure case. Faced with a predominantly single-track system, mounting losses, over 200 carriages, of which only two were modern, and a steam locomotive fleet that contained just one engine that was less than twenty years old, they recommended abandoning everything other than the 12 mile Bangor branch. The proposals were published on 10th March 1949, and after a Transport Tribunal hearing, where the UTA estimated that the BCDR section was losing over £180,000 a year, they were accepted. The entire Co Down, save for the Bangor line, closed between January and April 1950. The speed and ruthlessness of the closure left a suspicion that Frank Pope's desire to show quick results, and the prejudices of the bus men, meant that no serious consideration was given to any other option. On the other hand, the public was no longer prepared to travel in antiquated 6-wheelers, so new rolling stock was vital, and that would take several years, given the constraints on steel supplies. As it was, with just 12 miles to modernise, full dieselisation took until 1953,

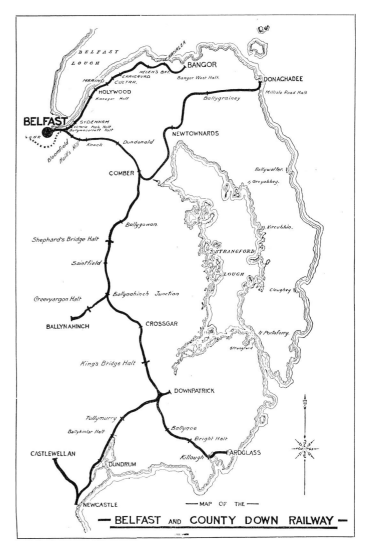

— MAP OF THE —
— BELFAST AND COUNTY DOWN RAILWAY —

although accorded a high priority. The seaside branches to Donaghadee and Ardglass carried few passengers in winter, whilst the Castlewellan branch, though part of the GN route to Newcastle, was useless to the Co Down, and there was no need for two competing routes. The line to Comber might have been saved, but whether a more ambitious survival plan was feasible is doubtful.

In later years, the UTA was anti-railway, but whether it was indifference in 1948, or a deliberate attempt to make the case as black as possible, is conjecture. Doubts have been expressed over the UTA's £180,000 loss in its first year. In 1946, when the BCDR had much to gain from good results, as it was trying to sell the line, it lost £50,000, despite reduced maintenance. On a sustainable basis it would have been £76,000, and experience elsewhere showed that losses accelerated rapidly, so the UTA figure is by no means impossible. I have covered the demise of the Co Down in depth because it was a small self-contained system, and offers detail that is lacking for the average BR branch line at this time. Events that are obscure on BR stand out in sharp focus on the Co Down.

7 · 'BUS OR RAILBUS, THAT IS THE QUESTION?'

Above: Was the County Down in a unique situation, with bad management, archaic stock, or hopeless routes compared to most railways? By itself, it is a pointer to wider trends, but if we look elsewhere, there is more to learn. Historically, County Donegal, which is the most northerly County in Ireland, was part of the Province of Ulster, one of the four ancient provinces into which Ireland was divided, but unlike the mainly Loyalist and Protestant population of the rest of Ulster, was largely Catholic, and in favour of Home Rule. When Ireland was partitioned in 1921, a referendum was held in each county, twenty-six of them, including Donegal, opting to join the independent Irish Free State, later Eire, the other six counties becoming Northern Ireland, and remaining a part of the United Kingdom. The railways of Ireland pre-dated this division, which caused much disruption to traditional trading patterns, as customs inspections now sprang up at the border. Three broad gauge and two narrow gauge companies were affected, gaining the unwelcome distinction of becoming International railways. The worst affected was the Londonderry & Lough Swilly Railway, whose lines radiated out north and west from the City of Londonderry into remote Donegal. Londonderry, or Derry to republicans, had always been the market town and supply centre for north and west Donegal, and with partition, a customs barrier was imposed on those crucial links. For the L&LSR, the result was bizarre. Of the 99 route miles worked by the company in its heyday, just a couple of miles were in Northern Ireland, but they included the terminus at Londonderry, and the loco and carriage sheds at Pennyburn. L&LSR No 2 came from Andrew

Barclay & Co in 1902 and was one of four identical engines delivered for the Letterkenny & Burtonport Extension Railway, which carried Swilly metals to the wild west coast of Donegal. It was an outside framed 4-6-0T, and was supplied to specifications drawn up by the Irish Board of Works, as the Burtonport Extension had been built with assistance from public funds. Not for the first or last time in railway history, civil servants decided that they knew better than railwaymen, although the Swilly protested vigorously that they were not up to the job on the long and heavily graded extension. Naturally, the bureaucrats ignored the protests of professional railwaymen. The engines, whilst unsuited for the road they had been built for, were ideal for shorter distance runs, as the Swilly soon realised, putting some of its own engines on the Burtonport line instead. This logical answer was an anathema to the civil servants. No 2 is seen at Londonderry (Graving Dock) terminus on 14th June 1948. The dismal iron shed in the background is the passenger shelter. No 2 was scrapped in 1954. *R E Tustin*

Opposite page top: Relations between the Lough Swilly and the government reached rock bottom over the Burtonport Extension, and the manager of the LSWR was appointed to investigate. His report highlighted defects with the L&LSR, but predominantly came down on their side, and granted them additional funds from a niggardly treasury, helping to get the ailing company back on its feet. A pair of 4-6-2Ts were ordered immediately, and in 1912, the Swilly purchased their final pair of engines from Hudswell, Clarke, and what engines they were! Weighing an incredible 58 tons 15 cwt in full working order, they were 4-8-4Ts, a wheel arrangement not found anywhere else in the British Isles. They were numbered 5 and 6 in the complex Swilly numbering system which went as high as No 17, and included A list duplicate engines at one time. Both survived until the end of Lough Swilly services in 1954. No 5 is seen at Letterkenny shed on 14th June 1948. Serving a desolate and under-populated area, with few industries, the Swilly had not been prosperous before 1914, but Partition of Ireland, with an intransigent and bureaucratic customs barrier, increased working expenses, and the disruption to traffic, plus the

growth of road competition, hit the Swilly hard. With losses from 1921, the directors even subsidised the line out of their own pockets for a time, but after 1924-25, the Swilly received grants from the Southern and Northern governments to keep the trains running. *R E Tustin*

Bottom: Early views show Swilly coaches in a smart two tone livery, but in later years, drab all-over light grey was used to save money. As with locomotives, there were separate Swilly and Burtonport Extension number series. Burtonport brake third coach No 9, seen on 14th June 1948, was supplied by R Y Pickering of Wishaw in 1902. *R E Tustin*

Above: In 1931, James J W Whyte, who had joined the Swilly in 1910, and had been accountant since 1921, was appointed secretary & manager, and a thorough review of operations was undertaken. Whyte felt that the railway had no long-term prospects and that passenger and freight traffic could be better moved by road. The two governments agreed that the Swilly would acquire competing road services in the area, with a view to eventual closure of the railway. The Carndonagh line, Ireland's, most northerly railway, closed in 1935. The western end of the Burtonport Extension closed in 1940, and the line was cut back to Letterkenny in 1947, leaving just 30 miles from Letterkenny to Londonderry in operation. By 1948, the Swilly's receipts from railway operations of £39,695 were less than a quarter of the receipts coming from road services, which stood at £174,393, but whilst bus and lorry operations produced a profit of almost £15,000, rail services lost £4,246. The bus fleet, which stood at 34 vehicles in 1947, rose to 42 vehicles in 1948 and to 52 by 1952. Lough Swilly AEC Regal 0662 single decker No 49, IH5619, is part of this post-war build-up, and is seen at Letterkenny on 15th June 1948, working on the rail replacement service to Gweedore. The roof-mounted luggage rack, piled high with suitcases, some of which seem perilously unstable, and even a pram, was a feature of Irish buses at this period. With sufficient buses and lorries to eliminate the railway, Whyte, prepared a report condemning rail operations as uneconomic, and recommended their final replacement. It was easy to see why. In the last full year of operations in 1952, rail services earned £23,537, but failed to cover costs by £6,244, whilst Road Transport had earned £229,810, yielding a profit of £11,940. Virtually all of the rail income came from freight, passenger numbers having dwindled to 2,811 in the entire year, with earnings of £128. Given the cost of running even a narrow gauge train in such desolate countryside, the Swilly had put its faith in road vehicles. The Act incorporating the Londonderry & Lough Swilly Railway had been passed in June 1853. A hundred years after the company's birth, the L&LSR Directors' Report for 1953 reported the death of the railway in a few lines.

DISCONTINUANCE OF RAIL SERVICES

The proposal to discontinue the remainder of our rail services – approved by an Extraordinary Meeting of the Shareholders on 27th March 1952 – was carried into effect on 8th August 1953, when all regular rail services were discontinued and substituted by Road Transport Services, the necessary authority having previously been obtained from both Irish Governments. The relevant Abandonment Orders have also been obtained and the salvage of the rail track is at present proceeding.

With the rail operations ended, the Swilly served its district by lorry and bus, and 150 years after the company was formed, the Londonderry & Lough Swilly Railway Co is still in the transport business, although its last train ran half a century ago. James J W Whyte, the architect of the demise of the railway, and the survival of the company, managed its affairs for 36 years, taking it from virtual bankruptcy to financial solvency. Was he right or wrong? Was he a good transport manager or a bad railway manager? I suspect it depends on your viewpoint.

Right: The Swilly's neighbour, the County Donegal Railways Joint Committee, was another international narrow gauge railway. The 110 route miles of the Donegal and the 19 miles of the Strabane & Letterkenny Railway, meant that at 129 miles in all, it was the largest narrow gauge system in the British Isles. The Donegal originated as a broad gauge line with a narrow gauge extension, but the whole system was later narrow-gauged, and various extensions were built. The main line commenced on the banks of the Foyle at Londonderry, and ran to Strabane, its original starting point, where there was an interchange station with the GNR(I). One line crossed into the Free State, and ran north to Letterkenny, whilst the main line ran west over the border to Stranorlar, headquarters of the CDRJC. A branch ran north-west to Glenties, whilst the main line continued on to Donegal Town where it split, one line serving Ballyshannon and another going to Killybegs. It was purchased jointly by the Midland Railway and Great Northern Railway (Ireland) in 1906, hence the 'Joint Committee' in its title. The Joint Committee's transfer was applied to locomotives and coaching stock, and consisted of the heraldic arms of the O'Donnells, Lords of Tyrconnel, within a circle, the title lettering being applied round the perimeter.

Below: Although the Donegal served a remote area, and trains were often lightly loaded, on fair days, public holidays and religious festivals, services were packed to capacity, so large engines were called for by British narrow gauge standards. In 1904, Nasmyth Wilson supplied four 4-6-4Ts to the Donegal. Accorded Class 4, and numbered 12–15 when new, they became 9–12 in 1937. No 9 *Eske* is seen at Londonderry (Victoria Road) terminus on 15th June 1948. With declining traffic, 10 and 12 went in 1952, whilst No 9 was scrapped in 1954. Although small by UK standards, Londonderry, with a population of 39,892 people in 1907, was a major city in Irish terms, and was served by no less than four railways, the NCC, the GNR(I), the L&LSR and the CDRJC. Geography, and the tangled nature of railway politics, meant that all four had separate termini, two being on the east bank of the River Foyle, the other two on the west bank. In many ways, it would have made economic sense if the lines could have been brought together in one central terminus, as this would have facilitated onward journeys and offered economies, but a similar picture was encountered in many towns and cities throughout the British Isles, much of the duplication being eliminated in the Beeching era on British Railways. *R E Tustin*

Above: The Baltic tanks were followed by eight Nasmyth Wilson 2-6-4Ts of classes 5 and 5A between 1907 and 1912. They were superb engines, especially after the earlier class 5 engines were superheated, and hauled the bulk of steam services until the demise of the system in 1959. No 19 *Letterkenny* is by the turntable pit at Londonderry (Victoria Road) station in 1932. Delivered in 1908, No 19 was involved in the Donemana accident in 1913. Her name and number were to have been altered during the 1937 changes to No 7 *Finn*, but she was apparently out of use, and scrapped in 1940. The existence of four separate stations was inconvenient, but a two level bridge, which carried road vehicles on the upper deck, and had mixed gauge 5ft 3 ins and 3ft 0 ins tracks on the lower level, permitted interchange via the lines of the Londonderry Port & Harbour Commissioners. The structure is visible in the background. Most photographs of the Donegal show engines in the geranium red livery adopted by the manager Henry Forbes, to produce a brighter image

in the 1930s, but from the MR/GNR(I) take over in 1906 and until 1937, Donegal engines were black, lined out in red. The Irish railways were more vulnerable to the winds of change than their British counterparts, due to the weak Irish economy. Joseph Tatlow, whom we met on the B&CDR, and who went on to a successful career on the Midland Great Western Railway of Ireland, made this perceptive comment in a letter written at Christmas 1927 when he was living in retirement at Dalkey, Co Dublin, 'Oh, the poor Irish Railways! Yours are suffering by the new Competition we know, but how much more the Irish lines, with Ireland's sparse population and limited industry! England has a big traffic – a big cake to share, and some of it can be spared, and the railways still be fairly fed; but in Ireland how different. Had the railways there all the traffic to themselves, it were not too much to provide, even with the best economies, more than a moderate dividend. Well the world rolls on, and in its changes, some must at times suffer, so philosophy must come to our aid.'
H J Stretton-Ward

Opposite page bottom: 2-6-4T No 8 *Foyle* shunts at Stranorlar on 17th June 1948. Built as a saturated class 5 tank, No 20 *Raphoe* in 1908, she was superheated in 1924, renumbered and renamed in 1937, and survived until 1955.

When this view was taken, the Lough Swilly was on its last legs, but the Donegal appeared to have a good future. Why was it that two adjacent lines fared so differently? To some extent, the structure of the two concerns mattered. The Swilly was an independent company, traditionally short of cash, whereas the Donegal was owned by the Midland Railway and the GNR(I) from 1906. This gave the Donegal a financial cushion that the Swilly lacked, and provided access to the technical skills of the GN works at Dundalk. Of even more importance was the human factor. In 1910, a young GNR(I) officer, Henry Forbes was sent to Stranorlar to reorganise the railway. It was a brilliant choice, and Forbes was to become one of the most outstanding railway managers of all time. He quickly opened halts to attract additional custom. Station and coach lighting was improved, and Forbes fought valiantly for 'his' railway. Fight is the right word; when civil war and 'The Troubles' came to Ireland, Forbes, an Ulsterman, respected by his own men on the Donegal, but hated by the insurgents, carried a revolver for his own protection. One day, he was a passenger on a train that was held up at gunpoint. Slipping out of the carriage on to the track, he crept up to the engine, exchanged fire with the raiders, captured one after a chase, and eventually handed his prisoner over to the police. *R E Tustin*

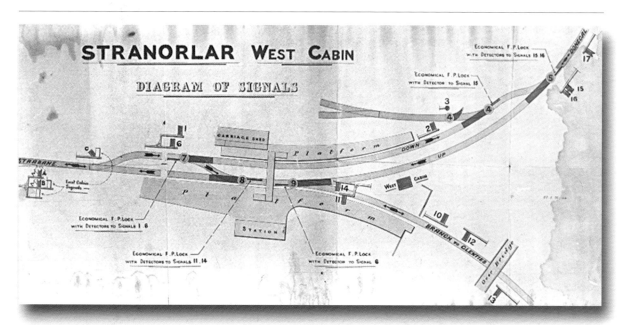

Above: The depressed state of the Irish economy in the late 19th century prompted endless government enquiries, and in 1888, a Royal Commission recommended the development of light railways to stimulate depressed rural areas. The Light Railways (Ireland) Act, 1889, allowed for interest-free government grants, and a dividend guarantee as well. An order was approved under the Act in 1891 authorising a three foot narrow gauge line, 24 miles in length, from Stranorlar to Glenties. The station at Stranorlar had been laid out with the Strabane-Donegal line in mind, but the Glenties branch had to diverge away sharply from the main line, and

cross over the River Finn on an impressive viaduct. As the junction points were too far from the main signal cabin, which controlled connections at the Strabane end of the station, to be worked mechanically, a separate 20 lever box was provided by Saxby & Farmer & Co in 1895, prior to the opening of the line. Although the Glenties line was built under a Light Railway order, the complexity of the junction reminds us of how costly railways were to build, and whilst a line such as this might serve a valuable social purpose, it was likely to be a millstone round the necks of those who built and ran it.

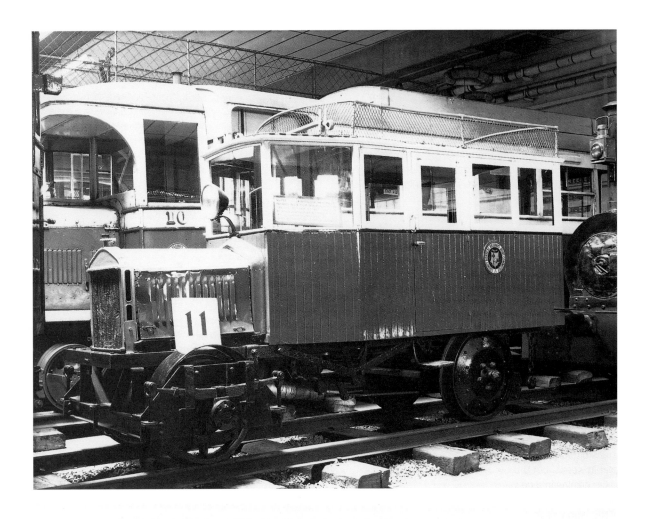

Opposite page top: With a population of 366 people in 1907, traffic was light at Glenties, and passengers could often be counted on the fingers of one hand. In 1926, the miner's strike, which triggered the short lived and abortive General Strike, caused severe disruption to all the railways of the British Isles. Not only did they lose millions of tons of traffic and revenue, but were short of coal for their engines. Forbes rose to the challenge. In 1907, the Donegal bought a small petrol-engined 4-w inspection car from Messrs Allday & Onions of Birmingham. For nineteen years, it saw little use, but with the miners strike, Forbes had to save coal, and the lightly-laden Glenties trains were an obvious economy. A steam train was cancelled, its place being taken by the diminutive railcar, which could seat 6-10 persons. Running over 6,000 miles in three months without problems, it proved its worth, and not only saved coal, but slashed operating costs as well. The GN works at Dundalk provided technical backup for the Donegal, and within weeks, Forbes wrote to the GN, suggesting a larger car for Glenties. Lightweight trailers, and even one-man operation were already in his mind. Two small standard gauge cars that used bus components came second hand from the Derwent Valley Light Railway near York, and were in service before the end of the year, but both suffered the fate of many road-rail conversions. On the roads, the cushioning effect of pneumatic tyres protects the lightweight axles of such vehicles from severe shocks that can cause fatigue fracture. On the railway, the track is smoother, but steel tyres have no resilience, so shocks are transmitted to the axle. Both cars fractured their front axles within weeks, but the experience Forbes and Dundalk works were gaining in a new field was to stand them in good stead, as they blazed a trail in railcar evolution. G B Howden of the GNR, who was to be involved with the dieselisation plans of virtually all the Irish railways, put the cost to the Donegal at £314 per car. Both were withdrawn in 1934, but No 1 remained in stock to the end of the Donegal, and was then retired to the Belfast Transport Museum, where it is seen on 1st September 1964. This diminutive four wheeler set the Donegal and its powerful parent, the GNR(I) on the road to diesel railcars. These developments were studied by the neighbouring NCC, which inaugurated its own railcar fleet. After the war, the GN and the UTA were more ambitious, and under Frank Pope, UTA engineers developed the wiring harness that made the modern DMU possible. In 21st Century Britain, the multiple unit dominates passenger services. They can trace their line back to Forbes and No 1.

Opposite page bottom: More railcars followed. The next car, No 4 used a Ford 30-cwt truck chassis with a locally built body, weighed 2 tons 12 cwt, seated 22 passengers and cost £522. Initially provided with the normal swivelling stub front axles of a road vehicle chassis, these were a source of weakness. Howden realised that the excessive flange wear on the leading wheels was due to oscillation of the steel wheels on a steel rail not being damped by a continuous axle. In 1933, No 4 received a solid front axle which cured the problem. Forbes idea of a light four-wheel trailer bore fruit in

1929, with railcar trailer No 5. Forbes and the Dundalk works team became more ambitious with the next trio of cars, 6-8, moving from the 4 wheel concept, to a leading axle and two powered axles beneath the passenger section. Forbes was also busy on the roads, but whilst James Whyte of the neighbouring Lough Swilly saw buses as a replacement for trains, Forbes saw them as a useful adjunct to his trains, and as a way of keeping competition at bay. Some second-hand buses came from the GNR in 1930. By 1933, they were no longer fit for road use, so two were converted into railcars 9 and 10. Smaller than No's 6-8, they reverted to the two-axle layout. They could carry 20 passengers plus luggage, and haul lightweight trailers. No 9 was broken up in 1949, but judging by this view, taken at Stranorlar on 17th June 1948, when she was lacking her engine, she had probably reached the end of her active career some time earlier. The lives of some of these cars may appear short, but when their ancestry, second-hand vehicles acquired at a fraction of their new cost, is taken into account, the savings they offered made their purchase well worthwhile. In the 1930s, steam haulage cost the Donegal between 10.6d and 13d per mile, whilst railcar costs were 3d to 4d per mile. These were old pennies, of which there were 240 to the pound. In modern currency, the figures would be 4-5p per mile with steam and 1 to 1.5p for the railcars. In 1925, motive power costs on the Donegal were £15,378 for 225,220 miles, with 100% steam traction. By 1935, train mileage had soared to 419,395, an 86% increase, but with railcars contributing over 75% of services, costs had fallen to £10,295. *R E Tustin*

Below: Excursion tickets were often colourful, as with this Stranorlar - Derry ticket which has three red stripes on off-white card. The Child's single, which is on pale brown card, is to Killens Signal, a name that reflects the desolate nature of the area served by the Donegal and Forbe's policy of opening halts wherever passengers wanted to board his trains. 4d is less than 2p in decimal currency.

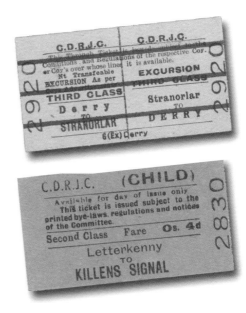

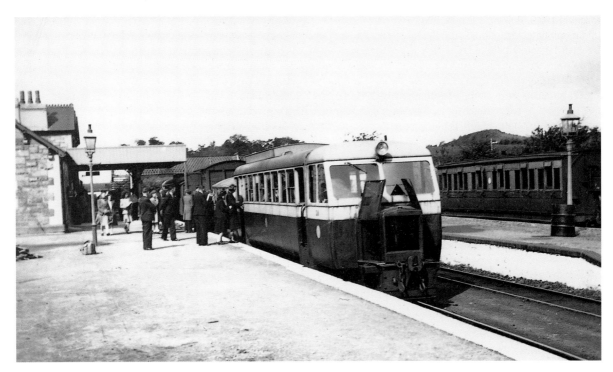

Above: Having moved from 4 to 6 wheeled cars, and from 6 to 32 seats, Forbes advanced to a bogie design in 1934. Using the dependable Gardner 6L2 diesel engine, Walker Bros of Wigan produced a power bogie with steam style coupling rods, and Dundalk works supplied a body that was articulated to the power bogie and cab unit. No 12 cost £2,281, and seated 41 passengers. Five similar cars followed between 1935 and 1938. No 16, of 1936 repeated the Gardner-Walker power bogie with a Dundalk-built body and cost £2,408. With a low top speed due to sharp curves and severe gradients, the Donegal cars had four forward gear ratios, giving speeds of approx 8, 13, 23, and 37 mph. They were driven from one end only, the reason being that because of the long journey times, using a locomotive turntable at the end of each journey was easier than designing a double ended unit with duplicate controls at the rear. This avoided overheating the engine when the vehicle was running in reverse, and the radiator was denied a direct supply of cooling air. The GN, which needed double ended cars, had trouble in ironing out this problem, and the LMS, in developing a sophisticated articulated unit a few years later, managed to place the radiators in such a sheltered position that they overheated, irrespective of which way it was going! Railcar No 16 is picking up passengers at Donegal Town station on 18th June 1948. Although partially obscured by passengers waiting to board, the roof of a small brightly painted wagon is visible behind No 16. This is one of the legendary 'red wagons', so called because of their geranium red paintwork that matched the red and cream of the railcars. They were special lightweight railcar trailers, an idea that had been in Forbes mind as early as 1926. Towering above the red wagon is a conventional Donegal van, for Forbes found that the big bogie cars could easily tow two or three wagons, or a full sized bogie coach, giving immense operational flexibility. Armed with his own imagination and flair, and backed with the technical expertise of the GN and of Walker Bros, Forbes had placed the Donegal at the forefront of railway technology, and staved off the fate that overtook many of the Irish narrow gauge lines in the 1930s. He had also provided an example that other companies might copy if they so chose.
R E Tustin

Opposite page: After over thirty years in office, Henry Forbes died on 7th November 1943. His legacy to the Donegal was remarkable. He had pioneered the railcars that had permitted a more frequent train service, whilst slashing operating costs by a third, and without his efforts, it is likely that the Donegal would not have outlived the Swilly, if it had lasted that long, for the LMS, when faced with losses on the Leek & Manifold Valley Light Railway, which had far more chance of success than the remote Donegal, had opted for the easy course of abandonment. Would the LMS have been more considerate over a remote line in far away Ireland that could bring little feeder traffic to its own system? It is unlikely, but the reverse side of the coin was that in Forbes' struggle to keep the line 'in the black', rolling stock and track renewals had been cut to an absolute minimum. His successor, Bernard L Curran faced wartime inflation, a shortage of material, and an ageing railway. Forbes had staved off closures of any part of 'his' railway by desperate economies. By 1947, rising costs and declining traffic forced Curran to accept the inevitable, and discontinue regular services over the hopelessly uneconomic Glenties branch. With several railcars worn out, Curran persuaded the GNR(I) and their new partner, which was the British Transport Commission, as successor to the LMS, to approve the purchase of a new diesel railcar in 1949. Built at a cost of £8,176 which was over two and a half times as much as any previous car, due to inflation, No 19 entered service in January 1950, being followed by a similar car, No 20 in January 1951. Traffic receipts hovered around the £100,000 mark each year from 1948 to 1952, but costs were rising, and from an £11,698 surplus in 1948, an amazing achievement given the remote and under-populated territory the Donegal served, and an operating ratio that was better than BR in its first year of operation, the surplus fell to just £4,265 by 1950, and losses were incurred thereafter, reaching £17,662 in 1952. With careful housekeeping, Curran cut the loss to a quarter of that figure the following year. The Londonderry section, which paralleled the GN line closed in 1954, and although it takes us beyond the period of this volume, losses mounted again, forcing eventual closure of the rest of the system in 1959. In 1961, at an auction at Stranorlar, the Isle of Man Railway Company, which was by now the last common carrier narrow gauge line in the British Isles, bought the two newest Donegal cars, No's 19 and 20. They were shipped to Douglas where they entered service, now running back to back, as the IMR needed a greater carrying capacity than the 41 seats of a single railcar, and lacked the numerous turntables of the Donegal. No 20 is the leading car as the two units take the crossover at the throat of Douglas station from the Port Erin line to the Peel line. Mention of the differing fates of the Manifold and the Donegal inevitably poses the question, 'If Forbes could keep the Donegal running, why did the LMS not do more with the Manifold, which had far better prospects than the Done-

gal?' Forbes was an autocratic ruler of his own railway, and the joint committee was content to follow his wishes. He was determined that the Donegal should survive, and would find a way to do so. He was totally focussed, as we would say. The Manifold was a tiny part of the LMS. The LMS had many difficulties, and senior officers such as Lord Stamp or Stanier rightly focussed on the big problems, such as adequate express power for the West Coast Main Line, or reducing the bewildering array of classes, to permit economies in motive power costs. The potential savings amounted to millions. A Forbes style approach on the Manifold could have staved off closure, but the savings would have been paltry, and involved a disproportionate amount of executive time that was better spent on more important matters. To use another modern phrase, he prioritised issues. The alternative, of devolving greater autonomy on local officers, risked fragmenting the LMS, and was alien to the big business ethic of centralised management. Even if adopted, it could only work if the LMS happened to put a Forbes in charge, as the differences between the Swilly and the Donegal reveal. By chance, the Donegal was a small semi autonomous unit led by the right man. The Manifold was not, so it closed down twenty-five years earlier than the Donegal. Size offered benefits, but they came at a price, and nationalisation carried an even greater risk that the inevitable centralisation would stifle innovation and imagination. The signs were there, had the politicians cared to study them. That they did not do so was hardly surprising. Nor is it surprising that it turned out to be an expensive mistake.

8 · THE HOWDEN TOUCH

Above: As a child, I liked to see a 4-4-0 at the head of a train, as their day as premier express engines was over. The Derby Compounds, 2Ps, and GW 'Dukedogs' I saw on the Cambrian, were all in BR lined black. Then we visited Dublin, and I saw a massive 4-4-0 adorned in azure blue, with black and white lining, vermillion footplate edging and tender frames. Emblazoned on the tender were letters of gold saying GN. That day marked the start of a lifelong affection for the Great Northern Railway (Ireland). Connecting Belfast and Dublin, it was Ireland's most prosperous railway. The engine reminded me of old colour postcards of Caledonian engines before 1914, though I was later to discover that it was a few months younger than I was. It was a class Vs 4-4-0, designed by H R McIntosh, the Scottish Locomotive Engineer of the GNR(I). McIntosh had succeeded Ireland's most celebrated railwayman, George B Howden, when the latter resigned the twin posts of Civil Engineer and Locomotive Engineer on becoming General Manager of the GN in 1939. Because of the war, nine years elapsed before McIntosh could order any new engines, but the GN was sufficiently prosperous by the late 1940s, to obtain fifteen new engines of three different types. Two were improved versions of pre-war designs, but instead of ordering more of the Glover class V compounds which had handled the premier Belfast Dublin trains since 1932, McIntosh preferred a simple version, to be called the Vs. It is said that at the board meeting at which the new engines were to be approved, McIntosh was looking increasingly anxious, when the chairman turned to him, telling him not to worry, as he was 'going to get his simples'. Five engines were built by Beyer Peacock, the first, GN No 206 *Liffey*, arriving in August 1948. No 206 is ready to depart from the Amiens Street terminus and headquarters of the GNR(I) a few years later. Dieselisation of the Belfast-Dublin expresses cut her career short, and she was withdrawn in 1960, a sad end for a magnificent locomotive. In retrospect, the decision to order these engines was surprising, for whilst BR was about to design new standard steam classes, and had just two main line diesel locomotives in service, the GN was already considering diesel multiple units. Three years earlier, George Howden had looked at how to improve services on the Belfast-Dublin main line. Before the war, five expresses ran each way daily, usually loading to eight coaches, with gaps between trains varying from 1½ to 4¼ hours. Diesel locomotives were still in their infancy, Howden commenting, 'The Irish railways cannot afford to embark on large-scale and expensive experiments in diesel traction, however desirable these may be', but he felt that ten 4-coach services a day would be better than five steam trains, 'On the service between these two cities, a diesel unit capable of dealing with about 200 passengers in comfort is a much more practical and attractive proposition than one dealing with 400 passengers'.

Below: As BR did not build the production HST until 1975-76, what gave George Howden the confidence to implement such ideas twenty-five years ahead of BR. In a word, 'Experience'. Although it was Henry Forbes of the Donegal who had the vision to introduce the first diesel railcar in the British Isles in 1931, the technical know-how came from the Dundalk works of the GNR(I), and the company introduced its first bogie railcars in 1932. 'Numbered' A and B, they seated 48 passengers, with car C1 following in 1934. Running costs were about 2.45d per mile, with maintenance and overhauls adding 1.79d per mile. Maintenance was relatively high due to the experimental nature of the cars, Car B being particularly troublesome, but even so, they offered a welcome saving compared to a steam train at 10-12d per mile. Howden, who had been civil engineer since 1929, added the post of Locomotive Engineer when G T Glover retired in 1933, and was an enthusiastic advocate of diesel traction. Railcars D and E of 1937 consisted of a 6-coupled power bogie and engine house, to which two passenger sections were articulated, being supported at the outer ends by a conventional 4-wheel bogie. By mounting the engine in a separate unit, passengers were spared the noise and vibration that characterised most diesel railcars built before 1970. D and E were powered by a Gardner 6L3 diesel engine developing 153hp. They seated 8 first, 50 second and 101 third class passengers, and cost £6,935. Both units ran well over half a million miles in service, but Howden discovered that a single Gardner bus engine was inadequate for a unit of this size, as speed was restricted to about 40 mph. He also concluded that coupling rods, though used on the smaller Donegal

units, were not ideal, and in the next two units, F and G, two Gardner 6LW engines were used, each developing 102hp. Cost increased to £7,279 per unit, but running costs, including repairs, were just 7.75d per mile. Railcar E, allocated to the service between Amiens Street and the popular residential and seaside community of Howth, is entering Sutton & Baldoyle on 30th September 1949. In 1938, shortly before he was appointed General Manager, Howden looked at diesel locomotives, comparing an estimate from Beyer Peacock of £7,500 each, for five 4-4-0s, with £20,000 for a similar batch of diesel locomotives. He felt that adopting diesel locomotives would be premature, as the technology was largely experimental and costly, whereas railcars could draw heavily on bus and lorry components. Howden remained in close touch with developments, and could cite American progress 'off the cuff'. Except for 1938, which was a bad year for railways in the British Isles, the GN achieved an annual surplus of about £100,000 every year between 1935 and 1939, on a turnover of £1.3m or £1.4m, but World War Two offered the same changes in the company's fortunes as it had to the BCDR. People left war-torn Belfast, for the safety of the neutral South. Revenue doubled from £1.4m to over £3m by 1943, and net receipts from 1941 to 1944 were in excess of £600,000 each year. The long-suffering shareholders who had foregone dividends year after year, received a modest reward, but money was set aside for long-deferred renewals, as UK government restrictions on steel made progress difficult. Desperate to make good the lean years, the GN had to place contracts years in advance.
R E Tustin

Opposite page top: Howden had served the North Eastern Railway and the LNER, before joining the GN, and would have been familiar with the petrol inspection railcars built by the NER before the First World War, and with a converted bus that ran on rail wheels until someone inspected the petrol tank with a naked flame! In 1933 two former GNR road buses that had been sold to the CDRJC were converted to railbuses, (see page 98) With some GN branches serving areas that were as impoverished as the wilds of Donegal, Howden explained 'It was thought that on certain branch lines in sparsely populated areas there was need to provide passenger services which could not be justified unless it were possible to devise some very cheap form of transport, something much cheaper than steam trains or even railcars of more or less conventional types. At that time, the Great Northern Railway had a number of ordinary road buses, which, because of their condition, the authorities would not permit to be used on the highways. It was necessary, if these vehicles were to be used, that they should be converted at a very low cost. Except for the front axle which replaced the stub axles, the provision of special wheels and a few minor details, the vehicles were adapted to rail work without alteration, and the total cost of conversion including new wheels was about £100. Earlier experience of the high stresses set up in wheels, axles and the underframe of a road vehicle when used on the railway track, made it obviously desirable that the wheels should be provided with some cushioning effect and pneumatic tyres were decided on'. A flanged wheel was required and Howden and R W Meredith, the Dundalk works manager, had the answer, 'bearing in mind that the area of contact between the tyre and the top of the rail was much reduced and that there was danger to the tyre from the sharp edges on the heads of the rails, it was decided to fit a steel tyre over a special tyre of pneumatic type'. The Howden Meredith wheel was the result, though problems with working track circuits later resulted in conventional wagon wheels being used for the front wheels. The GNR produced six railbuses, some of which went to the Sligo Leitrim & Northern Counties, and Dundalk, Newry & Greenore railways. Railbuses D and E entered service in 1934, but with the expansion of the railcar fleet, became D1 and E2 in 1936. E2 became No 1 in 1947, and was transferred to the Civil Engineer's department as 8178 in 1956. Covering 374,000 miles by the time the GNR was partitioned between the CIE and UTA in 1958, it was at Grosvenor Street Goods Yard, Belfast, when I photographed it on 30th August 1964. Happily this amazing machine is now on display at the Ulster Folk & Transport Museum.

Opposite page bottom: Railcars and railbuses suggested an ingenious company, but, as Howden reveals, that ingenuity was born of necessity. Many GN lines served remote communities and had been badly affected by partition, the GN having 17 border crossings, whilst road competition was a worry. Much was done, but elderly steam locomotives soldiered on in many places, hauling two or three varnished mahogany 6-wheelers. One such location was the Belturbet

branch, which diverged from the GN at Ballyhaise. Class JT, 2-4-2T No 91, built at Dundalk in 1902, is at Belturbet station in the early fifties. Belturbet, which was also served by the Cavan & Leitrim narrow gauge, had a population of 1,587 people in 1907, which comfortably eclipsed the 103 residents of the junction at Ballyhaise. Cavan and Clones, the other towns in the area, each held less than 3,000 people. By 1948, the improvements were dramatic, as major capital expenditure reached £412,563, including fifteen new engines. £501,379 went on permanent way and signalling repairs, and £573,283 on maintaining rolling stock, with a further £306,000 earmarked for a batch of 20 diesel railcars. Although revenue continued to rise, costs increased even faster, and from a net income of £502,323 in 1945, it had dropped to £29,338 by 1948, but government policy had forced the GN to commit itself to heavy capital programs, or lose its place in the queue. 1949 was worse, with expenses exceeding receipts by £118,293, and the deficit rose to £154,313 in 1950. Without dieselisation, the GN was doomed, but the railcar program cost over £200,000 in 1950 alone. By November 1950, the GN had run out of money, and on 6th December, the shareholders authorised the board to close the system as soon as possible. No one wanted this, least of all the GN management, but it was the only way to force the Irish and Ulster governments to act. Faced with a collapse of transport links, the two governments started to move, but only after the GN had given its staff in Northern Ireland a week's notice! The two governments agreed to underwrite losses to keep services running until the railway system could be transferred to a new statutory body, the Great Northern Railway Board, whose ten members would be appointed equally by the two governments. The loss of £154,313 in 1950 paled into insignificance in 1951, as the deficit quadrupled to £597,308, and to £871,441 in 1952, the last full year of operation under the company. The new GNR Board took over on 1st September 1953.

GNR(I) 1949 handbill. It is a mystery where the train even started from, let alone ran to!

Below: Howden's ideas for diesel trains came closer in 1948 when twenty power cars were ordered from Park Royal-AEC. Dundalk works would provide trailers from existing steam stock, or newly built, to create ten 3 or 4 coach trains, as the GN never used the term diesel multiple unit. Each power car had two 125hp AEC 9.6 litre engines, providing 500hp, which offered lively performance with 3 car sets, and allowed them to haul a fourth coach. Renumbered as UTA 115, and garbed in the short lived GN section blue and cream livery, GNR-AEC diesel car 611 entered service in November 1950, and is powering south near Adelaide on a Belfast-Dublin express on 25th August 1966. The AEC cars worked Dublin-Belfast expresses, secondary routes, or suburban services. Overnight, the GN had more diesel railcars than BR. It was an astonishing tribute to Howden, but as we have seen, the GN had little cause for joy.

Opposite page top: Howden had served the GNR(I) brilliantly, from the day he became Civil Engineer in 1929, and slashed the cost of the Boyne viaduct reconstruction. As Locomotive Engineer, and as general manager from 1939 until the take-over by the GNRB in 1953, he promoted dieselisation. His 1940s vision of frequent lightweight express units, instead of infrequent locomotive hauled trains, was visionary. Its achievement in 1950, placed the GN years ahead of BR, and it was only in the 1970s, with the HST, that BR implemented Howden's vision of 1945! If that had been the total of his achievements, his career would have been remarkable, but it was not. He managed the BCDR as well as the GNR(I) from 1944 to 1948, and conscious that railway operations in the south were disintegrating, the Irish government asked Howden to take over as general manager of CIE

as well from 1950 to 1953. The CIE benefitted from GN expertise, introducing its own AEC cars. Joint projects were facilitated, and in 1950, the Enterprise Express between Belfast and Dublin was extended to Cork, joining Ireland's three main cities. Due to lighter traffic, 4-6-0s were rare in Ireland, the ten B2s, built by the Great Southern & Western Railway between 1916 and 1923, being the most numerous type. Designed by E A Watson, they were unsatisfactory, and seven were rebuilt with 2 cylinders by Watson's successor, J R Bazin, from 1927. No 405, built by Armstrong Whitworth in 1923, and withdrawn in 1955, is at the GN Amiens Street terminus on a Dublin-Cork working in 1952. Howden stepped down from managing the GNR(I) and CIE in 1953, becoming full-time chairman of the Ulster Transport Authority from 1st April 1953. From September 1953, until its dissolution in 1958, when its assets were split between the UTA and CIE, Howden acted as joint chairman of the GNRB, representing the Northern Ireland government. He retired as chairman of the UTA on 30th September 1963, bringing to a close a unique career in which he had run virtually the whole of Ireland's railways.

Opposite page bottom: During World War Two, President De Valera kept Eire neutral, and even sent a message of condolence to Germany on the death of Hitler, though thousands of Irishmen fought valiantly against Nazi oppression. Given his attitude, the British government saw Ireland's needs for coal as a low priority, as Britain was suffering shortages. By 1942, many GSR secondary routes had closed, with passenger services elsewhere reduced to two days a week. Briquettes of coal dust and cement, peat and wood were used to keep trains moving. On 1st January 1945, Great Southern

Railways merged with Dublin United Transport to form Coras Iompair Eireann (Irish Transport Company). The coal situation became even more critical in 1945-46, and with Eire at the back of the queue, CIE tried oil firing, over 30 engines being adapted. So deplorable was the fuel situation, that trains often came to a stand for hours as the crew shovelled fused clinker from the firebox, and raised steam again. As the oil burners did not require long halts at stations, or out on the road, white circles were painted on the tenders to indicate oil-burners. Because oil burning was costly, a relaxation in the fuel supply position early in 1948 meant that locomotives were converted back to coal over the next few months. Class D4 4-4-0 No 338, was one of eight engines built in 1907-08 to the designs of Robert Coey, who succeeded Aspinall at Inchicore in 1896. No 338, still with a faded oil burner circle on the tender, is on a Limerick City train at Limerick Junction on 23rd September 1949. *R E Tustin*

Above: Because traffic was limited, and money tight, Irish locomotive classes were usually numerically small, but there was one notable exception, the '101' or later J15 class 0-6-0 goods of the Great Southern & Western Railway, of which 119 were built between 1866 and 1903, the last examples surviving for sugar beet specials until 1966! No 104, which was in service from 1873 to 1965, is the leading engine on a Killarney-Dublin express on 29th September 1949. The 101s, were designed by Alexander McDonnell, a brilliant locomotive engineer who transformed the locomotive situation on the Great Southern & Western between 1864 and 1882, when he was appointed to the North Eastern Railway. Killarney has long been a popular tourist destination, with through trains from Dublin in summer. Often these could be heavily laden, but after the fuel crisis of 1942-1947, it was not until 1949 that traffic returned to normal. However, all was not well with CIE. In 1945, CIE's first year of operation after the government-inspired merger with Dublin United Transport, which provided buses and trams in the capital, all divisions of CIE, except for road freight, earned an operating profit, the railways contributing £221,185. In March 1946, the former head of Dublin United, A P Reynolds, who was now chairman of CIE, announced plans to build five diesel shunters, and to obtain main line diesels from the UK and Switzerland. Differences between the busmen of DUTC, and the railwaymen from the GSR were kept out of sight, but DUTC officers were horrified at the chronic waste and inefficiency on the rail side. 1946 was not a good year for CIE, as rail traffic was hit by a prolonged strike of the sugar beet fac-

tory workers, whilst the resumption of branch line services that had been suspended during the war to conserve coal stocks, put up train mileage and operating costs, but contributed negligible revenue. Passenger train mileage increased by about 1m miles, but for every mile run in 1945, CIE had carried 5.66 passengers; for 1946, the figure was 3.80 passengers The railways division of CIE made a loss of £433,911, a stark contrast to the previous year, when a dividend had been declared, and discussions had taken place over quoting shares on the Dublin Stock Exchange! 1947 was a great deal worse, with passenger services at a standstill for weeks due to coal shortages, and the railway deficit doubled to £995,897. Profits on the buses and tramways were falling, and no longer covered the rail deficit, which soared to £1.3m in 1948, and the Irish government announced its intention to nationalise the failing company.

Opposite page: The GSR had been created out of railways operating wholly in the south in 1925. After the GS&WR, which was by far the biggest constituent, the next largest company was the Midland Great Western Railway, whose main line ran due west from Dublin to the Atlantic coast at Galway. Another important line ran north-west from Mullingar to Sligo. The best-known locomotive engineer on the MGWR was Martin Atock, who held sway from 1872 to 1901. His 'L' class 0-6-0 goods, later GSR class J18, was similar in size to the GS&WR J15 class, and almost as long-lived. CIE No 592 started life as MGWR No 138 in 1895, and remained in traffic until 1962. No 592, seen at Sligo Docks on 17th June

1948, carries the 'Flying Snail' symbol that had been used by Dublin United Transport before 1945, and became the CIE logo thereafter. Sir James Milne, the last general manager of the GWR, was asked to prepare a report on CIE in 1948. The average age of CIE's 491 steam locomotives was 51 years, a much worse figure than on the GNR or NCC, whilst the average age of passenger stock was 47 years. Most were 6-wheelers, many had no heating, a couple had no lighting, and some had not been overhauled since 1929! Wages and salaries had risen by 55% in three years, and staff levels seemed excessive. Despite A P Reynolds success with Dublin United, Milne concluded that running the combined organisation was beyond one man. He also felt that main line diesel locomotives were not a panacea, as they could not be used intensively enough on CIE to justify their high capital cost. He suggested that 50 new steam locomotives replace many of the antiquities from the Victorian era. Rather than adopting Milne's suggestion to support the existing company, the Irish government introduced nationalisation proposals in February 1949. The rail loss dropped from £1.28m to £1.09m in 1949, but Reynolds, out of favour with the politicians, and disheartened that his dieselisation proposals had been discarded, was forced out of office. *R E Tustin*

Right: This letter, from Hartnell Smith, of the Accountant's Office of Great Southern Railways, which was in the old M&GWR station at Broadstone, reflects the parlous state of GSR by 1941. The letter head is rubber stamped in violet ink, whilst the ragged edges show it has been creased and then torn by hand from a larger sheet of paper. It is in fact on the back of a previously used freight traffic return referring to manure, dead animals and potatoes. It hardly creates an inspiring impression, yet the company was so desperate that it scarcely mattered.

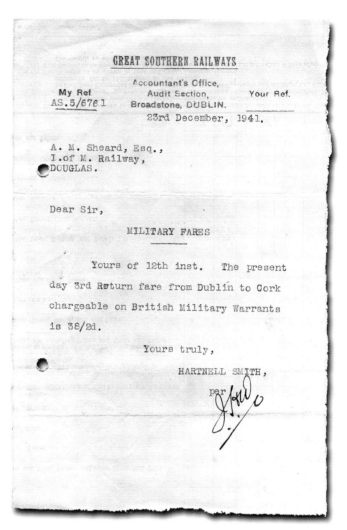

No................

Coras Iompair Eireann.

TRAIN STAFF TICKET

5

....Line or Branch

Train No........................ (UP or DOWN.)
To the Engine Driver.
        You are authorised, after seeing the Train
Staff for the Section, to proceed from........................

to........................ , and the Train Staff will follow.

Signature of person in charge........................

Date........................

Above: The infant CIE was as strapped for cash as the GSR had been, and rather than issue separate numbered and coloured train staff tickets for each single line section, as was usual on most railways, produced this blank ticket on white card that had to be filled in with both station names, the direction of travel, and sequentially numbered. Several of the safeguards that were inherent in the staff and ticket system were ignored or badly bent, to say the least. The BCDR train ticket on page 89 shows the normal format and explains the proceedure adopted on most railways.

Opposite page top: A P Reynolds faced a daunting task when he took over former GSR, with strikes, coal shortages, inflation and archaic equipment. Although partly to blame for the deepening crisis between 1945 and 1949, a shortage of capable deputies to whom he could delegate work, placed an intolerable load on his shoulders. Even so, he left a positive legacy to CIE, in the shape of five Class J1 diesel electric shunters and a pair of Sulzer engined main line Bo-Bo locomotives. The shunters came first, the Bo-Bo's not being delivered until after his departure. The first of the 0-6-0 shunters was completed at the CIE Inchicore works in December 1947, and was powered by a Mirlees 487hp turbo-charged diesel. The five engines were numbered 1000-1004, later becoming D301-305. They were intended for yard shunting and to work transfer trips between Dublin Kingsbridge and North Wall, and received a two-tone green livery. T C Courtney took over from Reynolds, and the final report and accounts for CIE as a company, covered the first five months of 1950, during which losses came to £561,900. CIE shareholders received Irish government Transport Stock in exchange for their holdings, and a new state owned CIE took over on 1st June 1950. A new management team was appointed, including George Howden as general manager, whilst Oliver Bulleid came from the Southern Region to head the Motive Power department. In 1951, the first CIE railcars, which were closely based on the GN

cars, arrived, permitting a welcome improvement in services. A P Reynolds, who had begun with one bus, and eventually led DUTC and CIE, had been a scathing critic of what he regarded as over-manning on the GSR, of branch lines that saw one or two trains a day, yet were fully staffed, and other costly practices. He would have liked to see many little used lines closed down and replaced by road transport, arguing that they served little purpose, and could never be made economic, but at the same time he realised the important role the railways served in moving Dublin's traffic and on the key main lines. Despite a parting shot when leaving CIE that passengers would 'not travel by train if any other form of transport was available', Reynolds was to return to political favour within four years, and with Howden, was appointed joint chairman of the Great Northern Railway Board.

Opposite page bottom: Brigadoon, the delightful Hollywood musical about the village that returns to life for a single day each century, has enchanted generations of film buffs. At the start of the 1950s, word filtered through to enthusiasts about a railway in the far west of Ireland with similar characteristics, although the time scale of one day each month was more manageable. The place was the hilly Dingle peninsula that juts out into the Atlantic. The Irish 5 ft 3 ins broad gauge metals of the Great Southern & Western Railway had reached Tralee, a market town of 9,867 people, and thus of considerable importance by Irish standards, but the cost of driving a broad gauge line for thirty miles through the Dingle hills was prohibitive. Instead, the independent three-foot gauge Tralee & Dingle Light Railway was formed, and with a Baronial guarantee, which was a subsidy by local ratepayers if the line was uneconomic, built the route, with trains facing climbs of 1 in 29 or 1 in 30 to two separate summits. The T&DLR opened on 31st March 1891, and soon needed the guarantee. The company limped into the 1920s, and was merged into Great Southern Railways, with the other lines operating solely in the south of Ireland in 1925. By 1939, the roads on the Dingle peninsula had been improved sufficiently to permit passenger services to be withdrawn, but a daily freight continued to run, as this extract from the Great Southern Railways working timetable of 22nd November 1943 reveals. The daily freight was scheduled to take over three hours for the 30 mile trip, the only intermediate stop for traffic purposes being Castlegregory Junction, where the abandoned branch to Castlegregory diverged from the main line. The freight service declined to 'as required' in 1944, and ceased in 1947. On almost any other railway, that would have been the end, but CIE was reluctant to abandon any lines at this stage, despite Reynold's condemnation of uneconomic branches. A once monthly cattle working ran in conjunction with Dingle Fair, and from 1950, the anachronism of a railway that came to life for one day each month became increasingly popular with enthusiasts who made the pilgrimage to the West of Ireland. A co-operative attitude by CIE meant that visiting enthusiast were allowed to travel with the train, and photograph it en route, and photos of the Dingle train are a treasured possession of those who made the trip.

Tralee to Dingle.   Dingle to Tralee.

Distance from Tralee	DOWN TRAINS.		WEEK-DAYS.			UP TRAINS.			WEEK-DAYS.			
				1. Goods.							2. Goods.	
				a.m.							p.m.	p.m.
	TRALEE ...	* dep.	...	7 30	...	DINGLE ...	... dep.	...	...	...	1 0	...
2¼	BLENNERVILLE HALT	N ,,	...	...	...	BALLINASTEENIG	... ,,	...	...	...	...	...
6	CURRAHEEN	N ,,	...	...	...	LISPOLE HALT ...	... ,,	...	...	...	1 29	...
7¼	DERRYMORE HALT	N ,,	...	...	...	GARRYNADUR	... ,,	...	...	...	...	...
10	CASTLEGREGORY JOT.	* arr.	...	8 10	...	BALLINASARE ...	... ,,	...	...	...	...	...
						ANNASCAUL ...	... ,,	...	...	...	2 10	...
						EMALOUGH ...	... ,,	...	...	...	...	...
	CASTLEGREGORY JUNCTION dep.		...	8 20	...	GLENMORE ...	... ,,	...	...	...	...	...
11¾	CAMP HALT	N ,,	...	...	...	GLENAGALT	... ,,	...	...	...	...	...
14	GLENAGALT HALT	N ,,	...	...	...	CAMP ...	... ,,	...	...	...	...	...
16	GLENMORE HALT	N ,,	...	...	...	CASTLEGREGORY JUNCTION	arr.	...	...	...	3 15	...
17¼	EMALOUGH HALT	N ,,	...	...	...							
20¼	ANNASCAUL ...	* ,,	...	9 40	...							
23	BALLINASARE HALT	N ,,	...	...	...	CASTLEGREGORY JUNCTION	dep.	...	...	...	3 25	...
24¼	GARRYNADUR HALT	N ,,	...	...	...	DERRYMORE ...	... ,,	...	...	...	...	...
26¼	LISPOLE HALT ...	,,	...	10 12	...	CURRAHEEN ...	... ,,	...	...	...	...	...
27¼	BALLINSTEENIG HALT	N ,,	...	...	...	BLENNERVILLE ...	... ,,	...	...	...	...	...
31¼	DINGLE ...	* arr.	...	10 32	...	TRALEE ...	... arr.	...	...	...	4 5	...

N.—No Telephone Communication.   * E Tablet.

Opposite page top: Because of the formidable 1 in 29 or 1 in 30 banks, the cattle specials were double headed, and a pair of the Hunslet 2-6-0Ts that provided the mainstay of Dingle motive power would be steamed at Tralee for the empty train to Dingle fair. There were five of them, 1, 2, 3, 6 and 8, the missing numbers covering other locomotives. They had 3 ft 0½ ins driving wheels, 13 x 18 ins cylinders and Walschaerts motion. Given a T suffix by the GSR after the 1925 take-over, No 3T had been transferred to the Cavan & Leitrim in the 1940s, and No 6T had gone for overhaul in 1950, and never returned, leaving just 1T, 2T and 8T. No 2T was the next casualty, failing in November 1952. With the cattle trains having months to run, it was not worth overhauling 2T, and she lay at the back of Tralee shed, where she is seen in April 1953. She was later scrapped at Inchicore.

Opposite page bottom: By 1952, CIE railways were losing £1.7m, and although CIE had ordered four diesel railcars for the West Clare narrow gauge section, followed by some B-B freight engines, it made little sense to do so for the Dingle, with its once monthly cattle train. No 8T is the pilot engine on the April 1953 empty cattle special to Dingle, and is taking water at Annascaul, one of the two principal intermediate stations on the T&DLR. It is 20¾ miles west of Tralee, and the deserted countryside gives an idea of the terrain that was crossed by the Dingle train. Water was always a problem and the second engine, 1T, will have a much-needed drink, as soon as 8T is replete. Although maintenance was minimal, the survival of a railway to carry one train a month was hopelessly uneconomic, and by 1953 it was clear that the end was near. The last cattle train ran two months later, on 26th June, and a month later a clearance special collected stock from Dingle and returned it to Tralee for disposal, and the railway that came to life for one day each month passed into fable. Maybe, like Brigadoon, it will return for one day in 2053.

Below: The Down cattle special has arrived at Dingle, (population 1,786 in 1907) and No 8T has already uncoupled, and run to shed, to water and turn, leaving the second engine, No 1T, to follow. The bowed frame on the leading open wagon, 36T, speaks volumes. Unroofed cattle wagons had been banned in England before World War 1, but persisted in the west of Ireland for over 40 years. The short canopy is a relic of the passenger service, but the last regular passenger train had departed in 1939. One more passenger train will come to Dingle, a special arranged by the celebrated enthusiast and writer J H Price, who was also editor of Cook's Continental timetables. It will bring a party of enthusiasts in June 1953 and the railway era at Dingle will come to an end. Sadly, I was too young to make the pilgrimage to far-off Dingle, but was fortunate enough to know at least five people who did so, and hear at first hand of the magic of the Dingle railway. No 5T, the only 2-6-2T was out of use after 1949, and went to the Cavan & Leitrim section of CIE, migrating to the USA, but returning to Ireland in 1986. A short section of the T&DLR was re-laid, and although this is at the flat Tralee end of the line, so lacks the drama of the 1 in 30 assault on the summit at Glenagalt, it was wonderful to see a Dingle locomotive in action.

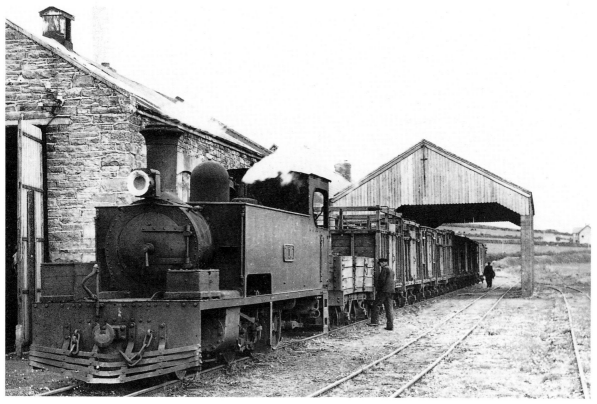

9 · CAITHNESS TO THE BORDERS

Prior to 1923, the Scottish railways had been as distinctive as their Irish cousins, perhaps even more so, for unlike Ireland, where the Midland and the LNWR both controlled subsidiary companies, the five Scottish lines were entirely independent. Each had its own individuality, but a common Scottish theme as well, and English influence was notably lacking. Indeed, it could be said that Scottish railwaymen had a greater impact on England, than vice versa, for had not James, Patrick and Matthew Stirling all migrated from Kilmarnock to south of the border? Dugald Drummond had made the same move, as had his successor on the LSWR, R W Urie. All had been attracted by the better prospects held out by the wealthier English lines, and herein lies the paradox of the Scottish railways. Forced to be frugal and efficient by the railway environment they were raised in, Scots railwaymen proved adaptable whether they worked in Scotland itself, in England, or across the globe, but the limited population, much of it crammed into the Clyde valley, meant that the Scottish companies, although stronger than their Irish counterparts, were financially weaker than the English lines. The most obvious manifestation of this came with the grouping in 1923. As the five Scottish companies, the Caledonian, the North British, the Glasgow & South Western, the Great North of Scotland and the Highland Railway were all independent, there would have been no problem in setting up a Scottish Railway Group, but parliament decided that its earning capacity would be insufficient, and Scotland's interests would best be served by merging its railways into the two Anglo-Scottish groups, the LMS and LNER, where profits earned in England could subsidise the weaker Scottish lines. Whatever the merits of the idea, Scotland felt slighted, and when British Railways was set up in 1948, a separate Scottish Region was created out of the LMS and LNER lines in Scotland. Fortunately both companies had a divisional structure that simplified the task, and there was an ample supply of talented Scottish officers from which to select the management of the new Region. The man selected to head the new region was T F Cameron, who had been the LNER Divisional General Manager in Edinburgh. As the BTC had objected to the idea of Regional General Managers, claiming it would impede integration, Cameron became Chief Regional Officer. In pre-group days there had been considerable rivalry between the Caley, the North British and the GSWR, and between the Highland and the GNSR, but in 1948, Scottish railwaymen realised that if they were to make a success of their new status as a separate region, they had to work together.

Opposite page: The 1,377 route miles of the North British Railway in 1915, made it the largest of the Scottish lines. The northern partner in the East Coast Main Line, the NBR tapped the West Coast Main Line at Carlisle, via the Waverley route. Other important lines connected Edinburgh and Glasgow and ran up the east coast. The way the Scottish Region blended its diverse heritage is apparent in this early post-nationalisation view. An LMS Black Five heads Gresley stock past the chaotic layout at Edinburgh St Margarets shed. The depot, one of the two principal sheds in Edinburgh, lay east of Waverley station on the East Coast Main Line, and had grown up piecemeal from the dawn of the railway age, with cramped and awkward facilities on both sides of the running lines. An NBR 0-6-2T is partially obscured by wagons on the right, whilst another NB engine, a J88 0-6-0T with outside cylinders, is near the sheerlegs. Loco depots required a constant stream of wagons to bring in loco coal and stores, and to take away ash. The wagons include a brand new 16 ton steel mineral, a former private owner coal wagon which still displays a faded Denaby inscription, but has been renumbered into the ex-Private Owner 'P' number series on the bottom plank, and an ex LMS open M22505.

Below: The most celebrated NBR engines, the Reid Atlantics, had gone by November 1939, leaving Reid's class K 'six foot' 4-4-0s as the premier surviving design. Given Glen names, and classed D34 by the LNER, thirty of the thirty-two engines came into BR ownership. Best known for their long stint on the West Highland Railway, from Helensburgh to Fort William, a distance of almost 100 miles, the Glens were at home on expresses or a pick-up freight. In 1953, eight Glens were sent to the Great North of Scotland section. 62493, *Glen Gloy*, which was stationed at the GNSR Kittybrewster shed in Aberdeen, has arrived with an express from the Great North, and is blowing off at the north end of Aberdeen Joint Station, as she waits a path back to shed. Built in June 1920, and carrying the first 'Bicycling Lion' device, 62493 lasted until June 1960. Motive power transfers had long been a feature of the Scottish railways, with Caley engines displacing Glasgow & South Western classes, and NB 4-4-0Ts going to Kittybrewster. In BR days, many transfers took place, with Caley and NB engines venturing far from their home metals. Whilst the new BR 'Standards' and DMUs became common elsewhere, the Scottish Region often seemed reluctant to discard the ageing pre-group classes that reflected its Scottish heritage, and the restoration of several engines to pre-group liveries in the late fifties, including a Glen, reinforced this impression. The Region's attitude to closing lines was also different to other areas, as was evidenced on the Great North section. Many lines served remote communities, and a few closures of hopeless routes, such as the Old Meldrum and Boddam branches had occurred before the war. The Scottish Region ended passenger services to Alford in January 1950, and from Inveramsay to MacDuff in 1951, but with these chronic loss-making lines eliminated, the region was reluctant to prune further, despite pressure from the BTC. A dislike of direction from across the border, and the reassuring remoteness of BTC headquarters from Scottish Regional headquarters, a blessing that none of the other regions possessed, may have strengthened resistance. In the end, the closures came, and between 1964 and 1968, the Lossiemouth, Banff, Fraserburgh, Ballater, Portessie and Craigellachie lines all closed, but this was years after comparable or more heavily used lines had closed in the south.

4-6-0 with maximum accessibility, that could replace the surviving pre-group 4-6-0s, such as the Robinson designs we have already encountered, and eventually all other 4-6-0s, large 4-4-0s such as the GC directors or D49s, the remaining Atlantics, K2 and K3 2-6-0s, and fitted 0-6-0s. The first of an initial batch of ten engines, which became class B1, appeared in 1942, followed by the first of 400 production engines in 1944. To ease pressure on the LNER workshops, one of the great Scottish locomotive manufacturers, NBL of Glasgow was contracted to build most of the new engines, and NBL turned out No 1197 (NBL works No 26098) in May 1947. This brand new locomotive has just left the Forth Bridge, and is approaching Dalmeny station on the south bank of the Firth of Forth on 27th June 1947 with a stopping passenger train, recognisable by the single headlamp on the bracket below the chimney. With 36 B1s allocated to the Scottish area by the end of 1947, the B1s were a familiar sight on passenger workings from Edinburgh up the bridges route to Dundee, to Glasgow, and on the East Coast Main Line to Newcastle. When delivered from NBL, new B1s were mostly based at Eastfield for a short time for running in turns, before being dispatched to their home shed. 1197 became an Eastfield engine, and already sports the shed inscription on her buffer beam. The B1 4-6-0s finally provided the LNER with an equivalent to the Stanier Black Five, and after the fusion of the ex LMS and LNER lines into the Scottish region, were to appear on former Caley and GSW metals as well. They were popular and well-liked engines, and a feature of the Scottish railway scene for over twenty years. *R E Tustin*

Above: After Gresley's death in 1941, Edward Thompson became Chief Mechanical Engineer of the LNER. Gresley's engines, though magnificent, required careful maintenance, if they were to perform well, and Thompson realised that under modern conditions, a small number of simple low maintenance types had become essential. A new 2-cylinder

Opposite page bottom: Dominating the 'Bridges Route' on the east coast between Edinburgh and Aberdeen, the Forth Bridge became the icon of Scottish railways. The original design was worked out by Sir Thomas Bouch, designer of the ill-fated Tay Bridge, but the loss of a complete train, when the Tay bridge fell in December 1879, shattered Bouch's dreams, and the design of the Forth bridge was handed to Sir John Fowler and Sir Benjamin Baker instead. It was built between 1882 and 1890. The two main spans are 567 yards long, and the height to the top of the structure is 361 feet. Clearance at the centre of the main spans for shipping is 150 feet, a height demanded by the Admiralty so that the largest warships could have access to the Forth at any state of the tide. Even the approach spans are massive, and at the South bank, there are ten spans, each of 168 feet, some of which are visible in the view taken at South Queensferry on 18th September 1951. Queensferry, as the name implies had been the site of a ferry across the stormy waters of the Forth long before the railway age dawned, but with the appearance of railways, train ferries crossed the Forth and the Tay until the bridges were built. As there was still be a need for ferry connection after the bridges were opened, parliament insisted that the NBR should continue to provide ferry services. In 1933, the LNER decided to lease out the Queensferry passage to Denny of Dumbarton. Two new vehicle and passenger ferries were built at the Denny yard in 1934, and named *Robert the Bruce* and *Queen Margaret*, and the latter is depicted at South Queensferry on 18th September 1951. Primarily intended for road vehicles, space for foot passengers was limited to the poop and forecastle ends of the vessels. They were the first diesel electric paddle vessels built for service in the British Isles. Her Majesty Queen Elizabeth II sailed on P M V *Queen Margaret* on the final sailing on the Queensferry passage, when the Forth Bridge opened in September 1964. Under the 1934 agreement, British Railways were required to buy the ferries from Denny, if the service ceased. Three of the four ferries, including the 1934 twins, were broken up in 1965, the survivor being sold to Holland. Even in the fifties, the ferries were hard pressed to cope with demand, and the road bridge provides a faster and more convenient crossing, but so long as you weren't in a hurry, waiting at Queensferry, with shipping entering or leaving the Forth, the ferries arriving and departing every few minutes, and steam trains rumbling over the bridge itself, was a lot of fun. The crossing, sailing within a few yards of the bridge, was fascinating, and I am glad I experienced it.

JOINT CIRCULAR.

GLASGOW,
17th May, 1948.

Standard Instructions for the Reservation of Seats on Trains.

Commencing on 31st May, 1948, the following arrangements for the reservation of seats in trains for individual passengers will apply. All previous Circulars will be cancelled.

(a) Charting Arrangements.

The reservation of seats is restricted to the following trains and care must be taken to keep this information up-to-date from advices received from the Operating and Commercial Superintendents. Seats can only be reserved at the starting points of trains on through coaches.

WESTERN SIDE.

Stations from which reservations can be made.	Train (Weekdays unless otherwise shown).	Destinations to which seats can be reserved.
ABERDEEN. Reservation and Enquiry Office. Telephone 3103 (Ext. 6).	9-40 a.m. to Glasgow (Buchanan St.) 1-10 p.m. to Glasgow (Buchanan St.) 5-30 p.m. to Glasgow (Buchanan St.) 1-20 p.m. (Sunday) to Glasgow (Buchanan St.). 5-25 p.m. (Sunday) to Glasgow (Buchanan St.).	Stirling and beyond. Do. Do. Do. Do.
EDINBURGH (Princes Street). Enquiry Office. Telephone 23276.	10-10 a.m. to Birmingham ... ... 10-40 a.m. to Liverpool (Exchange) 10-40 a.m. to Manchester (Victoria) 4-5 p.m. to Liverpool (Exchange) ... 4-5 p.m. to Manchester (Victoria) ... 9-35 a.m. (Sunday) to Birmingham 10-30 a.m. (Sunday) to Manchester (Victoria). 10-30 a.m. (Sunday) to Liverpool (Exchange).	Crewe and beyond. Beyond Carlisle. Do. Do. Do. Crewe and beyond. Beyond Carlisle. Do.
GLASGOW (Buchanan Street). Enquiry Office. Telephone : Douglas 2900 (Ext. 71 and 113).	10-0 a.m. to Aberdeen ... ... 1-35 p.m. to Aberdeen ... ... 11-0 p.m. **SX** to Aberdeen ... ... 10-10 a.m. to Inverness ... ... 10-20 a.m. **SO** to Inverness ... ... 1-45 p.m. **SX** to Inverness ... ... 1-52 p.m. **SO** to Inverness ... ... 10-20 p.m. **SX** to Inverness ... ... 8-0 a.m. to Oban ... ... 12-12 p.m. to Oban ... ... 10-0 p.m. **SX** to Oban ... ... 10-15 a.m. (Sunday) to Aberdeen ... 11-10 p.m. (Sunday) to Aberdeen ... 11-25 p.m. (Sunday) to Inverness ...	Bridge of Dun and beyond. Do. Dubton and beyond. Aviemore and beyond. Do. Do. Do. Do. Dalmally and beyond. Do. Do. Dubton and beyond. Do. Aviemore and beyond.
GLASGOW (Central). Enquiry Office. Telephone : Douglas 2900 (Ext. 91, 92 and 273).	10-5 a.m. to Birmingham ... ... 10-30 a.m. to Liverpool (Exchange) 3-55 p.m. to Liverpool (Exchange) 10-0 a.m. to London (Euston) ... 1-15 p.m. to London (Euston) ... 10-40 a.m. to Manchester (Victoria) 4-12 p.m. to Manchester (Victoria) 9-30 a.m. (Sunday) to Birmingham 10-0 a.m. (Sun.) to London (Euston) 10-10 a.m. (Sun.) to London (Euston) 10-25 a.m. (Sunday) to Manchester (Victoria). 10-50 a.m. (Sunday) to Liverpool (Exchange).	Crewe and beyond. Beyond Carlisle. Do. London (Euston) only. Crewe and beyond. Beyond Carlisle. Do. Crewe and beyond. London (Euston) only. Crewe and beyond. Beyond Carlisle. Do.

Below: I have to confess a bias when it comes to Scottish railways. One of my father's patients, a Scotsman by the name of Arthur Forsythe, had been brought up alongside the Calendar & Oban section of the Caledonian Railway. He had a clockwork O gauge layout representing the Caley, on which lovingly built Caley locos performed. By modern standards, track and scenery were rudimentary, but when the Connel Ferry bridge was put across the shed door, and trains started running, we were not in a small garden shed, but on the windswept moors of Perthshire and Argyll. It was great fun, and Arthur's reminiscences of the 'Perth Blue' engines of the Caley, delivered in his own soft Scots brogue, enchanted me. The Caley was conscious of its own superiority, calling itself 'The True Line', and adopting the Royal Arms of Scotland for its own. Its 4-6-0s were impressive looking machines, though like many pre-group 4-6-0s, were disappointing on the road, but its 4-4-0s were magnificent. J F McIntosh's Dunalastairs, and their Pickersgill successors, provided the Caley, the LMS and BR with dependable engines that lasted into the 1960's. in the case of the final series of engines. Caley No 79, LMS 14484, seen at Perth shed, was a Pickersgill '72' class superheated 4-4-0 built at St Rollox in 1920, and lasted until November 1959. My last glimpse of a Caley 4-4-0 was at Edinburgh about 1958 or 1959, and I still recall being fascinated by the large driving wheel splashers and the smaller coupling rod splasher that is so prominent in this view. The mix of LMS, LNER and BR Standard classes, leavened by engines I only saw on visits to Scotland, made trips north of the border a treasured memory. The 1,118 route miles of the Caley put it behind the North British in mileage, but its 1000 plus engines put it within fifty or so of its rival, and its profitability and dividend record was far superior. The Scottish region was to adopt Caley blue as its house colour in 1948, and for the Blue Trains that introduced electric workings to the Clyde.

Above: Splendid though Arthur Forsythe's Calendar & Oban line was, the Caley earned its money from its main lines from Carlisle to Glasgow and Edinburgh, from the busy industries of the Clyde valley, and its route to Perth and up the east coast to Aberdeen. Perth itself was a busy location, with the main line services between Aberdeen and the south, and the Highland trains coming across the rugged Cairngorms from Inverness to Stanley Junction, a few miles north of Perth. Going north, it was the gateway to the Highland, going east it heralded the start of the coastal route to Aberdeen, whilst the industrial heartland of Scotland lay south of this city of 40,000 people. Outside cylindered 0-6-0Ts have been relatively rare in British railway history, but the twenty-three examples of McIntosh's 498 class 'Dock Tanks', including LMS 16173, seen at Perth, were an attractive addition to the breed. The first pair were built in 1912, later examples coming out under his successor, William Pickersgill. 16173 was the final engine, appearing in 1921, and when she was withdrawn exactly forty years later, she was one of the last two survivors. Although called dock tanks, they were built for the sharply curved goods yard and private sidings in the industrial heartland of Scotland. The combination of a compact ten-foot wheelbase and outside cylinders meant they lurched alarmingly from side to side at any speed, but pace was not their metier, and for heavy haulage in a tight location they

were splendid. The combination of cinder ballast on yard tracks, tall lattice post signals, and an old NBR coal wagon, still bearing its NB lettering, helps recall the Scottish scene that the Railway Executive was heir to. The tall chimney in the background belongs to Perth Dye Works.

Opposite page top: The Caledonian and the North British have always attracted a legion of admirers, whilst the Highland Railway had the romance of serving the rugged terrain of the north of Scotland. Perhaps the least appreciated of Scotland's railways was the Glasgow & South Western Railway. In terms of mileage, its 492 route miles in 1915, placed it behind the HR, but with the busy Clyde suburban services, and the Ayrshire coalfield, it carried far more passengers and freight traffic than the longer Highland Railway, and its 529 locomotives were more than three times as numerous as the Highland loco stud. One reason why the 'Sou-West' has fared so badly in enthusiast eyes was that at the time of the grouping, many of its engines were elderly, whilst the newer designs by Peter Drummond, the younger brother of the legendary Dugald, and by R H Whitelegg, were few in number, and were to fall foul of the LMS standardisation drive. Although a variety of G&SWR engines could be found as late as 1931, within five years, the survivors had declined to just 36 locomotives, and only one engine entered BR stock. This was one of Peter Drummond's 0-6-2Ts, of which twenty-eight were built between 1915 and 1919. They were intended for coal and ironstone trains on the steeply graded Ayrshire mineral lines, and in the use of an 0-6-2T, Drummond copied the Welsh Valleys railways, and anticipated the 56xx tanks of the GWR by more than a decade. No 16901 is at Hurlford shed, which boasted an allocation of these powerful tanks for many years. Starting life as GSWR No 2 in 1919, and becoming 16401 after the grouping, a second renumbering followed, to make way for a batch of LMS 'Jinties' that were briefly numbered in the 16xxx range. By the time of its demise in February 1944, Sou-West engines were down to single figures and the last survivor of all, sister engine, 16905 went in April 1948 without carrying its allocated BR number. A Hurlford resident that met its fate a few months earlier was a large trout that lived in the 50 foot x 10 foot water tank at the shed. Lacking any predators, and feeding off a plentiful supply of minnows that were drawn into the tank via the supply pipe, the trout had reached 23 ins and 4½ lbs in weight, when the tank was cleaned out in 1947, and it made a welcome addition to the rations of some of the shed staff. Although the mineral branches in Ayrshire were to succumb in later days, the Sou-West main line from Carlisle to Kilmarnock and Glasgow has survived, along with the coast line to Stranraer, and the suburban lines to Ardrossan and Largs. *H J Stretton-Ward*

Opposite page bottom: The River Clyde was the cradle of steam navigation from the day when Henry Bell's primitive steamboat *Comet* first took to the water in 1812. Within ten years, fifty paddle steamers had been launched, and as Glasgow expanded and became a great manufacturing and ship building centre, ordinary Glaswegians sought relaxation along the shores of the Clyde, whilst the wealthy moved out from the centre of the city to the more salubrious coastal communities on the north and south banks of the Clyde. Going 'Doon the Watter', for business or pleasure, was a part of everyday Glaswegian life by 1860, and the tradition

endured for over a century. The three great railway companies that served Glasgow, the North British, the Caledonian, and the Glasgow & South Western, all took to the water, vying with one another, and with independent operators, to open up new routes and provide faster and better steamers. Eventually the three railway companies dominated the Clyde, and from 1901, the paddlers had a rival in the shape of the revolutionary new turbine screw ships. However the paddle steamer never lost its hold on popular sentiment, and its incredible ability to manoeuvre by putting one wheel ahead, and one astern, meant it remained competitive on many routes. Savage competition and rising costs hit profits, and a pooling arrangement evolved before the First World War. The amalgamations of 1923 merged the Caledonian and G&SWR fleets, whilst the NBR steamers became LNER property. Many of the steamers were elderly by the Thirties, whilst others had been lost during the First World War, and both companies added fine new vessels from time to time. In 1934, one of the best loved of the Clyde paddlers joined the LMS fleet. The P S *Caledonia*, commemorated an earlier ship of the same name. She was 623 gross register tons, 230 feet overall, by 62 feet over her paddle boxes, but half that width over the hull, with a draught of 7 ft 6 ins. She was built by Denny of Dumbarton, and was powered by a 3 cylinder compound engine developing 1800ihp, which was capable of driving her at 16¾ knots. As she was intended for shorter runs that required her to turn in restricted waters, paddle wheels were preferable to turbines, but the LMS wanted a modern look, so her paddle sponsons were disguised to resemble the hull. She saw war service as HMS *Goatfell* in the Clyde minesweeping flotilla. *Caledonia* is seen at Dunoon Pier on 15th September 1951, and continued to delight travellers until the 1960s, and the drastic changes brought about by the Transport Act 1968. This transferred the Scottish Bus Group, David MacBraynes, and the railway owned steamers to a newly formed Scottish Transport Group. The new owners made pious comments about fostering Clyde cruising, but 1969 marked the end for PS *Caledonia*. She was sold for use as a floating restaurant on the Thames where she caught fire, a sad fate for a beautiful ship that I recall with affection.

Caledonian Steam Packet and LMS monthly season ticket.

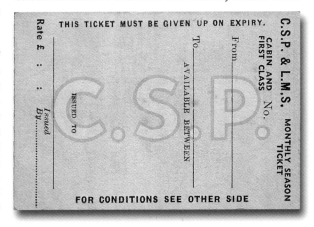

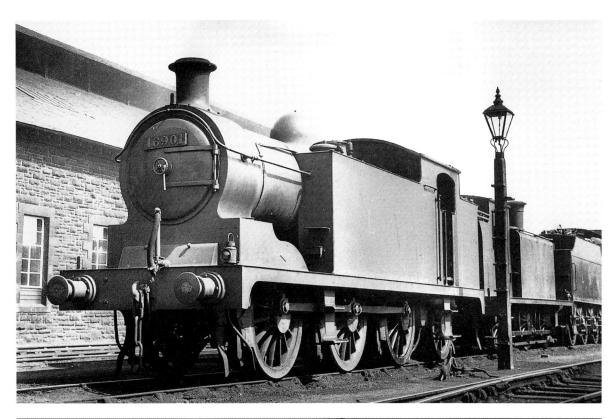

Opposite page top: On 17th March 1949, agreement was reached between the BTC and the Scottish Motor Traction Co Ltd, as a result of which SMT buses were transferred to the Commission, along with the group's interests in various subsidiaries, including Western SMT, Rothesay Tramways (which had long since ceased to operate trams) and W Alexander & Sons Ltd. Alexander's had been formed in 1923, coming under control of SMT in 1929, and built up a dense network of routes in Fife, across the Scottish Midlands, from Grangemouth to Oban, and in the north, from Dundee to Aberdeen and Peterhead. As with the Bristol Group, Alexander's operated their own body building plant, though they did not manufacture their own chassis. In the last days before the BTC take-over, and for another year or so afterwards, Alexander's standardised on the Leyland PS1 Tiger for their single deckers, providing smart coach or bus bodies from the Alexander works. CWG275, which is carrying Alexander's fleet number plate NPA173, was a 1950 PS1 Tiger with a 35 seat front entrance Alexander coach body, and when Alexander was reorganised in 1961, was allocated to W Alexander & Sons (Northern) Ltd. A vivid new Yellow and cream livery was adopted, along with a script Northern title. NPA173 is seen at Aberdeen bus station in July 1969, on route 38 to Stonehaven, and bears the S allocation plate of Stonehaven garage above the fleet number. With a considerable volume of parcels traffic, Alexander's had retained crew operation on some routes, rather than opt for one-man-operated under-floor-engined single deckers, and the beautifully turned out PS1s were a joy to behold, as half-cab single deckers were a rarity by the late 1960s. Equally pleasant to behold were Northern's conductresses or clippies, as the company seemed to have a policy of only selecting the most lovely Scots lassies, and then turning them out in an elegant uniform. I suspect that many a romance must have blossomed on the No 38 bus, and the other routes operated by Northern.

Opposite page bottom: At the dawn of railways, when primitive plate ways were laid down to serve coalmines, small chauldron wagons were moved by manpower or by horse, but with the success of the iron horse, many enthusiasts assume that the equine variety quickly passed from the railway scene. This was far from the truth. Tucked away on page 321 of the BTC Annual Report for 1948 is a return for Road Vehicles and Horses. On 1st January 1948, the Railway Executive was the proud possessors of no fewer than 8,793 horses, of which 8,555 were used for road vehicles. The remaining 238 horses were shunting horses, one of which was 'Mac', seen at work at Kyle of Lochalsh on 24th June 1947. In a number of locations, where wagons needed to be moved a few at a time, or intermittently, the horse was cheaper than its steam powered rival, and the last shunting horses lingered in BR service into the 1960s. It was not only remote outposts where they were found, Rugby, for example having Up side and Down side shunting horses. Many years ago, my father and I spoke to a retired railwayman who had vivid memories of horse shunting at Rugby. They were limited to a maximum

load of three wagons, and one horse, with a highly developed sense of horse rights, would look behind him when starting, and if a fourth wagon had been attached to the rake, would stop until it had been detached. Whether 'Mac' had similar principles, I do not know, but the thought of a horse checking its load to confirm its rights had been respected, adds a pleasing touch to railway history. Over the years, I have often thought how pleasant it would be to replicate horse shunting on our layout, but I have never worked out how to do so convincingly. A powered goods van would present no problems, but getting the horses' legs to move convincingly would be difficult, and what happens when the wagon is to be moved in the other direction? *R E Tustin*

Below: This LMS handbill was to inspire the Scotsman to travel to far-away London for the Bakers' and Confectioners' Exhibition on Monday 4th September 1939. Alas, the Second World War broke out at 11.00am the previous day.

Above: Running north from Stanley Junction to Inverness, stretching part way to Aberdeen, and with lines reaching the west coast at Kyle of Lochalsh, and as far north as Thurso, on Scotland's rugged northern coast, which is washed by the restless waters of the North Atlantic, the Highland was a railway of Romance. With 506 route miles at the grouping, it came third in Scotland, and just ten of the English railways exceeded it in mileage, but traffic was light and trains infrequent. Its 150 engines were exceeded by the Taff Vale Railway in Wales, which was less than a quarter of its size. Its most northerly outpost was Thurso, some 688 miles from London, with a population of 3,203 people at the start of the 1950s. A main platform face, protected by a short train shed, a bay platform open to the elements, a modest goods shed, and a single road loco shed comprised the station facilities, as we see in this study dating from 19th June 1947. The station was controlled from a small open air ground frame, visible to the left of the loop points. Trains were infrequent. In September 1949, there were two passenger trains each day, leaving Thurso at 8.30am and 3.35pm, with workings arriving from the south at 1.30pm and 4.35pm. They ran to Georgemas Junction, seven miles to the south, where they combined with workings to and from Wick, for the remaining 147 miles to Inverness. Apart from Dingwall, with a population of 3,453 people, the remaining communities in that immense tract of country varied from a few hundred people to a couple of thousand. It was amazing that anyone had built a railway in such remote terrain, or that the Highland Railway managed to work it profitably, but in the years before 1914, the HR not only worked it, but paid a small dividend to its shareholders. Although the section was a chronic loss maker

by the 1950s, Scottish Region's resistance to closures meant it hung on year after year. When Dr Beeching proposed abandonment of everything north of Inverness, strong pressure was exerted, and the proposals rejected by the Minister of Transport. Happily the line survives. *R E Tustin*

Opposite page top: The Highland bequeathed over 150 engines to the LMS in 1923, and whilst HR engines did not suffer the same horrendous attrition as the 'Sou-West', just 29 were active by January 1948. The ten surviving members of the 'Small Ben' class 4-4-0s were the most numerous. Peter Drummond had built twenty of these small boilered 4-4-0s for the Far North Line between 1898 and 1906, whilst he was on the HR. Some of them were still there almost fifty years later! HR No 41, *Ben Bhach Ard* of 1906, became LMS 14415, and is seen at Thurso shed on 19th June 1947. She entered BR stock, but was withdrawn in May 1948. The small stone loco shed dated from 1874 when the line was opened from Georgemas Junction to Thurso. The 45-foot turntable was later provided with extensions to allow it to turn the 'Small Bens', the rails projecting beyond the end of the turntable pit, and being strengthened by L-shaped plates. Ash and coal sidings were provided off the turntable, but wagons had to be moved by hand to and from these sidings, as the turntable was not long enough to accommodate a wagon and a loco. Just one engine, usually a 'Small Ben' was shedded at Thurso. A quiet backwater for most of its life, Thurso carried an immense traffic during both world wars, as it was the gateway to the important naval base at Scapa Flow in the Orkneys. *R E Tustin*

Below: The Far North line was unlike any other railway in the British Isles, traversing the almost treeless northern plains. An Inverness 'Black Five', LMS 4772, approaches Georgemas Junction from Wick, with the 3.30pm Wick to Inverness stopping passenger, due into Inverness at 9.25pm on 19th June 1947. Georgemas, which was 7 miles south of Thurso, was the most northerly railway junction in the British Isles, and with few dwellings in the vicinity, functioned as a junction, rather than to meet local needs. From 1941 until June 1947, when he retired on health grounds, Malcolm Spier, whom we have met on the NCC, was the LMS Chief Officer for Scotland. Appointed in wartime, he was not able to effect the same changes in Scotland that he had achieved on the NCC, but between the end of hostilities and his retirement, he improved Lanark, Kyle of Lochalsh, St Rollox, Polmadie and Irvine, and enhanced the docks at Troon and Grangemouth, and refurbished hotels at Edinburgh, Gleneagles, and Perth. His successor as Acting Chief Officer Scotland was T H Moffat, who became deputy to T F Cameron, on the formation of the Scottish Region in 1948.

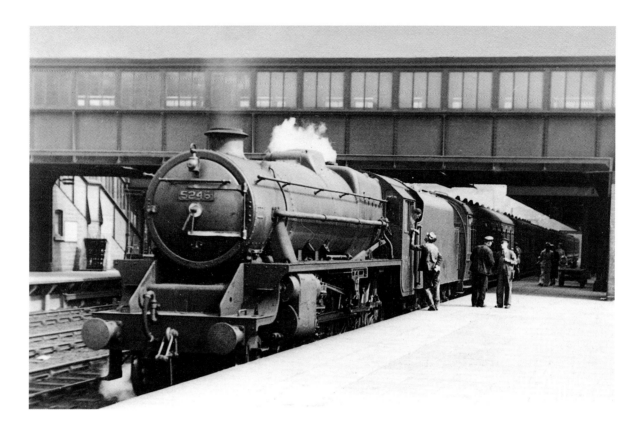

10 · CROESO Y CYMRU

The question is sometimes asked why the BTC set up a Scottish Region, but not a Welsh Region. In Scotland, the railways had been separate companies from the outset, and although merged into the LMS and LNER in 1923, rather than formed into a separate Scottish Railway, both companies operated a divisional structure, and the new Scottish Region was easy to assemble from the LMS and LNER Scottish areas in 1948. By contrast, the LNWR Holyhead main line and branches dominated North Wales, whilst the GWR main line to Newport, Cardiff and Fishguard was the premier route in the south. In Central Wales the LNWR and GWR vied for power. The only sizeable Welsh company was the Cambrian Railways, with a main line which ran from Whitchurch, a few miles west of Crewe, to Pwllheli and Aberystwyth, plus the small but very busy South Wales Valleys coal lines, such as the Taff Vale or the Rhymney, all of which were eventually absorbed into the GWR. Without appropriating parts of the LNWR and GWR in 1923, a Welsh Railway was pointless, and would have suffered the same economic problems as a Scottish Railway. In 1948, a Welsh Region could have been created, but unlike Scotland, where the border was the divisional boundary as well, the for-mer North Western lines were merely a part of the Western Division of the LMS, and similar problems would have existed had any attempt been made to unravel the ex-GWR lines. As there were significant traffic flows from North Wales to Chester, and the LM Region, and from South Wales to the GW main line, but traditionally there had been very little north-south movement, a Welsh Region would have been a political gesture, rather than an operational unit. Operationally the decision not to create a Welsh Region made sense, but the lack of a Welsh regional voice meant that local interests counted for less than in Scotland. Closures seem to have bitten in Wales much sooner than in Scotland, and this may have been one legacy of this decision, though it is hard to blame the railway managers of the day for not seeing that a Welsh voice might have staved off an as yet unseen threat. I have used the contemporary spelling of place names in this section, e.g. Towyn rather than Tywyn.

Opposite page: Good communications between London and Dublin was a perennial government preoccupation, but became especially significant following the Act of Union in May 1800, after which Irish MPs sat in Westminster. Thomas Telford refurbished the Holyhead road between 1815 and 1819, but the coming of railways offered better and more convenient facilities. The Chester & Holyhead Railway was incorporated in 1844, and with the completion of the Britannia bridge over the Menai straits in 1850, through communication was possible between Euston and Holyhead, where ships belonging to the City of Dublin Steam Packet, and to the LNWR, took passengers and mails across the water to Ireland. From the outset, the C&H was worked by the LNWR, and taken over a few years later. With the rise in traffic to and from Ireland, and the growth of North Wales coast resorts such as Llandudno, Colwyn Bay and Rhyl, parts of the C&H were quadrupled, a rarity in any of the Celtic fringe countries. The 'Irish Mail' became one of the prestige trains on the North Western, worked for many years by LNWR 'Prince of Wales' 4-6-0s in their own link at Rugby steam shed. This arose due to a 19th century agreement whereby 150 miles was a day's work for an express crew, and Rugby to Holyhead was just over the 150 miles, giving good value to the LNWR, and a short working day for the men, compared to the standard 10 hour pay day. After the grouping, rules changed, and 'Royal Scot' 4-6-0s, some of them based at Holyhead itself, took over. In due course, Stanier 4-6-0s appeared on secondary turns, and 'Black Five' No 5246 is seen on a Down semi-fast at Bangor on 23rd August 1937. Bangor station itself was the result of a major reconstruction commenced by the LMS in 1924, but inherited from the North Western. The existence of the largest and most pow-erful of England's railways, the mighty LNWR, and then the LMS, astride the North Wales coast, stamped one of Wales' busiest lines with an unmistakably English appearance which owed little to Welsh tradition or opinion, as this view of an LMS engine in an LMS station reveals. *R E Tustin*

Below: Bangor station occupied a site that might not appeal to a professional railwayman but could have been designed with the railway modeller in mind. A ridge at each end of the station meant that the line plunged into tunnels at each end of the station. We are looking from high ground to the west of the station, through which the 648 yard Belmont tunnel burrows, towards the platforms, and the portal of the 890 yard long Bangor tunnel on 27th August 1952. Bangor No 1 signal box can be seen to the right of Bangor tunnel, whilst the roof and cast iron chimney of No 2 box appear in the foreground. The steam shed parallels the platforms to the right of the station, and for many years was under the charge of a well known North Western railwayman and author, J M Dunn. To the right of the shed is the combined water tank and coal hole, the carriage sidings and the goods depot, part of which is at right angles to the running lines. LNWR and LMS loco types can be seen in the loco yard and goods depot. The existence of this LMS station, which was actually designed at the close of the North Western era, and of an LNWR running shed and coal hole, emphasises the English nature of this Welsh main line. The same combination of motive power, station buildings, signal boxes and other structures could have been found anywhere from Euston to Carlisle. Administered as a part of the Western division of the LMS, the Chester & Holyhead passed to the London Midland Region of British Railways, being administered from the district offices at Chester.

Opposite page top: Located a few miles west of Bangor, and just across the Menai straights in Anglesey, the Welsh influence was more obvious. Llanfairpwllgwyngyllgogerychwyrndrobwllllantysiliogogogoch had achieved fame in North Western days, and the station name was set out in full on a gigantic version of the standard London Midland region enamelled station sign. A smaller board that broke down the Welsh name into syllables, provided a convenient translation into English. This revealed that it was an essay on geography, explaining the name of the local church, and where it was located. In the 19th century, North Wales was still a predominantly Welsh speaking area, and apart from the place names, another concession to local feeling was to cast the standard LNWR trespass notices in Welsh, as well as in English.

Opposite page bottom: In pre-group days, branch lines were often thrown off trunk routes to tap local communities, and to protect vital routes from 'poaching' lines constructed by rival companies. As a coastal route, the C&H branches mostly ran south, the only notable exception being the Llandudno branch. A GWR line meandered through the mountains some 20 to 30 miles south of the C&H from Wrexham to Bala and Dolgelly, and whilst the GWR would have liked to reach the North Wales coast, the LNWR came out on top, every one of the north-south routes being staked out by the North West-

ern. Today, Denbigh is at the heart of a 'rail desert', but had been reached from three directions in Victorian times. The oldest line, the Vale of Clywd, came in from the north, where it joined the C&H, and opened in 1858. The Denbigh, Ruthin & Corwen Railway carried North Western influence south to tap the GWR at Corwen, and opened in stages between 1862 and 1865. The final link, the Mold & Denbigh, came in from the east, and opened in 1869. All three lines have long gone, the DR&C being the first to go in 1953, the Vale of Clwyd following in 1955, and the Mold line losing its passenger services in 1962. When Fairburn 2-6-4T No 42053 was photographed running into Denbigh with a 3 coach local from Chester on 8th September 1955, the DR&C had already lost its passenger service, and the same would happen to the Vale of Clwyd trains in ten days' time. Even so, the station is still well maintained, with a well-tended flowerbed in the foreground, whilst two other locomotives are visible in the distance. The illusion, that all was well, with a sizeable station staff and plenty of motive power, presented a reassuring picture, but one wonders if a more economical approach, with an unstaffed station, DMUs rather than costly steam trains, or even a GNR(I) railbus, together with a more critical look at motive power needs, might have offered worthwhile economies. Did a town of 8,127 people, with an infrequent train service, actually need three engines in steam?

Above: Of the several communities in the British Isles to be called Newport, the largest was Newport (Mon), so called from its location in Monmouth, a county that has always enjoyed an ambivalent 'Is it; Isn't it' English or Welsh status. With a population of over 100,000, it was one of the largest cities in the United Kingdom, and its location astride the GWR South Wales main line, ensured it of a good train service and plenty of railway activity. At the start of the fifties, the goods depot adjoining the station still proclaimed its GW & LMS joint ownership, for although this was GW territory, 'foreign' or joint goods depots had sprung up in many cities. 5685 is one of the celebrated 56xx tanks, which were developed by

C B Collett shortly after the grouping. The design was a Swindon version of existing 0-6-2Ts used by the valleys railways on the steeply graded branches that served the coal mining communities that flanked the main line, most of the lines having been independent until the grouping in 1923. 5685 bears the lamp code of a parcels, fish, fruit, or livestock train, and parcels are being unloaded from the leading BG. Just as the Chester & Holyhead proclaimed its LNWR/LMS parentage, Newport station was a classic Great Western creation, and this scene could have been repeated anywhere on GWR metals.

Below: One of the little railways absorbed into the GWR in 1923 was the Burry Port & Gwendraeth Valley Railway. Rather than the 0-6-2Ts that abounded on the valleys lines, the 15 BP&GV engines that came to the GWR were 0-6-0Ts. No 8 *Pioneer*, came from Hudswell, Clarke of Leeds, in 1909. Unlike the LMS, which disdained small non standard classes, GWR policy was to send absorbed engines to Swindon, where any well designed types with a reasonable life expectancy would receive standard GWR fittings. BPGV No 8, which became GWR 2197, and was withdrawn in October 1952, is seen at Swindon. In the halcyon days of the South Wales coal trade, when annual production figures rose to an amazing 56.8m tons in 1913, ownership of shares in the more prosperous of the valleys coal railways was virtually a licence to print money. The Rhymney Railway paid 8.5%, whilst the neighbouring Barry Railway did better than that,

with 9.5% dividends. Much of the South Wales output went for export, and the disruption of World War One led to increased foreign competition, a loss that was never recouped. The switch from coal to oil fuel for shipping, and to motor ships, was another body blow to the industry, whilst the 1926 Miners' strike added to the misery. The shareholders in the Valleys lines that had once been so profitable, must have thanked their lucky stars that parliament had insisted on transferring their lines to the GWR when they were still riding high. The decline continued after the war, and the switch from coal to other forms of domestic heating saw the South Wales coalfield dwindle to insignificance. Robbed of their traffic, the Valleys railways had little purpose, and by the 1980s most of the competing lines that gave the area one of the most dense rail networks in the world had long gone. *H J Stretton-Ward*

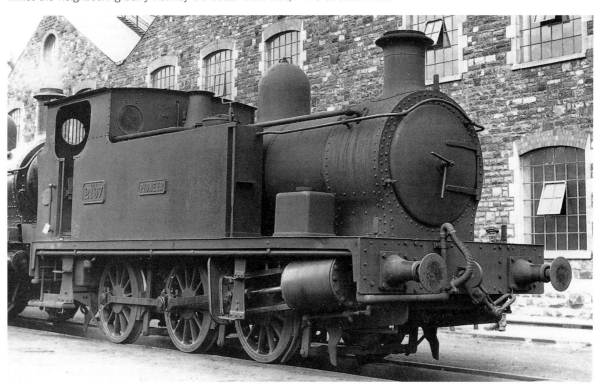

Opposite page top: The only Welsh line of 'national' size was the Cambrian Railways, which was an 1860s merger of impoverished local companies in mid Wales. The Cambrian main line tapped the GWR and LNWR at Wrexham, at Whitchurch, and at Buttington Junction, and ran via Welshpool and Machynlleth to Dovey Junction, where one line ran south along the coast to Aberystwyth, and another line turned north, passing Towyn en route to Pwllheli. Machynlleth, a town of 1875 people, would count as little more than a village in the south east of England, but in Central Wales, was a regional centre. By the 1940s, it had gained fame as the junction for one of the few surviving narrow gauge railways in the British Isles. We will visit the Corris railway later on, but here we will explore the Cambrian station, which was on an embankment some feet above the adjacent Corris sta-

tion. The main buildings, a handsome two story stone structure, were built for the Newtown & Machynlleth Railway in 1863, with three gables fronting onto the railway. The buildings were on the Down platform, the line being carried over the main road on a girder bridge, one of the bridge girders being visible in the distance. The main and loop lines merged beyond the bridge, but in mechanical signalling days, the points were too far away to be worked by the main box, which served the yard connections at the east end of the station, so a small West Signal Box was provided on the Down platform. *H J Stretton-Ward*

Opposite page bottom: The Aberyswyth and Pwllheli lines split west of Machynlleth, the Pwllheli line providing superb seascapes for the rest of the journey. At Towyn, the line

diverged inland, and the Cambrian station was located off the end of the main street, not too far from the sea, making it useful for townsfolk and holidaymakers alike. The seaside traffic, though trivial compared to Blackpool, Southend, or Brighton, brought welcome cash into the Cambrian coffers, as the company was habitually hard up, and ordinary shareholders did not have to worry about how much their dividend would be, as it was nothing, year after year. The Cambrian was not a good investment, but served a vital transport need in central Wales and along the coast. To many of its shareholders that mattered more than dividends, as they were local people who had invested in their local community. The station buildings at Towyn were more modest than at Machynlleth, but boasted a similar short canopy, the ornately carved wooden support spandrel being visible. In latter years, BoT rules required a minimum distance of six feet between a roof support, nameboard or lamppost and the platform edge, so that a standing passenger could not be crushed between the fixed obstruction and an open door on a moving carriage. Stations built prior to this rule were not affected, giving an idea of the antiquity of this structure, and the poverty of the Cambrian. *H J Stretton-Ward*

Opposite page top: Near Barmouth, the Cambrian coast line crossed the tidal Afon Mawddach on a long viaduct, before running parallel to the coast again. Where a passenger line is built to less than 10 chains radius, Board of Trade rules required that it should be checkrailed as a safety precaution, and subject to rigid speed limits. I could not resist this lovely portrait of 55xx 2-6-2T No 5517 squealing round the continuously check-railed exit curve from the 800 yard long Barmouth bridge on 23rd June 1954. A few yards beyond the bridge, the train will plunge into a short tunnel, then run within reach of the waves up the coast to Portmadoc, and finally to Pwllheli. Barmouth bridge was a composite structure, with two steel spans that date from 1906, one of which opened across the navigable portion of the estuary on the north bank, and a long viaduct of 113 sections, each supported on timber piles. Often described as Bowstring girders, the Barmouth spans are technically hogbacked, as the curved top chord joined the horizontal bottom chord in a true bowstring, but is separated from it by a short vertical member in a hogbacked girder, as at Barmouth. The bridge, which was built in 1867 to the designs of Benjamin Piercy, is the only substantial timber viaduct surviving on the rail network today, but nearly met its fate some years ago, as the timbers had been under attack by the Teredo Navalis worm for many years. This had not been a hazard when the bridge was built, but had arrived in the Afon Mawddach in the timbers of ships returning from warmer waters long ago, the worms finding the tidal waters of the estuary, and the bridge timbers a pleasant home from home. The bare slopes rising up to the gaunt summit of Cader Idris are a reminder of how mountainous this part of Wales is, and how railways must thread their way through the valleys, or along the narrow strip between the coast and the mountains. It also helps explain why so much of the rail network of Central Wales disappeared between the 1950s and the end of the 1960s.

Opposite page bottom: Often, stations were far from the towns they served, but the Cambrian coast stations were mostly well placed. Barmouth was right in the heart of town, within yards of the main street, and the seashore. Although displaying a local passenger headcode, 'Dukedog' 4-4-0 No 9024 is on the Up Cambrian Coast Express on 23rd June 1954. Intended for the lightly laid Cambrian section, their outside frames and archaic 19th century appearance made them firm favourites with enthusiasts, but the appearance of BR Standard 78000 2-6-0s in the early fifties suggested their days were numbered, though it was not until 1957 that the axe fell, with half of the survivors going in three months, including No 9024. This view, with the Dutton signal box, footbridge, the Dukedog, traditional advertisements, including Players and Gold Flake cigarettes and NIP-A-KOFS, which were 'Fine for Throat and Chest', epitomises the closing years of an era in which holidays did not mean going to Heathrow or Gatwick to catch a plane, but a summer Saturday express to the coast at Blackpool, Barmouth or Bournemouth, or a myriad of other coastal resorts. Well into the sixties, when jet travel was bringing Spain and other continental resorts within

reach of many people, over 75% of families holidayed by the seaside. Even allowing for many more 'second' holidays, this had dropped to a little over 40% by 2003. The signal box, which was built by the Worcester signal engineers, Dutton & Co in 1890, when the Cambrian upgraded its signalling to meet BoT requirements, survived until the introduction of Radio Electronic Token Block on the Cambrian Coast in 1988. As a listed building, it could not be demolished, so was later moved to the Llangollen Railway.

Below: If, instead of journeying north from Dovey Junction, we had travelled south, we would have reached Aberystwyth, a thriving seaside resort of some 9,000 souls, with its own long established and highly regarded university, and the National Library of Wales. Once upon a time, no fewer than three lines served Aberystwyth. The Cambrian Railways came in from the north, whilst an impoverished concern called the Manchester & Milford Haven Railway, which reached neither of its name towns, entered from the south. A two-foot gauge line (actually 1 ft 11½ ins) ran due east from Aberystwyth for a distance of twelve miles into the hills, as far as Devils Bridge. Built to open up the valley, and handle mineral traffic as well as tourists, under a Light Railway order of 1897, the Vale of Rheidol Light Railway opened in 1902, was

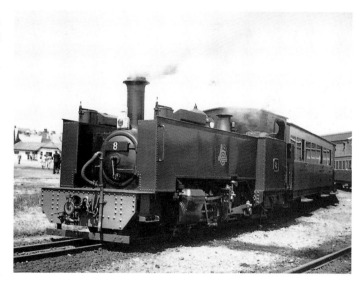

merged into the Cambrian in 1913, and taken over by the GWR in 1923. Until 1968, when it took over the disused Manchester & Milford platforms in the main station, VoR trains used their own ground level platform adjoining the standard gauge station. Provided with a pair of 2-6-2Ts by Davies & Metcalf Ltd prior to the opening, both were in poor condition by 1923, and to stave off a motive power crisis, Swindon built a pair of Westernised 2-6-2Ts in 1923, giving them no's 7 and 8, both of which were blank at the time in the GWR loco lists. No 8 is seen at the VoR terminus at Aberystwyth on 22nd June 1954. In 1956, the Western Region decided on a brighter image for the VoR, putting the engines in lined-out green livery and naming them, No 8 becoming *Llywelyn*.

Above: The GWR had two other freight only narrow gauge feeders that were inherited by BR. The Corris Railway had started life as a 2ft 3ins gauge horse worked tramroad as early as 1859, running from a wharf on the River Dovey at Machynlleth, and later from the Cambrian main line, to slate quarries north of Corris, a distance of some 6½ miles. It was laid in light bridge rail, but in the 1870s, passed into the control of what was to become the Bristol Tramways & Carriage Co. Steam freight services began in 1879, soon after the delivery of three small locomotives. A passenger carriage was also delivered, but this was horse drawn, and proper passenger services were not authorised until 1883. Although passenger trains ran between Machynlleth, Corris and Aberllefenni, the lines from Maespoeth Junction to Upper Corris, and from Aberllefenni to Ratgoed quarry remained mineral only. Although the Iron Horse supplanted its equine cousins on the main line, the branches were not relaid, and the equine variety remained in charge, and whilst the Upper Corris line was lifted during World War Two, the Ratgoed tramway, above Aberllefenni remained open, worked in its declining years by a magnificent white 'shire' horse, which is hauling an empty wagon up Ratgoed tramway embankment en route to the quarries on 25th March 1947. Although many horse worked tramways existed at the dawn of the railway age, most had succumbed by the mid-nineteenth century, and the survival of horse working at Corris was remarkable at this late date. Even the demise of steam work-

ing on the main line in August 1948, did not spell the end, as there was no road up to Ratgoed, and the only way coal, stores and quarry traffic could be moved up the valley was by the tramway, which remained in existence until 1952. *R E Tustin*

Opposite page top: The Bristol Omnibus Co grew into one of the giants of the road industry, with its own bus building plant, and affiliated bus companies, and by the late 1920s, its railway appendage in rural Wales was an embarrassment, especially as slate traffic had long since reduced to a trickle. The main line railway companies had invested heavily in bus services, and in 1930, rail and bus interests were re-organised, the Corris Railway being handed to the GWR in the process. Although the GWR withdrew passenger services in 1931, a daily freight continued to creep over the deteriorating track, and this view of Corris station, taken on 11th April 1946, shows surprisingly few changes in the fifteen years since passenger trains last ran. The main line, which continues on to Aberllefenni, runs beneath the wooden train shed on the left. Oil lamp cases survive on the platform, but without the burners, and some of the heavy slate slabs that make up the platform have been removed over the years. The two road structure to the right of the station is the carriage shed, which ceased to be required when passenger services ended and the coaching stock was sold off, but has survived, albeit rather neglected. The line to the right loops round the back of the buildings to rejoin the main line, but was used for unloading freight rather than as a running line. *R E Tustin*

Opposite page bottom: In 1948, the Corris passed into the BR fold. The railway crossed the River Dovey just outside Machynlleth, but severe flooding, to which the Dovey is susceptible, progressively undermined the south pier of the viaduct, and by the summer of 1948, most of the stock was stabled at Machynlleth in case of trouble. In August 1948, a new inundation made the Dovey viaduct unsafe, the last train running on 20th August 1948. BR had decided that repairs were uneconomic, and demolition of the line began in November 1948. Although standard gauge engines that had been withdrawn were being broken up relatively quickly, no effort was made to break up the Corris stock at Machynlleth. This was surprising, as BR had no other 2 ft 3 ins lines of their own, and the only possible user was another equally obscure railway in Wales that was built to the same odd gauge. However, it was virtually moribund by 1948, and hardly seemed likely to be a customer. No 4, which was the last engine built for the Corris, and came from Kerr, Stuart & Co as late as 1921, is 'in store' at Machynlleth, a process that involved throwing an old GWR wagon sheet over the cab and saddle tank. Open wagon No 31987, and the shrouded cab of No 3 are visible beyond No 4. It is hard to imagine that anyone on the Western Region could seriously have expected that any of this stock would find any purchaser bar the scrap merchant, but fate was to play a strange trick, and all were to be rescued in 1951. *H J Stretton-Ward*

Below: If a passenger left the Cambrian line train at Towyn, and walked across town, he would have found the only other surviving 2ft 3ins gauge line in the British Isles, which ran from Towyn to Abergynolwyn, a distance of just over 6½ miles. It was located less than six miles west of the Corris railway, though there was a mountain range in-between. The railway was incorporated in 1865, and opened the following year to serve the slate quarries above Abergynolwyn. It acquired two locomotives from an obscure manufacturer called Fletcher, Jennings, and four diminutive passenger coaches that carried very few people, but were ample for the regular traffic. Slate was its mainstay, and when the slate quarry closed down in 1910, it looked as if this obscure railway was doomed. Mr Henry Haydn Jones, a successful local businessman, who planned to contest the Merioneth seat in the forthcoming elections, felt something should be done for the unemployed quarrymen. Unlike most politicians, who promise the earth, though not out of their own pockets, and then forget their promise as soon as they have been elected, Haydn Jones bought the quarry and the railway himself, a philanthropic gesture that could only have done him good in local eyes! He was elected, and held the seat for the Liberals until 1945. He kept the quarry going until 1946, by which time it was worked out, but Sir Henry Haydn Jones, as he was by now, did not have the heart to close the railway he had saved half a lifetime previously. He said it would continue to run during his lifetime, even though it now only ran on two days a week. Except locally, and when it was inspected prior to its opening, the Talyllyn Railway, for such was the name of the line, was virtually unknown to enthusiasts and civil servants alike. Whilst many narrow gauge lines fell into the net at the Grouping in 1923, the TR chugged on, oblivious to the changes surrounding it. When the civil servants trawled through lists of railways, hunting down the most obscure of the Colonel Stephens lines, they either overlooked the Talyllyn Railway, decided it was already closed, or was so close to doing so, that it was not worth nationalising. Whatever the story, the TR escaped. Today, we are used to a myriad of railway books on offer, and to the information explosion on the internet, but it was different in 1948. As on the far away Dingle peninsula, news filtered through about this astonishing independent railway that survived on the Welsh coast. A handful of visitors made their way to Towyn for the trip up the line to Abergynolwyn. By now, the railway's fate hung in the balance, for No 1 *Talyllyn*, which had been delivered by Fletcher, Jennings in 1865, still carried her original boiler, and had last run in 1945. She was unfit for further use, requiring a new boiler, saddle-tank, bunker and cylinders, the cost of which was far beyond Sir Henry's eighty-year-old pocket. She was pushed to the back of the loco shed at Towyn (Pendre), where she is seen on 6th October 1950. *H J Stretton-Ward*

Above: On 3rd June 1950, at the age of 86, Sir Henry Haydn Jones passed away, but in deference to his wishes, his executors ran the line until the end of the season on 6th October 1950. It looked as if the thread that had kept the TR alive had snapped. One of the enthusiasts to hear of Sir Haydn's death, was a Leamington businessman called Jack Stretton-Ward, who had been photographing railways since 1911, and taking cine film from the 1920s. Although in poor health, he journeyed to Towyn for the last day, and travelled up and down on the morning and afternoon trains. With the demise of No 1 *Talyllyn* in 1945, just one engine was runnable. This was No 2 *Dolgoch*, an 0-4-0WT delivered by Fletcher Jennings in 1866. She was to a peculiar patented design, with a long wheelbase to accommodate the inside valve gear and firebox between the frames. By the 1940s, she was in deplorable state, and Haydn Jones twice paid for frame repairs, but with the demise of No 1, she was all that kept the TR alive. In the late 1950s, it was usual for last trains to attract numerous locals and visiting enthusiasts, and to be strengthened to cope with the large number of would-be passengers, but when Stretton-Ward filmed No 2 on the last Up train from Towyn Wharf, the train consisted of just one coach and the unique combined brake van and travelling booking office. Edward Thomas, the long serving manager felt that one coach would be ample, and he was right, for apart from a handful of local housewives on shopping trips and Edward Thomas, making a last sentimental trip, Stretton-Ward had the train to himself, making these views an important record of what seemed likely to be the last train, but turned out to be something very different. *H J Stretton-Ward*

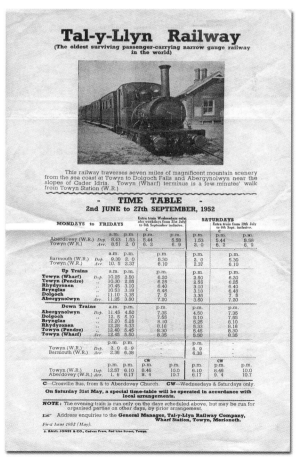

Opposite page top: In 1950, there were no watering facilities at Abergynolwyn, engines using the water tank on the disused mineral extension part way towards Nant Gwernol. Jack Stretton-Ward photographed *Dolgoch* before the engine crew had uncoupled and gone for water. Other enthusiasts had heard of this enchanting railway and wondered it could be saved. There were many sceptics, as the idea of a railway being run by amateurs was novel, and the only precedent in the United States had ended in abject failure within months. An enthusiast with an engineering background called Tom Rolt felt it was possible, and he and a few like-minded people formed the Talyllyn Railway Preservation Society, and with the co-operation of Sir Haydn's widow and of the executors, rescued the TR. In doing so, they not only saved the line for posterity, but gave birth to the railway preservation movement. It is a curious thought that this diminutive engine, built in 1866 by an obscure maker in far away Whitehaven, and running for over 80 years in obscurity, gave birth to a world-wide movement that has given pleasure to so many, and saved so much of our heritage. As these views offer a unique record of the last day of operation in pre-preservation days of the railway that gave birth to the preservation movement, they merit extended coverage. *H J Stretton-Ward*

Opposite page bottom: This scene was taken on the afternoon on 6th October 1950, and when it appeared in print some 30 years later astonished TR devotees. At first sight, No 2 *Dolgoch* seems to be entering Abergynolwyn station, but the brake van/travelling booking office, coach No 5, ALWAYS ran at the lower, or Towyn, end of the train, and NEVER ran at the Abergynolwyn end, regardless of whether the train was proceeding up hill, or back to Towyn, so the van is at the wrong end of the train. As well as stills, Jack Stretton-Ward also took a 16mm cine record of the event, and at the request of Roger Whitehouse, the chairman of the TRPS at the time of the 50th anniversary celebrations in 2000, we were invited to show the film after the TRPS AGM in 2000. The reason for this strange train formation then became clear. The Abergynolwyn end of the van contains an aperture for the brake handle, and Jack Stretton-Ward had observed this, and realised that he could film out of the brake handle opening on the return trip, if the van were at the upper end of the train. He spoke to the obliging Edward Thomas, and the train was re-marshalled to this unique formation, and Stretton-Ward photographed the train being shunted back into the station after the coaches had been re-arranged for filming on the return journey. For the 50th anniversary re-enactment, Roger Whitehouse insisted that the same procedure be followed, with the van at the upper end of the train, and invited my wife and I to film from the brake aperture, just as Stretton-Ward had done fifty years earlier. In the older

record, the camera was not pointed correctly at times, and I discovered why. The brake aperture is waist high, and it is necessary to bend or crouch to see through the viewfinder. We were using a modern lightweight video camera; Jack Stretton-Ward was using a heavy 16mm cine camera, and had to rewind the clockwork drive regularly. I realised the effort he put into creating his unique film record, which has subsequently appeared in a video, 'TR 50', which is available through the Talyllyn Railway Preservation Society, or via the producers, Hillside Publishing. *H J Stretton-Ward*

Below: With the co-operation of Sir Haydn's widow, the TRPS took over the railway early in 1951, and under the leadership of Tom Rolt, prepared for the first season under preservation. TRPS members inspected the disused Corris locos that had been stored at Machynlleth since 1948, and then visited Swindon to negotiate their purchase, coming away with both engines for £50. The engines and some freight stock arrived at Towyn on standard gauge wagons in March 1951, and were unloaded at Wharf station, but neither engine was fit for immediate service, so TR No 2 *Dolgoch*

limped through the 1951 season. The new engines retained their Corris numbers on the TR, No 3 being named in Sir Haydn's memory, and No 4 after the long serving manager, *Edward Thomas*. Although Corris No 3 was in better condition than No 4, her wheel treads were narrow, and on trial trips she dropped between the rails on the disintegrating TR track far too often, so could not run in 1951-52. By 1953, the track was much better, and No 3 entered service. When delivered to Wharf station, she had been put on the line in the traditional TR fashion, i.e. facing chimney uphill to Abergynolwyn, so that the firebox was at the lower end when the engine was climbing, providing a deeper head of water over the crownsheet. Because the vacuum brake reservoir was on the left side of the cab, there was no opening in the sidesheet, so crews had to enter her from the opposite side to the other TR engines. To obviate this, No 3 was turned to face the downhill, and is seen with brake van No 5, at Abergynolwyn on 22nd June 1954. No 3 *Sir Haydn* ran like this until 1957, when she was stored, pending a new boiler.

11 · A WEST COAST PERSPECTIVE, 1948–1953

When the BTC and the Railway Executive formally took control of the Nation's railways on 1st January 1948, some politicians hailed it as a 'new beginning', but Eric Gore Browne, the chairman of the Southern had put it more brutally, but more realistically, back in 1946. Angered at snide remarks by government ministers that under private enterprise, trains ran late and that the upholstery was dirty, he had retorted, 'Do they really believe, the one whose train was late that day, that when the railways are nationalised then will be the time for punctual running, and the other, that ladies will be able to sit down in railway carriages without making their clothes dirty when the railways are owned by the State?' Gore Browne realised that it would take more than state control to improve punctuality or cleanliness. It needed new locomotives, rolling stock and track, and above all, a higher priority for steel, timber, paint and cloth, which were restricted, due to the government's rationing priorities, to make a difference.

Although British Railways did not inherit a clean slate, as the exigencies of war and the different policies pursued by the companies would be crucial for some time, they had considerable scope for shaping the railway network that would emerge over the next decade. In this section, we will examine how one of the princi-

pal trunk routes in railway history, the West Coast Main Line, evolved between 1948 and 1953.

In drafting this section, my original plan was to take material from the whole of BR, but with over 50 views short-listed for a section that could not run to more than a fifth of that, I faced a problem. Did I take a couple of views from each region, and provide the impartiality that has the benefit of not offending anyone, or did I select one route and examine it in more depth? As I studied the photos of the West Coast Main Line, I recalled the old adage that 'the sum of the whole is greater than the sum of the individual parts', and when I looked at comparable Western or Southern region material, the same held true. In the never-never world, where an author could write a book of 5,000 pages, each region would be covered in this depth. In the real world, I decided that an in-depth study of one route had greater impact. The West Coast Main Line may not be your favourite, but if you lived through that era, I hope it will rekindle your memories and help put them in perspective. If you did not experience these fascinating times, then this portrait of the 299 miles between Euston and Carlisle, which actually embraces some 15% of the total mileage of BR, though selective, acts as a pointer to what was happening in Penzance, Perth, Lowestoft or Llandudno.

Opposite page: Sir Nigel Gresley, conscious that the only stationery locomotive testing plant in the British Isles was the GWR establishment at Swindon, campaigned for many years for a national locomotive test station, and a joint project was agreed between the LMS and LNER in 1936. Construction on LMS land adjoining the West Coast Main Line at Rugby began shortly before the war, but was suspended for the duration. One reason for this location was that it was also within yards of the GC London Extension, which was carried over the WCML on a lattice girder bridge, and there was some talk of providing a connection on to the LNER as well. Work resumed after the war, and the Minister of Transport, Alfred Barnes, officially opened the Rugby Locomotive Testing Station on 19th October 1948. As a fitting tribute to Gresley, who had been the mainspring behind the project, but had not lived to see it come to fruition, the engine that was 'on the rollers' for the opening ceremony was Gresley's A4 Pacific, 60007, *Sir Nigel Gresley*. A series of locomotives were tried out on the Locomotive Testing Station, the exterior of which displayed a gigantic version of the British Railways 'Totem', that was to become familiar on paperwork, on timetables and on station signs. For the first time, it was possible to try out many different variables in a strictly controlled environment. A 'Royal Scot' 4-6-0, and a former Great Eastern Railway J19 0-6-0, No 64669 are outside the Test plant. Although the sidings sometimes housed engines destined for test, they were adjacent to the loco shed, and were also used as a convenient stabling road.

Above: When the new British Railways Standards appeared, an early visitor to the Test plant was 'Britannia' Pacific No 70005, *John Milton*, which is seen outside the test house,

with the pressure reservoirs and water lines attached to the smokebox. The water line that sends pressure data to the control rooms is draped along the side of the boiler and diagonally across the cabside. When the locomotive is placed on the rollers, this will be connected to the permanent line to the instrument panel in the control room. My father was shown round the Test house soon after it opened. A locomotive was actually on test at the time, and on a later occasion, I was taken along as well. It was an extraordinary experience to see and hear a steam locomotive travelling at high speed, but standing still. The brick viaduct on the left reveals the proximity of the test house to the GC section of the LNER, but as the GC was carried over the former LNWR lines with no connections between the two, it was as isolated as if it had been 50 miles away from the nearest section of the LNER! Indeed, the test plant was in the order of 50 miles distant from LNER metals, as the nearest LNER access was from the East Coast Main Line at Peterborough, via the Rugby & Peterborough branch, or south on the GCR to Culworth Junction and Banbury, and then north, via Leamington, to Rugby! Used for a number of tests between 1948 and 1955, the death sentence passed on BR steam as a result of the 1955 Modernisation Plan meant that steam testing petered out thereafter, and although used as a store shed for some time, the building was eventually demolished.
P S Parish

Top: Inside the test house, the locomotive was held in place by a drawbar that replaced the usual tender drawgear, and supported on rollers, the position of which could be adjusted to suit the wheelbase of the locomotive. Seven pairs of rollers were provided as leading and trailing truck axles were also supported, and provision had been made for an additional roller if required at a later date. Five of the rollers could be connected to Froude hydraulic brake units, one of which is visible in the foreground. This allowed the test plant to be used for any steam locomotive up to a 10-coupled type. To prevent an excessive rise in water temperature in the Froude units, heated water was pumped from the drums to a cooler outside the building and then back to a 1000 gallon supply tank.

Below left: The drawbar that held the locomotive in position was connected by a sprung coupling to an Amsler hydraulic dynamometer, one end of which was secured to a steel beam set into the foundations to resist the pull of the locomotive. The oil pressure fluctuations in the dynamometer, which is seen here, were transmitted to the measuring cylinder of the recording table, which was in the control room. Results were recorded on moving paper rolls on a time or distance basis, the latter being preferred at Rugby. With measurement of coal and water consumption, speed and distance 'travelled', the power output via the dynamometer, and of exhaust gases, a great deal of data could be accumulated. Adjusting the resistance on the hydraulic brake units could simulate different loads, and variations could be made to the locomotive, for example the draughting arrangements, and the test repeated with identical load factors, allowing each variable to be tested independently. Similar facilities had been developed by the GWR at Swindon, and in France, Germany, and the USA. By the fifties, test data from all of these sources permitted designers to eliminate much of the guesswork that had existed in the past. The magnificent 9F 2-10-0s, which benefited from this scientific approach, showed that Riddles and Cox had all the data they needed to go straight from the drawing board to operational use with one of the most efficient steam locomotives ever built. It was the greatest irony of the steam age that just as steam locomotive engineering became scientific in approach, it also became obsolete, and the data that had been so carefully amassed became of interest to the historian, rather than to the design engineer.

Opposite page bottom: The glamour of the express train, and the charm of the branch line have always attracted more than their fair share of interest, but freight had been the lifeblood of Britain's railways since the dawn of the railway age. In 1948, average receipts per loaded train mile of 11s 1d (55p) for passenger trains, but no less than £1 10s 9d (154p) for freight trains emphasised the importance of a healthy freight business. The Big Four had realised the need to improve freight facilities, and new motive power, such as the Stanier 2-8-0s, had appeared between the wars, whilst the benefits of hump shunting, where wagons are pushed over a raised track or hump, and allowed to run by gravity into sorting sidings, had led to a multiplication of hump yards during the grouping. Some schemes, such as Toton, involved a massive yard on a green field site, and BR were to commission more hump yards in the early days, but the hump also earned its keep at smaller yards. One such location was Nuneaton, on the Trent Valley line. The yard was on a cramped site on the Up side, hemmed in between non railway property and the West Coast Main Line, so the hump was quite low, and provided with steep approach and exit ramps. At large yards, humps were often worked by dedicated shunting engines, but at smaller yards, where there might not be enough work to keep an engine employed continuously, train engines might do so. Stanier 8F, No 48437, which has just pushed a coke wagon over the hump at Nuneaton on 28th June 1950, had been shedded at Bolton at the start of the BR era, but later moved to Rugby, which was the parent shed for Nuneaton. As coke was lighter than coal, it took up more space for a given weight, so coke wagons often had extension railings. The wagon has a P-prefixed private owner number at the bottom left, but traces of the old private owner title still run diagonally from the bottom left to the top right of the body side. It seems to be a Whitwood Chemical Co wagon with a diagonal SMOKELESS FUELS inscription. Charles Roberts built forty-five wagons to this design in 1930. Whatever its antecedents, they are all but obliterated, due to wear and tear, and this was common with surviving private owner stock by the early fifties.

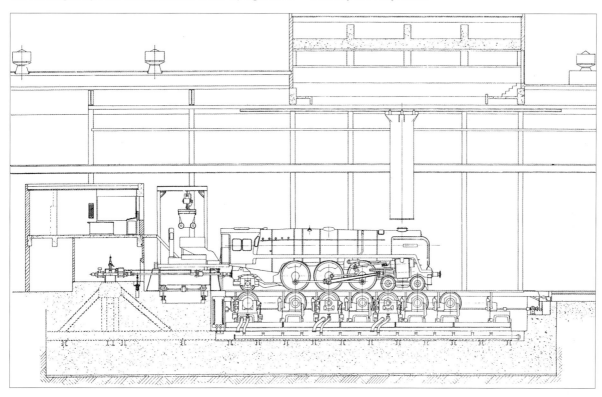

Above: The construction of the Trent Valley line between Rugby and Stafford in 1846, removed Birmingham from the West Coast Main Line as such, but many Anglo-Scottish services were routed via Birmingham (New Street), making it a part of the West Coast for practical purposes. It merits inclusion, and reminds us that although more than a quarter of a century had elapsed since the demise of the LNWR, that its locomotives still played a significant role well into the 1950s. No 58900, was one of the Webb 4' 5½" 0-6-2T's, commonly known as 'Coal Tanks', as they were derived from a similar small wheeled 0-6-0 tender engine. Three hundred were built between 1881 and 1896, and although the first withdrawals took place in 1921, a fifth of them entered BR service. They were accorded BR No's 58880 to 58937. No 58900 had begun life as LNWR No 156 in 1884, becoming LMS 7699 after the grouping, and acquiring its BR number in February 1950. It is seen at Birmingham New Street in March 1951. New Street was joint property until 1923, being owned by the LNWR and the Midland, the two sections being operationally distinct. Most enthusiasts will recognise the two lamps, one above each buffer, as denoting an express passenger service, but appearances can be misleading. Two white lamps so displayed were indeed an express passenger service, but station pilot engines carried a white headlamp above one buffer and a red tail lamp above the other buffer. 58900 is on pilot duty on the stock roads between platforms 3 and 4 on the North Western side of New Street station. The individual canopies over the platforms dated from 1947, when the 1854 overall trainshed roof on the North Western

side of the station was removed, due to age and decrepitude. 58900 was shedded at Monument Lane, which adjoined the main line a short distance west of New Street station. In latter years, the shed handled 0-6-0s and 4-4-0s for secondary work, a few 2-6-4Ts on suburban trains, and until its withdrawal in 1954, provided No 58900, which was its last Webb locomotive, as one of the New street pilots.

Opposite page: After the war, tragedy dogged the West Coast Main Line with uncanny persistence. The ill luck started when the peace papers had hardly been signed, with a high-speed derailment at Bourne End on 30th September 1945 in which 43 people died. Twenty more lives were claimed at Lichfield on 1st January 1946. A derailment at Bletchley on 29th May 1947 took no lives, but on 21st July 1947, the Polesworth derailment left five people dead. A collision at Winsford on the night of 16/17th April 1948 led to 24 fatalities. A period of immunity came to an end on the morning of 21st September 1951, and left Stanier Princess No 46207 *Princess Arthur of Connaught* lying on her side in a field alongside the West Coast Main Line just south of Weedon, and 15 people dead. 46207 had been travelling about 65 mph with the late running 8.20am Liverpool Lime Street to Euston express, when the driver felt vibration at the front end, and realised the bogie had derailed. He began to close the regulator, but it was too late. The entire engine became derailed, careered to the left, rolled over a shallow embankment and came to a rest lying on its left side. Out of the fifteen-coach train, just the rear two vehicles remained on the rails, and the first nine coaches suffered varying degrees of damage. Col G R S Wilson, the chief inspecting officer of railways, was called in. 46207 had run almost 1m miles since new, and had put in 81,000 miles since a wheel profiling in May 1950. Marks on the track showed that the leading bogie wheels had derailed almost a mile earlier, but that the engine had stayed on the rails until it had reached a section of bullhead rail. Although there were minor track defects, it was clear that the bogie was at fault. The leading bogie wheels had suffered more flange wear than the trailing wheels, and normal railway practice was to exchange them to even out wear. This had been done at Edge Hill mpd, where 46207 was based, on 19th September 1951. When carrying out such work, the fitter had to check that the clearance between the sides of the axleboxes and the horn faces in which they slide was correct. If it was too much, the axle box would be loose in the bogie frame. If it was too tight, it could jam. Clearances of 10 to 17 thousands of an inch were normal. In metric terms, this is between 0.25 and 0.5 of a millimetre. Unknown to the fitter, the clearance between the front horn faces was on the tight side and the rear horn faces on the generous side. When the axleboxes of the leading wheels were transferred to the rear, they were a sloppy fit, with up to 2.5mm play, but when the old rear axle was moved to the front, the clearance was too tight, but variable wear on the horn faces allowed the bogie frames to drop on to the axlebox. The fitter had checked the measurements with callipers, but had mixed up the figures. This error, coupled with the differential wear, and lax inspection, permitted 46207 to leave Edge Hill shed with a potentially fatal defect. If the leading bogie axleboxes rode up to the top of the permitted travel, they could jam, and the wheels would then leave the track. A minor track irregularity could now be lethal. The 08.20am from Liverpool Lime Street was 46207's first train after this work; about a mile before she left the track, there was such an irregularity, and the leading axle box jammed in the horn faces, and then dropped free by which time the wheels had mounted the rail. Rescue work concentrates on freeing the victims, and then clearing wreckage from the line so it can be re-opened, and if a locomotive or carriage is clear of the track, it may be some time before it is recovered. 46207 is lying on her side, and partially covered with wagon sheets, on 6th October 1951. Fifteen lives had been lost because of a defect of less than half a millimetre. A year later, all of the accidents on the WCML were to pale into insignificance, with the horrendous double collision at Harrow & Wealdstone that claimed over 100 lives. Today we are used to hearing of emergency plans to cope with civil disaster or terrorism, but this was not the case in the fifties. These accidents prompted my father to campaign for disaster contingency planning, and to take part in an early disaster exercise with the co-operation of BR. It was filmed for instruction purposes, copies of the film going as far afield as the United States Marine Corps and to the Australian government. *R E Tustin*

Above: Euston was the first main line terminus in London when it opened in July 1837. It grew piecemeal over the years, being massively enlarged between 1870 and 1892. With mechanical signalling, there were limits on the distance that points could be located from a box, and in April 1891, a new cabin, Euston No 2 box with two separate lever frames, each of 144 levers was opened. Under Lord Stamp, the LMS planned a massive remodelling of Euston, and work started just before the war, but was suspended for the duration. Some ideas were shelved until the BR rebuilding, prior to the introduction of 25kV electric services in the 1960s, but the signalling needed urgent work, and on 8th March 1951, the LM Region announced that work would begin on a £300,000 scheme which would be completed in two years, under which a new power-operated lever frame would replace the existing No's 1, 2, and 3 boxes. The Westinghouse Brake & Signal Co was to provide a 227 lever Type L miniature lever frame with all-electric locking. It would be extensively track circuited, but rather than use the old style separate track circuit indicators with an arm contained within a separate casing, two illumi-

nated track diagrams were planned, each fifteen feet long. A number of illuminated diagrams had been provided on the LMS before the war, the lines being shown in white on a black ground, but the Euston diagrams adopted the newer idea of a light toned ground, with tracks coloured in. The actual diagram was reproduced photographically on a rolled plastic surface, so represented state of the art technology. A pair of red bulbs indicated each track circuit. They were unlit, except when a train occupied the track, in which case, they were illuminated. Plug in relays on steel racking in a separate relay room replaced the old mechanical interlocking. The new box was commissioned over the weekend of 4/5th October 1952. By this time, my father had developed a substantial O gauge layout in our home, which was worked by a team of operators using our own miniature interlocked lever frames, with correct block working. He arranged a visit for members of the team to Euston, where one of our operators P S Parish, took this view. My father is standing in characteristic pose with his hands clasped behind his back to the right of centre. Sadly, at four years of age, I was too young for this trip. The North Western mechanical boxes gave over sixty years of service, but the new box with its miniature levers was soon overtaken by technology, and the first stage in its replacement with a modern power box took place in April 1964.
P S Parish

Below: Britannia Pacific 70044, with Westinghouse pumps, enters platform 3 at Euston with the Up Mancunian Express. In the early days, railways termini were laid out with arrival platforms on the right hand side as you looked towards the country, and the departure platforms on the left, inbound trains backing out to carriage sidings for servicing, before being returned to the station by a pilot engine to make up a

departing service. The old Euston was like this, with Platforms 1 to 6 handling Up expresses, and platforms 12 to 15 dealing with departures. The intermediate platforms were shorter and handled local services, postals, parcels and other traffic. This view, which is taken from platform No 6, shows platform 3, and the approach fan to the shorter platforms 4 and 5. Part of the reason for this chaotic layout was that the 1830s Great Hall projected into the middle of the site, hence the shorter platforms in the centre of the station, and this was why the Great Hall was swept away in the BR rebuilding. The old Euston was confusing, and the narrow alleyways from the Great Hall to the departure platforms were tawdry, but the splendour of the Great Hall made up for it. When we went up to London, we would visit the Great Hall, partly to imbibe the wonderful atmosphere of this palatial structure, but also to use the station cafeteria, where BR provided a splendid steak pudding at low cost. Some readers may recall James Robertson Justice, the celebrated actor whose flowing beard and dignified presence contributed much to the British cinema in the 1950s. Although the Euston cafeteria was self-service, tables were cleared by waiters, one of whom had a beard and a presence that would have rivalled the celebrated actor. I wonder if the two ever met? The modern Euston is more efficient, but lacks a soul, and I am glad I knew its predecessor. 70044 was one of a pair of 1953-built Britannia Pacifics that received Westinghouse pumps for comparative trials between vacuum and air brakes. The compressors and air reservoirs were draped around the smokebox, which precluded the fitting of the usual smoke deflectors. They were used on freight trains on the Midland main line during the trials and on WCML expresses, 70044 being a regular performer on the Mancunian. They later lost their air brakes. 70044 was named *Earl Haig*.

Opposite page top: We will journey 299 miles to the north, for our next glimpse of the WCML. The double-headed Up Thames-Clyde express makes a vigorous departure from the south end of Carlisle station just after mid-day in July 1952, the pilot engine being Carlisle Kingmoor's 2P No 40602, whilst the train engine is Leeds Holbeck's Rebuilt Scot 4-6-0, No 46103 *Royal Scots Fusilier*. The Thames-Clyde express, which was due out of Glasgow St Enoch station at 9.20am, and took about two and a half hours to reach Carlisle, touched West Coast metals at Gretna, where the old Glasgow & South Western Main Line joined the Caley. A few hundred yards south of the station, it would diverge off to the Midland Settle-Carlisle route, and continue south via Leeds, reaching London St Pancras just before 7.30pm. Although a Scottish region Kingmoor engine, with the typical Scottish feature of the smokebox number plate edged in white, and the shed name CARLISLE (KINGMOOR) emblazoned on the buffer beam, the Derby designed 2P will assist the Scot over 'The Long Drag' as the S&C was known, returning to her home shed later in the day. One of Upperby shed's 'Jinties', 0-6-0T No 47340, blows off lightly in the adjacent platform. Used as station and yard pilots throughout the LMS, the 'Jinties', as they were known to enthusiasts, were common until the sixties, when they fell victim to the ubiquitous English Electric 350hp diesel shunter, known today as the 08. The magnificent train shed screen in the Old English Perpendicular style at the South end of Carlisle station made one of the finest backdrops for railway photography in the British Isles, and Carlisle could truly be called a Citadel, or even a Cathedral of steam. This view, with numerous panes of glass missing or broken, and the tracery damaged in places, indicates the level of wartime and early post-war neglect. It was an ominous sign, and was to pave the way for a ruthless act of vandalism, when the entire screen was replaced by a tasteless expanse of plate glass. The grimy and decaying train shed screen, the fouled ballast and the general aura of grime were a legacy of wartime neglect, but this picture, after seven years of peace, was unimpressive, although to be fair, neither the companies nor BR were given the priority for materials they warranted, and repair programmes had to be curtailed time after time, until railwaymen accepted that this was inevitable.

Opposite page bottom: The characteristic 3 cylinder bark of Manchester Longsight's No 45638, *Zanzibar*, erupts from beneath the bridge carrying the Midland Birmingham & Derby line over the West Coast Main Line at Tamworth (Low Level) station, as this Stanier 5XP Jubilee hurries the Up 'Mancunian' southbound towards Euston in 1953. By this time, minor alterations had transformed the 'Jubilees' from being the uncertain performers of their early days to magnificent machines that were at home on the most prestigious services. The Up Mancunian, which was due out of Manchester London Road station at 9.45am, arrived at Euston at 1.05pm, and allowed northern businessmen five hours in the city, before catching the return working, which left Euston at 6.00pm, arriving back at London Road at 9.30pm. The

restaurant car served a plain breakfast for 3 shillings (15p) or a Full breakfast for 5s 6d on the Up journey, and a full dinner for 7s 6d (37.5p) on the return journey. Running non-stop between Manchester and Euston on the southbound leg, the Down Mancunian called at Wilmslow at 9.08pm to let businessmen who resided in the affluent stockbroker belt south of Manchester alight. Although a Brake third corridor or Brake composite corridor was normal at the head of an express, the Mancunian was an exception. It loaded to 12 coaches (391 tons), the first two cars being 42 seat FKs or First Corridors, which gave the businessman a quick exit from the platform at Euston, and an easy chance to pick up a taxi. The third vehicle was a BCK, or Brake composite corridor with 12 first class and 18 third class seats. Another all-first, this time a 42 seat FO, or first open, was marshalled next to the restaurant car. This high proportion of first class accommodation was usual on trains serving the business traveller. By contrast, the 9.10am London Road to Paignton (Saturdays only), which left London Road with 11 carriages, and picked up two more at Stockport, conveyed a CK or composite corridor with 18 first class seats, a BCK, or brake composite corridor with 12 first seats, and another CK with 12 seats, its 42 seats being equal to just one of the all firsts on The Mancunian. The explanation was quite simple. One train catered for the business elite; the other was for the less affluent holidaymaker en route for the family's week or fortnight at the seaside, and anxious to save his pennies.

The Royal Scot
Refreshment Car Express
LONDON (Euston) and GLASGOW (Central)
WEEKDAYS

			am						pm
London (Euston)	..	..dep	10 0	Glasgow (Central)	..	..	..dep		10 0
			pm						am
Glasgow (Central)	..	..arr	5†30	London (Euston)	..	..	..arr		5†30

†—On Saturdays arrives 6.0 pm.

The Mid-Day Scot
Refreshment Car Express
LONDON (Euston) and GLASGOW (Central)
WEEKDAYS

	Mons. to Fris.	Sats.					
	pm	pm					pm
London (Euston) ..	..dep 1 30	1 15	Glasgow (Central)	..	..	..dep	1 30
Rugby (Midland) ..	.. „ 3 1	2 52	Motherwell	..	..	.. „	1 50
			Carstairs	..	..	.. „	2†25
Crewe	.. „ 4 22	4 19	Carlisle	..	..	.. „	3†47
Carlisle	..arr 7 15	7 15	Lancaster (Castle)	..	..	.. „	5§15
Carstairs ..	.. „ 8 48	8 48	Preston	..	..	.. „	5§44
Motherwell	.. „ 9 14	9 14	Crewe	..	..	..arr	6 54
Glasgow (Central)	.. „ 9 35	9 35	Watford Junction	..	..	.. „	9 29
			London (Euston)..	..	..	.. „	9 55

†—Does not call at Carstairs on Saturdays commencing 27th June.
§—On Saturdays commencing 27th June departs Carlisle 3.41 pm, Lancaster 5.9 pm and Preston 5.38 pm.

The Thames-Clyde Express
Refreshment Car Express
LONDON (St. Pancras) and GLASGOW (St. Enoch)
WEEKDAYS

			am						am
London (St. Pancras)	..	..dep	10 0	Glasgow (St. Enoch)	..	..	..dep		9 20
Leicester (London Road)	..	.. „	11 52	Kilmarnock	..	..	.. „		9 59
			pm	Dumfries	..	..	.. „		11 15
Chesterfield (Midland)	..	.. „	12 55	Annan	..	..	.. „		11 35
Sheffield (Midland)	..	.. „	1 20					pm
Leeds (City)	..	.. „	2 39	Carlisle	..	..	.. „		12 5
Carlisle	..	..arr	4†55	Leeds (City)	..	..	..arr		2 21
Annan	..	.. „	5†26	Sheffield (Midland)	..	..	.. „		3 40
Dumfries	..	.. „	5†46	Trent	..	..	.. „		4 50
Kilmarnock	..	.. „	7† 1	Leicester (London Road)	..	..	.. „		5 18
Glasgow (St. Enoch)	..	.. „	7†41	Kettering	..	..	.. „		6 1
				London (St. Pancras)	..	..	.. „		7 28

†—On Saturdays arrives Carlisle 5.9 pm, Annan 5.38 pm, Dumfries 5.58 pm, Kilmarnock 7.14 pm and Glasgow (St. Enoch) 7.55 pm.

Seats on these trains are reservable in advance for passengers travelling from London and Glasgow on payment of fee of 1s. 0d. per seat.

LONDON MIDLAND REGION

TRAIN SERVICE ALTERATIONS

between
28th September and 30th October
1953

in connection with

ENGINEERING WORK IN KILSBY TUNNEL

ENGINEERING WORK IN KILSBY TUNNEL

It has become necessary to carry out extensive repair work to the railway tracks through Kilsby Tunnel (1 mile 666 yards long) on the London Midland main line from London to the North. To enable the work to be carried out quickly and confine to the minimum period of time the unavoidable disturbance to train services, the tunnel lines will be closed entirely between the 28th September and 30th October inclusive 1953.

During this period the following alterations will be made to main line and local train services :—

All main line trains except those shown in the next paragraph will travel via the Northampton line, which will cause some lengthening of over-all journey times.

Certain trains will be diverted to London St. Pancras or otherwise altered as shown on page 3.

No passenger trains will stop at BLISWORTH, WEEDON (except those to and from the Leamington Spa line) and WELTON STATIONS. Services between BLISWORTH and NORTHAMPTON will be suspended. Alternative bus services for the holders of rail tickets will be provided as shown in this leaflet.

British Railways regret the inconvenience to passengers using these services and will endeavour to keep to a minimum the delay to trains caused by this essential work in Kilsby Tunnel.

2

Opposite page top: When the 1 mile 666 yard long Kilsby tunnel opened in 1838, it was one of the engineering wonders of the age, and although eclipsed in size by later tunnels, it remained famous throughout the steam era, not least because of the legends that grew up around its construction. The tunnel was lined with Staffordshire blue brick, and over the years this suffered from smoke and chimney blast, and from water percolating through the rock. The tunnel always featured in the Civil Engineers programs, but by 1953, arrears of maintenance called for more work than was feasible with a weekend possession. Nowadays, we are used to lines being shut at bank holidays and weekends, or for weeks on end for civil engineering work, but in the old days, railwaymen made valiant efforts to keep trains running. It was therefore a surprise when BR announced that Kilsby Tunnel would be closed to all traffic from 28th September to 30th October 1953. For a whole month, over 250 men worked in shifts, lifting the old track and formation, removing the old brick culvert, installing a new concrete drain, putting concrete rafts beneath the two main ventilation shafts, and then relaying the track, which was slightly realigned at both ends of the tunnel to ease p.w. speed restrictions. Work was paid on a daily basis, at rates well above ordinary p.w. work, and many of the local p.w. men had booked their holidays for this period, so they could be taken on as day labourers. During the work, the tunnel was illuminated by 'Tilley' lamps, and the light shining on the strangely discoloured mineral deposits that coated the brickwork with a wrinkled skin created a weird impression. My father said it resembled a crocodile's back, and as it was chipped away during the work, the men who did so complained that it was as hard as steel! Mineral impurities in the water and smoke blackening had created such a strange blend of colours, that the broken deposit was in keen demand by local gardeners for their rockeries. Sadly I never had a bit! One unexpected find at the time was a scale model in stone of one of the portals of the tunnel. This had lain in the garden of Cedar Lodge in Kilsby for generations, and may have been used by Stephenson during the building of the tunnel. Although there is a fault in this view, its historic importance makes it worth including. Access for the work was from the north end, and by the time No 48131 was photographed outside the north portal of Kilsby Tunnel at the head of some Engineers Department drop side ballast wagons on the Up line on 7th October 1953, the project was well advanced, although the Down line had yet to be reinstated. Thousands of tons of new stone ballast was going in, and a procession of engineers specials with stone, sleepers, rails and fastenings arrived and departed. Ballast for the London Midland Region lines in the London area and the Midlands traditionally came from Brandon Ballast Pit near Coventry until its closure, from Jee's quarry at Hartshill, or Judkins quarry, which was adjacent to the ex Midland Railway station at Nuneaton Abbey Street. The train engine, Stanier 8F, No 48131 was a Kettering engine, but motive power for the relay was drawn from as far away as Willesden. The Tilley lamps inside the tunnel can be see glowing in the darkness, whilst a row of lamps provide lighting at the approaches as well.

Opposite page bottom and above: An 8-page booklet was produced for the public, outlining the changes. The majority of main line services were diverted via the Northampton Loop, adding a few miles and a few minutes to journey times. A few through trains terminated at Crewe, or were diverted to the Midland Main Line, arriving at St Pancras instead of Euston. Because of the additional traffic that would flow through Northampton, the Blisworth-Northampton local service was suspended, and Blisworth, Weedon and Welton stations would lose stopping passenger services on the main line during the work. Replacement bus links to and from Northampton or Rugby catered for local users. One such note for Welton station typifies the changes, '7.08pm From Rugby and beyond depart Rugby Midland at 6.57pm to Long Buckby Station due 7.13pm, thence by special bus, due Welton 7.25pm'. For staff, a much more comprehensive Special Notice was produced. This was supplementary to the usual weekly special notice, although to a similar format, and provided details of cancellations and alterations, and comprehensive notes on where fresh ballast and supplies would be sourced from and where foul fill would be disposed of. Reading the Special Notice gives some idea of the administrative problems of managing a railway.

12 · 'A MILLION TONS OF STEAM'

On 1st January 1948, The Railway Executive inherited 20,023 steam locomotives, 16 electric locomotives, 52 diesel shunters, 1 main line diesel locomotive, 2 petrol engines, 7 narrow gauge locomotives and 47 departmental service locomotives, giving an overall total of 20,148 locomotives. They weighed a staggering 1, 071,859 tons. The oldest locomotive dated from 1858. The newest locomotive dated from December 1947, and the Big Four all had orders outstanding for further locomotives. The man in charge of one of the largest motive power fleets under unified control in the world was Robert 'Robin' Arthur Riddles. His career on BR, and the motive power policy of the RE, has been the subject of controversy for more than half a century. Hailed by some as the last great steam engineer, and by others as a blinkered reactionary, it is necessary to understand the man and the forces that moulded him, if we are to gain an insight into what happened after 1948.

Robin Riddles was born on 23rd May 1892, and joined the LNWR as an apprentice in 1909, serving as a fitter at Rugby by 1914. After war service in the Royal Engineers, he was appointed Assistant to the Works Manager at Crewe in 1920, and Progress Assistant in 1925. After Stanier's arrival on the LMS, he became Locomotive Assistant to the CME, and in 1937, moved to Glasgow to become Mechanical & Electrical Engineer, Scotland. In 1939, Riddles was seconded to the

Ministry of Supply as Director of Transportation Equipment, and in 1941, also became Deputy Director General, Royal Engineer Equipment. Having experienced the supply problems in World War One, Riddles was determined that the Army would not be hamstrung again. Despite adopting the Stanier 8F as a war locomotive, he realised that its sophisticated design required too much workshop time and resources. In his Austerity 2-8-0 and 2-10-0 designs, Riddles created a basic locomotive, in order to get them into service as quickly as possible, reasoning that the army needed an ample supply of simple engines quickly, rather than a few sophisticated engines later on. When told that the engines were so crude that they would not be accepted by any CME to run in Britain after the war, Riddles' reply was brusque. He retorted that so long as they did their job during the war, he did not care if they were thrown into the sea afterwards. As Riddles saw it, his job was to give the army the tools it needed to win the war. Riddles returned to the LMS as Chief Stores Superintendent in 1943. When C E Fairburn, who had succeeded Stanier as CME, died suddenly in 1945, the LMS was in the enviable position of having two outstanding locomotive engineers, Riddles and H G Ivatt. Riddles, as a Chief Officer, was technically senior in the LMS hierarchy, but had been away on war service, and as Chief Stores Superintendent, was outside the direct line of promotion. Ivatt who was six years older than Riddles, had a similar career until 1939, but had remained with the LMS, as Assistant to Stanier, and then Fairburn. It was a hard choice, but the board appointed Riddles as Vice President for Engineering, and Ivatt as CME in 1946. Given the small age difference between them, it seemed that Riddles' direct hand in motive power design was at an end, but his appointment to The Railway Executive as member responsible for mechanical engineering in 1947 placed him in charge of the unified motive power fleets of all four companies.

Riddles' career up to 1946 had shown him to be decisive and focussed, characteristics that were supported by a clipped moustache and military bearing. His drive had been apparent as a young man. Many years ago, I interviewed a retired railwayman called Lew Walton, who had trained on the London & North Western Railway at Rugby. To my surprise, he spoke of Robin Riddles with obvious personal regard. As a young apprentice, Walton had worked with Riddles, and remembered him as a capable and practical young man, determined to get the job done. Speaking to Walton and other ex North Western men of his generation, I realised they had a shared belief in using proven technology. They were not averse to progress, but had seen many promising ideas that did not work out in practice. Riddles would have seen the LNWR steam railcars as a young man, and although the LNWR cars, along with the LYR counterparts, were the longest lived of the spate of railcars designs that appeared in the early 1900s, he must have reflected that the sudden craze had produced little of real worth. He would have seen the pioneer LNWR internal combustion engined railcar, which was even less useful, and in the 1920s, he would have witnessed the experimental high pressure engine Fury and its tragic end. Practical and hard headed though he was, Riddles was no reactionary. If the words of the politicians in the run-up to nationalisation in 1948 meant anything, then the public good must come first, and investment that might be eschewed by private enterprise, as not offering a sufficient return on capital, would be guaranteed under public ownership, where the public interest would be included in the equation. The political climate fitted in with Riddles' own strategy, which was to electrify the East and West Coast Main Lines, the GWR Bristol line, and other key routes. His long term goal was clear, but the problem facing Robin Riddles on 1st January 1948 was how to get there? There were several different things he could have done, and a lot of questions that had to be decided.

Opposite page: Robin Riddles, and Stuart Cox, who was 'Executive Officer, Design', had started their respective careers on the LNWR and the LYR. Both recalled the bitterness when Midland ideas were tactlessly stamped on the infant LMS, without consideration as to their suitability. They realised that old company loyalties were strong, and that to a Great Western man, only GW engine design was sound, whilst an LNER man would prefer LNER practice. Riddles and Cox rejected the 'horses for courses' argument that some types were specially suited to some regions, but it was another matter to convince others. To avoid a repeat of the LMS experience, and to select the best practice from the different regions, Riddles set up a locomotive components committee to report on which fittings should be adopted as standard components across the regions, and to recommend existing locomotive types for future construction, until a range of standard engines had been developed. Placing the chairmanship of the committee in Western Region hands was a shrewd move, as it helped avoid accusations of an LMS bias. A locomotive testing committee was set up to hold Locomotive Exchange trials as soon as possible. From 1870, periodic exchanges of locomotives had taken place between different railways, so that Locomotive engineers could assess the benefits and shortcomings of different ideas. The trials commenced in April 1948, and continued until September, and involved reciprocal transfers of engines between different regions. Trains on the LM Region were to be hauled by an A4 or a Merchant Navy, whilst a Stanier Duchess would haul the Atlantic Coast Express out of Waterloo. The 'competitors' on the West Coast route included Merchant Navy Pacific, 35017 *Belgian Marine*. As the Southern did not use water troughs, preferring to stop to pick up water, its engines were at a serious disadvantage on the West Coast. As there was no time to fit water pick up apparatus to a Bulleid tender, the malachite green liveried 35017, which retained the SOUTHERN smokebox roundel, but had received its new BR number, was paired with a black painted Stanier tender ex an 8F. This created an odd ensemble, but meant that the Bulleid engine could pick up water. 35017 appeared on LM metals at the start of May 1948, and is powering north through Brinklow, the curved cab profile making a strange contrast with the straight sided Stanier tender. The former GWR, LNER and LMS dynamometer cars were used to obtain comparative data during the exchange trials, but as the engines were driven by their own crews, who were working on unfamiliar metals, a number of familiarisation runs took place before any results were recorded. On this occasion, the leading coach is not one of the dynamometer cars, so this is probably the familiarisation run on 5th May 1948.
H J Stretton-Ward

Above: The Eastern Region sent a Gresley A4 Pacific, to the LMR. No 60034 *Lord Faringdon*, is at Rugby on 29th May 1948, the leading carriage being the ex LMS Dynamometer car. Owing to loading gauge restrictions, the GWR contender, a 'King' class 4-6-0s, could not run on the West Coast, but did perform on the East Coast Main Line, and on its home metals. In general, engines did best on home ground, the crews being used to their own routes, but the visitors put up many stunning performances. The A4 performed superbly, but the Gresley conjugated valve gear needed careful maintenance, and in post war conditions, this was not always possible. Three failures occurred on the West Coast, two prior to the runs, and one on a test run. Devotees of each company could point to particular virtues, but as Riddles and Cox expected, the results showed that the differences between modern well-designed engines were small, and the official report on the Exchange Trials condemned the 'horses for courses' argument. Although Hurcomb had told Missenden that the RE's job was 'to unify the four railways in a real and operating sense', and Riddles was seeking the best standards, without repeating the Midlandisation era on the LMS, when the BTC heard of the Exchanges, a tart letter went from Hurcomb to the RE, demanding that a committee be set up to examine different forms of traction, and that a representative of the BTC should sit on it. A few months before, the BTC had vetoed RE proposals that the regions should have considerable autonomy and their own general managers, preferring the less impressive title of Chief Regional Officer. Although Riddles favoured centralisation, the BTC was still unhappy. Their objection was the RE had not adopted dieselisation at once, but in doing so, the BTC muddied the muddy waters of a badly drafted act. The Transport Act had never

clearly spelled out the responsibilities of the BTC or the RE. If motive power policy was within the remit of the BTC as grand policy, and they were dissatisfied with the RE, their duty was to issue policy directives. If motive power policy was within the ambit of the RE, BTC meddling in duties it had delegated to the RE was counter productive. The BTC did neither, and the RE, aware of the creaking nature of the BTC, and lack of leadership, ignored them. *H J Stretton-Ward*

Opposite page top: Railway investment cannot be turned on or off like a tap, although some politicians have done so with dire consequences for the rail industry. The Big Four drew up construction programs long before anyone started 'cutting metal', and Riddles inherited them on 1st January 1948. He could have cancelled them, whilst a new motive power policy was developed, but that would have wasted resources, and with the backing of the WR-led committee on pre-nationalisation designs, he wisely allowed the existing programs to continue. When Edward Thompson had retired from his post as CME of the LNER in 1946, thirty-nine 6ft 8ins Pacifics to a new design to handle the heaviest East Coast trains had been authorised, although the design was not complete. His successor, Arthur Peppercorn, revised the plans, and frame designs were not finalised until October 1947. Although the first engine did not enter service until August 1948, Riddles had no qualms about them, and even agreed to another ten engines, boosting the class to 49. They appeared at a time of austerity, and the initial intention, was that with one exception, they should be unnamed. The exception was a well-merited tribute to W P 'Bill' Allen, who had joined the GNR as a cleaner, and progressed to fireman and then driver. Allen had been active in ASLEF, the Associated Society

of Locomotive Engineers and Firemen, and with the wish to have a working railwayman within the RE, Bill Allen became a member of the executive, a far cry from his day as a cleaner. It was a fitting tribute to this old railwayman that an engine that worked on the GN main line should receive his name at a ceremony at King's Cross on 28 October 1948, No 60114 started life at 'The Cross', moving to Copley Hill and Grantham, before reaching Doncaster in 1957, where she is seen on 11th August 1963, just over a year prior to withdrawal. By 1950, it had been decided to name all the Peppercorn A1s, and other distinguished railwaymen to be honoured included Ivatt, Sturrock, Stirling, Fletcher, Raven, and Worsdell. The Great Western Railway had included William Dean amongst its 'Saint' class 4-6-0s, so it was only fair that the Eastern Region included Saint Mungo amongst some fine locomotive engineers, though I am unaware of any locomotives that are attributed to the said gentleman.

Right: Despite the original intention not to name them, the Peppercorn A1s eventually carried a fine selection of names, including distinguished railwaymen, racehorses, literary characters, birds, places and constituent companies of the LNER. No 60157, which had been built at Doncaster in November 1949, was named *Great Eastern* in November 1951, the plates including a hand painted reproduction of the GER crest. Only four companies were so honoured, the GCR, GER, NBR and NER, the name Great Northern already being carried by a Gresley Pacific which had been rebuilt by Thompson. Because the plates were the work of one skilled painter, the naming was protracted, but they were some of the most eye-catching plates on BR.

Above: Although losing Scotland to the new Scottish Region, Riddles' old colleague, H G Ivatt, the last CME of the LMSR, became Chief Mechanical Engineer of the London Midland Region, a post he held until his retirement in 1951. Ivatt and Riddles held similar views on maximum accessibility of components, outside cylinders and valve gear, taper boilers and self-cleaning smokeboxes. Unlike the GWR, which was building the 2251 class, which was an updated version of the 19th century Dean goods, the LNER, which was thinking of resurrecting a GC 0-6-0, and the Bulleid Q1, which despite a revolutionary appearance, was a traditional inside cylindered 0-6-0 goods engine, Ivatt felt that a leading truck was vital to provide good riding for mixed traffic duties, and in his Class 4 design of 1947, produced a 2-6-0 that was suited to a pick up goods or a semi fast passenger. Twenty had been ordered by the LMS, but just three appeared prior to nationalisation. Once again, Riddles was happy to let construction continue, multiplying the design until 162 had been completed by 1952. As the Ivatt engines, in their original guise with massive double chimneys, had proved to be deplorable performers, a problem that was rectified by substitution of a single chimney, this suggests that Riddles was not the bigot that some writers have inferred, but a shrewd engineer who saw the inherent worth of the design. He also saw the need to conciliate the regional locomotive departments, and if building more engines to their designs helped the process, and made good use of works facilities, then it made sense. This pair of Ivatt class 4s at the north end of Leicester London Road station on a Birmingham – Lowestoft express, due away from Leicester at 3.15pm on Thursday, 23rd July 1953, recalls the days when seaside specials were an important part of the British holiday tradition, and reveals the underlying worth of Ivatt's design. The leading engine, No 43143 carries the lamp code of an express passenger train, and in common with the train engine, No 43104, is shedded at South Lynn on the erstwhile Midland & Great Northern Joint line. Although the peak traffic was on a Saturday, when hundreds of extras would run, a profusion of mid-week excursions took thousands of people from the Midlands to the North Norfolk resorts served by 'The Joint'. Running by way of Syston and Little Bytham, excited kids from my generation, the so-called post-war baby boom, will be heading for the beaches. Maybe some readers of this book travelled on this very train. If so, I bet you had a great time, and have happy memories of the times when you caught the train to have a day beside the seaside.

Opposite page: Apart from 20,023 standard gauge steam locomotives, Riddles inherited 52 diesel shunters. Most came from the LMS, though the other three companies contributed a few. It was Sir Josiah Stamp, President of the LMS from 1926, who had instituted an enquiry into 'economical shunting units'. Stamp found that the 8,680,603 freight shunting hours in 1929 comprised 50.02% of total freight engine hours, and realised this was a heavy drain on profits. Shunting and traffic analysis led to improved yard design and the multiplication of hump yards, and the first pioneer LMS diesel locomotive appeared in 1931, built on a chassis derived from a retired Midland Railway 0-6-0T. Over the next five years, several more experimental locomotives appeared, during which time, a detailed examination of shunting needs took place under Sir Ernest Lemon. At large yards, where shunting went on continuously, the longest time that a steam engine could remain in traffic was about 24 hours, due to fire cleaning and coaling. Without a replacement, shunting had to be suspended whilst the engine was serviced, whilst halts for watering throughout the day delayed work. Steam and smoke could obstruct visibility, and where engines stood for any length of time, fuel was still consumed. At hump yards, fine control of speed was difficult. A demanding specification was drawn up, calling for an engine with at least a week's fuel capacity, minimal requirements for lubrication and water, exhaust fumes to be discharged high up to avoid inconveniencing drivers and shunters, recessed steps at the front for shunters to ride on in safety, a hotplate to give the driver warm food, either side controls, good visibility and a cab radiator for warmth at night or in winter. The first production 0-6-0 shunters took to the rails in 1936, with small batches being supplied by Armstrong Whitworth, Hawthorn Leslie and English Electric. Their success meant that as far as the LMS was concerned, the production of the traditional 0-6-0T for shunting duties was at an end. Had war not intervened, hundreds would have been built by the late forties. As it was wartime disruptions retarded new construction, and many existing engines were requisitioned by the War Department. In 1945, the LMS began construction of an improved version of the pre-war 350hp English Electric diesel shunter, but only six engines appeared that year, and it was not until 1947, that another four were completed. BR 12045, shunting at

Nuneaton, had been ordered as LMS 7132, but did not appear from Derby until April 1948, by which time the 12000 series had been allocated to diesel shunters, 12045 being the first engine to bear its BR number from new. Readers familiar with the British Railways 350hp shunter, known today as the Class 08, will see few difference between this ex-LMS engine and the machines we still see in service. Further BR orders were placed, and by the time construction ended in December 1952, over 100 had been completed. The final examples were built at Darlington, as Derby had completed its last LMS/English Electric shunter that June. In October 1952, Derby began turning out the first of their successors, which were to become the 08s. Using the same EE6K engine, the principal difference was an increase in driving wheel diameter from 48ins to 54ins. This was to permit a higher maximum speed, as the 20mph favoured by Lemon, though suited to freight work, was inadequate for passenger station shunting, and the wider range of duties now envisaged. Almost 1,200 had been produced by the time construction ended in 1963, making them the most numerous class of engine ever to run on Britain's railways, a record that is unlikely ever to be surpassed. Although Riddles permitted the Western Region to build more of its beloved Pannier tanks, including completely new designs, and to allow the Eastern Region to resurrect a North Eastern Railway 0-6-0T for further construction, this alleged 'steam diehard' authorised the most numerous class of diesel engines ever to run in the British Isles.

Opposite page top: It was clear to Riddles that the 350hp diesel electric shunter, although ideal as a general-purpose type, was too large, and too heavy for dockyards, some private sidings and lines such as the Wisbech & Upwell Tramway in East Anglia. Having established a diesel policy for shunting locomotives, Riddles turned to the Drewry Car Co, which had a long history of producing small diesel locomotives, for the first in a long line of 204hp diesel-mechanical shunters. The first four engines, 11100-11103, were ordered in 1950, arriving in May/June 1952. All four were provided with side skirts and cow catchers, as 11101 and 11102 were allocated to March, for the roadside Wisbech & Upwell tramway, whilst 11100 and 11103 went to Ipswich and Yarmouth. They were highly successful, and the class was eventually multiplied to 142 examples, later becoming D2200 – D2341. They were allocated TOPS code 04, but withdrawal took place between 1967 and 1972, largely because the lightly laid lines they had been built to serve had vanished. I only saw the Wisbech & Upwell line in operation once. It was in the late summer of 1952, when a trip to the beach at Hunstanton was interrupted to pay a visit to this astonishing railway. It was an overcast day, and whilst I can remember a strange engine that apparently had no wheels, shunting by the roadside, my main memory was of something that I was told was a steam engine, but which appeared to my youthful eyes to be a brake van. Closer inspection revealed that some demented soul had truly planted a locomotive boiler in the brake van, so I was reluctantly prepared to believe that it might be an engine. It was years before I realised I had seen 68222, one of the Holden class J70 tram engines built for the Upwell tramway. After the arrival of the Drewrys, regular steam services on the tramway ceased in July 1952, making it one of the first sections of BR to be dieselised, but 68222 was retained as a spare until March 1953. I was allowed on the footplate to convince me that it really was an engine. I was also allowed on the footplate of the diesel, and this must have been my first diesel footplate ride.

Opposite page bottom: Apart from 52 diesel shunters, The RE inherited one main line diesel locomotive, No 10000, which had been rushed into service by the LMS, to produce the first main line diesel locomotive in Great Britain. In a scene that captures the evolving character of the railways at this time, we see 10000 and 10001 racing south through Nuneaton with the Up Royal Scot. The locomotives typify post war LMS thinking, whilst the station buildings and canopies recall the capacious buildings provided by the LNWR at its principal stations. The footbridge is a double structure, half being for passengers and the other half for mail, parcels and luggage. Lift towers exist at each end, the right hand tower being conspicuous. The signal box is a late LNWR design, but is unusual, as it consists of two type 5 boxes mounted back to back. The huts are standard LNWR prefab buildings which were churned out by the hundred, whilst the lattice post signal reminds us that the LMS used lattice steel posts for a time in preference to wood, before adopting the familiar tubular steel post. Although the LMS had built a prototype

main line diesel, Riddles preferred electrification for the trunk routes, but this was a long-term solution. With the rundown state of many older steam locomotives, BR faced a short-term motive power crisis. Riddles either had to devote resources to rebuilding elderly steam locomotives for further service, build new steam power, or opt for main line diesels. The 0-6-0 diesel electric shunter had a proven record going back more than a decade, and Riddles had no hesitation in consigning the steam shunting tank to history, but 10000 had no such background. Although a stunning technical achievement, both locomotives suffered a lot of down time. The steam heating boiler was so unreliable that the engines tended to work passenger trains in summer when the steam heat was not needed, and freight trains in winter. Another drawback was that their power output of 1600hp was only comparable to a class 5 steam locomotive. Both engines were required to work a heavy Anglo-Scottish express. Their maximum axle load of 22 tons 4 cwt restricted them to a few routes. Although a dramatic step forward, and capable of useful work, the capital costs of using two locomotives, which cost several times the price of a new Pacific, eroded the theoretical savings, whilst the down time and limited route availability meant that 10000 and 10001 were not worth multiplying, even if electrification had not been a long term goal. With electrification in mind, the prospects of moving a large class to other routes, had they been multiplied, would be poor, given the high axle loading. As it turned out, electrification was so protracted that this would not have mattered, but in 1948, it is doubtful if Riddles believed that electrification of the West Coast Main Line would not be completed until the 1960s and 1970s', that the East Coast Main Line electrification would drag on into the 1990s, and that the Great Western electrification would not even have commenced fifty years after he had retired.

Below: Sir George H. Nelson, F.C.G.I., M. I. Mech. E., M.I.E.E., chairman of English Electric at the time that LMS 10000 was built, and a firm advocate of the project.

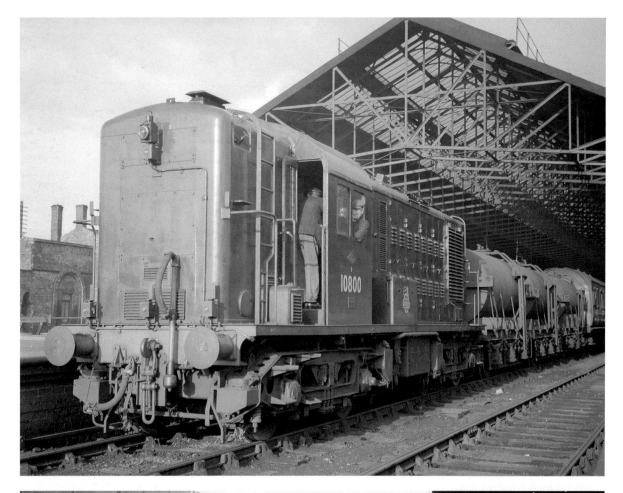

Opposite page top: In the United States, technical journals ran regular articles on progress in dieselisation. The diesel lobby in the BTC imbibed such material, without appreciating that US railroads enjoyed several advantages not open to the RE. When England went to war in 1939, America had a significant lead in dieselisation, and that intensified in the two years that elapsed before Pearl Harbor. Whilst US industry contributed massively to the war effort, it was not so single-mindedly directed to war-work as had been the case in the UK, and the US lead increased. One solution would have been to import proven US technology. This would not have been popular with the Treasury due to the drain of foreign currency. It would have aroused the wrath of the British diesel manufacturers, who were keen on building up home orders to help their export business, and would have enraged the National Union of Miners, a key backer for the Labour Party. Even then, it might not have worked. US railroads enjoyed a more generous loading gauge than their UK counterparts, and the size and axleload of the low horsepower first generation US diesels would have presented severe problems, had such designs been imported. With low priced indigenous sources of fuel oil, the financial case for dieselisation was stronger in the US than in Britain. From his time at the MoT/MoWT, Hurcomb had been used to issuing policy directives, but had never had to worry how practical they were, as the oil firing fiasco for steam locomotives had revealed. Riddles had to provide an adequate supply of reliable engines in a tight timescale. If 10000 and the US experience were not the answer, what other main line diesel experience could Riddles use? We have seen BCDR No 28, which was the only other road diesel in service, but with just two powered axles, it was too weak for BR needs. At the start of 1948, the RE inherited further diesel projects from the LMS and Southern Railway. The LMS project had started as far back as 1945, when H G Ivatt considered a small Bo-Bo diesel to do the work of a class 3 steam locomotive. Rated at 827hp, 10800 entered service in May 1950. It was built by NBL, one of the great steam locomotive manufacturers, as a first step into the new diesel market they saw opening up. Because NBL's expertise was in steam construction, they subcontracted the main diesel engine to Davey Paxman, who supplied a 16-cylinder engine, whilst the British Thompson-Houston Co, a leading electrical engineering company, supplied a BTH main generator and BTH traction motors. Using specialist contractors sounded wise, as all the firms had a high reputation, but the multiplicity of contractors was disastrous. As failure followed failure, an acrimonious correspondence grew up between the Railway Executive, NBL and the sub-contractors, and when the BTC, irritated with the apparent inability of the Railway Executive to make progress, demanded the file, the RE was only too happy to present the paperwork to them. BTC had no more success. 10800 ran its initial trials in Scotland, to keep it near to NBL, and was then sent to the Southern Region, next to the Eastern Region, and finally to Rugby, where it was in close proximity to the large BTH works. One of its duties when at Rugby was on milk, parcels and passenger turns on the old Midland Railway line between Rugby

and Leicester, which had the benefit of keeping it away from the main line for most of the day. 10800 is in the Leicester 'Bay' at Rugby Midland station, on a local passenger working, the leading three vehicles being 6-wheeled milk tankers. Whatever problems 10000 and 10001 might have had, they paled into insignificance compared to the attractive but virtually useless 10800, which had taken five years to build.

Opposite page bottom: If 10000 did not offer a way forward, and 10800 was even worse, although that did not become apparent until 1950, what about the Southern project? The Southern had achieved a dramatic lead in electrification, but this would never be viable in the West Country, and Oliver Bulleid realised that dieselisation might eventually be preferable to his own West Country Pacifics. Even before the LMS had approached English Electric, Bulleid had asked them to produce a suitable power unit. Although using the same 16SVT engine, by not imposing the same tight timescale on English Electric, Bulleid benefited from an increase in power output from 1600hp to 1750hp for the first two engines, and to no less than 2000hp for the third locomotive. With a more restricted axle loading than the LMS, Bulleid added an unpowered axle at the outer end of the bogies, creating a 1Co-Co1 arrangement, but achieved a respectable 18 tons 12 cwt axleloading, giving the locomotives greater route availability. Thus far, the benefits were obvious, but unlike the LMS engine, which was rolled out of Crewe works in December 1947, construction did not begin on the first two engines until 1949, with the first machine, 10201 being completed in November 1950. The second and third engines entered traffic in May 1951 and March 1954. To gain experience on a variety of routes, 10201 was tried on the St Pancras – Derby line before going to the South Western main line working between Waterloo and Exeter, where it was later joined by the other Bulleid and LMS diesels. Eventually the whole group migrated to Willesden shed and the West Coast Main Line. 10203 is ready to depart from platform 3 at Birmingham New St station with an Up Express. Riddles' problem was that whilst the BTC might pontificate about the benefits of dieselisation, he needed dependable motive power in a hurry. After the reliability problems with 10000, the Bulleid engines, which shared many components, would need adequate testing, which would take at least two years, and unless they were successful, any fresh design would also need testing before production engines could be ordered. Unless proven US technology was imported, the minimum time scale before reliable main line diesels could appear in any numbers was at least six years, and serious economies would only result when complete sections were dieselised, as maintaining steam and diesel facilities in the same area was inefficient. When the Southern engines entered traffic, Riddles' caution was justified, as all three spent a good deal of time awaiting attention, but experience gained from them stood BR in good stead, as the unusual 1Co-Co1 arrangement, and general layout provided the basis for the English Electric D200 series and BR/Sulzer D1 'Peak' classes introduced from 1958.

Top: 10100, the 'Fell' locomotive, seen here at Derby, was another pioneer diesel. It was a valiant attempt to avoid the weight problems associated with a diesel electric locomotive, which consists of a diesel engine that is coupled to an electric generator, the power output of which is fed to traction motors that drive the axles. Diesel mechanical transmission is much lighter, and is ideal for DMUs, or for small diesel locomotives such as the Drewry 204hp shunters, but is not suitable for power outputs associated with main line engines. Lt-Col L F R Fell designed an ingenious mechanical transmission that offered a way to build a high powered main line diesel, and hoped to see it adopted by BR. 10100 was authorised early in 1948, and built at Derby, being financed by BR, Ricardo and Fell. Unlike the other prototype diesels, it was powered by four Paxman 12 cylinder diesels, each developing 500hp. The individual diesel engines drove via fluid couplings to a common gearbox, which was connected to the driving wheels. Unlike conventional diesels, the Fell locomotive comprised an 8-coupled driving section, with 4 wheel unpowered trucks at each end, creating a 4-8-4. Two additional 150hp AEC 6 cylinder diesel engines powered auxiliaries, the transmission, and train heating, giving the locomotive the incredible total of sixty cylinders! It was completed at Derby in July 1950, but did not enter traffic until January 1951. A series of failures ensued, the engine eventually

catching fire at Manchester Central in 1958, after which it was withdrawn and broken up. Other experimental engines that Riddles could have developed included Bulleid's revolutionary steam powered 0-6-6-0 'Leader' and the two prototype Western Region gas turbine locomotives, but all suffered from serious teething troubles. With reliable diesel engines six to ten years away, unless the RE was given permission to buy American General Motors diesels, and with the government cutting back on allocations of steel to the railways, electrification was another long-term solution, it is hard to fault Riddles' decision to 'play safe', by building steam, as large scale dieselisation without proper testing risked saddling BR with a fleet of machines like 10100 or 10800. *P S Parish*

Left: Apart from the various prototype diesels, the Railway Executive inherited two projects for gas turbine locomotives. Both originated with the Great Western Railway, which had ordered its first experimental engine from the Swiss company, Brown Boveri as early as 1940. With wartime problems, the locomotive was not completed until 1949 and then carried out trials in Switzerland before being shipped to the UK. Early diesel locomotives offered a very low power to weight ratio, and even with the more generous American loading gauge and axle loadings, presented problems. With the more restricted British loading gauge, these were exacerbated, and the GWR was attracted to the theoretical benefits of the much more compact and therefore lighter gas turbine. Compared to the 131 tons of the 1600hp LMS diesels 10000 and 10001, the Brown Boveri locomotive delivered 2,500hp for an all-up weight of 115 tons. Metropolitan-Vickers provided a second British-built gas turbine locomotive, 18100, which entered service a few months after 18000. Given their experimental nature both locomotives performed acceptably, but apart from the inevitable high costs associated with any prototype and lack of crew familiarity which restricted their use to a few specially trained drivers, they suffered from what was to become the Achilles' heel of all gas turbine locomotives. Unlike a diesel engine, where fuel consumption is related to power output, the gas turbine is most efficient when working at a high load factor. Fuel consumption when working at lower power outputs is disproportionately high. In marine applications and many other fields, this is of no importance, as a constant output for long periods is desirable, but with a railway locomotive, acceleration and braking, station stops and gradients cause wide variations in power needs. The fuel consumption of the steam locomotive or the diesel will vary, depending on the route and demands on the engine, but the gas turbine, despite its weight benefits, is not fuel efficient when working below optimum output. Gas turbines have been used on a number of railways, most notably the Union Pacific RR, which replaced its Challenger 4-6-6-4 and Big Boy 4-8-8-4 steam locomotives with a fleet of gas turbines, but in the longterm, operating costs have proved to be the downfall of the gas turbine. This view of 18000 is from the No 2 end, the rectangular frame below the cab windows being for the GWR steam era train reporting numbers.

Below: Riddles had two options. He could continue to build steam locomotives to existing designs, and the last LMS and LNER designs were very good, or he could use the results from the locomotive exchange trials, the Rugby Test plant and from the components committee, to create go-anywhere standard engines that could operate on the main lines until they were electrified, and then be switched to other areas to replace older pre-nationalisation designs that might not be so flexible, due to loading gauge or other problems. Either policy was tenable, and H G Ivatt in the short time left prior to his retirement, favoured continued production of existing company designs. Riddles asked Stuart Cox, his 'Executive Officer, Design', to prepare a report, listing the standard types that would be required. In June 1948, Cox proposed twelve types, four of which were entirely new, four being developed from existing types, and the other four being existing LMS types with minor alterations. Although the details underwent considerable revision, the Cox Report formed the basis of the Standard classes. Cox and Riddles realised that with the Stanier Pacifics on the LMS, the Merchant Navy Pacifics on the Southern, and the array of LNER Pacifics, there was no immediate need for a class 8 top link Pacific, so this was put to the back of the queue, but given the desire to accelerate trains on several sections, most notably the ex Great Eastern lines in Norfolk, a light Pacific with 6 ft 2 ins wheels, and a 20¼ ton axleload would be useful. A 4-6-2, although adding to first cost, compared to the 4-6-0s that had handled such turns in the past, would permit a wide firebox and larger grate, which would facilitate burning the lower grade coals that Riddles and Cox realised were likely to be available in the future. Hindsight has shown that they were entirely correct in this assessment. Although the new Class 7 Pacific was given priority, work went ahead with other standard types on Cox's list. To avoid giving too strong a regional bias to any particular class, by entrusting the entire design to one drawing office, the work was shared between Derby, Swindon, Doncaster and Brighton, one drawing office becoming the parent for a specific class, whilst each drawing office specialised in certain components, Doncaster, for example, looking after coupling rods and connecting rods for the whole series. This plan worked well, and the first of the new class 7 Pacifics, No 70000 *Britannia* appeared in January 1951. It was an auspicious moment. In 1851, the Great Exhibition took place in Hyde Park, and to celebrate Britain's recovery from war conditions, and to mark the centenary of that event, the Festival of Britain took place in 1951. A Britannia class Pacific, No 70004, *William Shakespeare*, received a special exhibition finish at Crewe, before being sent to the BR pavilion at the South Bank near Waterloo station. The locomotive was a firm favourite with children, though I suspect that many children who visited the Festival of Britain, as I did, would have clearer memories of Heath Robinson's 'Far Tottering & Oyster Creek' fantasy engines that ran on a circuit in the exhibition grounds. The public could visit the cab of this exciting new locomotive, which, with its high running plate, was visually very different to its predecessors. Many enthusiasts disliked the lines of the Standards, adding to the bias against Riddles, but they were a practical engineering response to the new conditions in which steam locomotives had to operate.

Above: 70032 *Tennyson* is backing into the North end bay at Rugby Midland Station, prior to heading a Manchester semi-fast. The 'Britannias' were spread out across the regions, most of the early engines going to the Eastern Region, though 70004 and 70014 went to Stewarts Lane for the Golden Arrow services. 700015 to 70029 were given names from early Broad gauge engines, and dispatched to the Western Region. 70030-70049 became LM engines, and 70050-54, with 'Firth' names, went to the Scottish Region. In later years they moved around a good deal.

Opposite page top: A lot of thought went into designing the cab for the new Standards, and an instruction diagram was produced. Riddles and Cox felt it was essential to provide better crew comfort, including a seat. A mock-up was built, and shown to wives and families of the design team, and then to a wide selection of railwaymen to seek their opinions. On one occasion when my father was in London, I was taken to see the cab. For a small child it was a great thrill to sit in the driver's seat, and even to work some of the controls, although it was a shame that the cab was not attached to a full sized locomotive as well! Having seen the crude cabs on engines such as the Johnson 0-6-0s, which were still plentiful at the time, the padded seat particularly impressed me.

Opposite page bottom: In 1948, the railway network included many routes where something more powerful than a Black Five or a Thompson B1 was needed, but where the 20-ton axle load of a 'Britannia' was excessive. Riddles and Cox decided to marry a Britannia chassis with a smaller boiler and smaller cylinders to produce a Light Pacific with a wide route availability, and a tractive effort of 27,250 lbs. Numbered in the 72000 series, and given the names of Scottish Clans, as they were intended for the Highland section, they were actually put to work on services from Glasgow to Liverpool and Manchester, where their light axle loading was of no help. This squandered their only advantage, but the engines themselves lacked the crispness and liveliness of the rest of the Standard range. Stuart Cox himself said so, after taking the regulator on a working between Carlisle and Shap summit. Cox put their disappointing performance down to draughting proportions, and this was altered, improving their performance, but by the time this had been done, several of the lines they had been built for had been upgraded, so the need for the 'Clans' as they became known, had vanished. The class was not multiplied beyond the initial ten engines built at Crewe in 1951-52. No 72001 *Clan Cameron* shows its obvious Britannia affinities, despite the smaller boiler. With the exception of the one-off No 71000 *Duke of Gloucester*, the 'Clans' were the least numerous of the Standards, and the least successful. It is fair to say that the concept of carefully graduated classes was sound, but the gradations were too fine, and the Clans offered no worthwhile advantages over the Stanier Black Five or the equally successful BR Class Five. Had the prospective life for steam not been cut short,

they could have been rebuilt with new cylinders and Britannia boilers, transforming them into more useful engines, but they were not sufficiently bad to call for such treatment until their original boilers and cylinders were in need of major work, and by that time, steam had no future anyway.

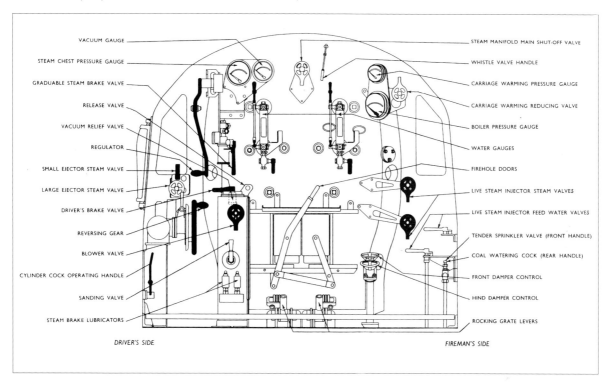

VACUUM GAUGE
STEAM CHEST PRESSURE GAUGE
GRADUABLE STEAM BRAKE VALVE
RELEASE VALVE
VACUUM RELIEF VALVE
REGULATOR
SMALL EJECTOR STEAM VALVE
LARGE EJECTOR STEAM VALVE
DRIVER'S BRAKE VALVE
REVERSING GEAR
BLOWER VALVE
CYLINDER COCK OPERATING HANDLE
SANDING VALVE
STEAM BRAKE LUBRICATORS

STEAM MANIFOLD MAIN SHUT-OFF VALVE
WHISTLE VALVE HANDLE
CARRIAGE WARMING PRESSURE GAUGE
CARRIAGE WARMING REDUCING VALVE
BOILER PRESSURE GAUGE
WATER GAUGES
FIREHOLE DOORS
LIVE STEAM INJECTOR STEAM VALVES
LIVE STEAM INJECTOR FEED WATER VALVES
TENDER SPRINKLER VALVE (FRONT HANDLE)
COAL WATERING COCK (REAR HANDLE)
FRONT DAMPER CONTROL
HIND DAMPER CONTROL
ROCKING GRATE LEVERS

DRIVER'S SIDE

FIREMAN'S SIDE

Opposite page top: No such doubts existed over the 73000 series Class 5 mixed traffic 4-6-0s, of which 172 were built between 1951 and 1957. The cylinders, motion and wheels were identical with the 'Clans', so shared many common features with the 'Britannia', but the boiler was based on the final Stanier Black Fives as produced by H G Ivatt. Although most illustrations in this book have been contemporary with the events described, I have made an exception for this view of the class leader, No 73000, which I took at Banbury on 30th October 1965. It is good to have rules, but it can be fun to break them occasionally, and this view has been a favourite since the day I took it. Of greater relevance, it shows the condition that the Standards had reached by the end of their lives, but also recalls that Riddles' policy of building 'go-anywhere' engines worked. At the start of 1960, No 73000 was shedded at Grimethorpe, moving to Canklow in January 1961. This was not a big move, but in January 1962, 73000 was transferred to Derby, but this was a short-lived posting, as Woodford Halse on the GCR became home from September 1962 to January 1965. The run down of the GC meant she was surplus at Woodford, so in January 1965, she joined the predominantly GWR stud at Wolverhampton Oxley shed. After just three months at Oxley, 73000 was moved to Shrewsbury, staying there from April 1965 to April 1966. This photograph was taken whilst 73000 was carrying a 6D Shrewsbury shed plate. By 1966, Western steam was on its last legs, and 73000 moved north to Agecroft in April, and to Patricroft in October 1966. This was to be her last home, withdrawal coming in March 1968. This record, eight sheds in eight years, was not uncommon, as the Standards were moved from area to area as steam working contracted. I always regarded the '73000s' as amongst the best looking of the Standards, and their performance did not belie their looks. They were good engines, and a fundamental change in conditions, rather than any design fault, signalled their premature end. In terms of numbers, the only post-grouping 4-6-0s to eclipse them were the GWR Halls, the LMS Black Fives and Jubilees, and the LNER Thompson B1.

Opposite page bottom: Although the 19¾ ton axleload of the Standard Class 5s gave them wide route availability, Riddles and Cox wanted a locomotive with a 17¼ ton axleload to replace the mixture of 4-4-0s and Moguls inherited from the Big Four. It was an ambitious target, but the 75000 Class 4 was one of the most successful of the Standards. Eighty of these light 4-6-0s were built at Swindon between 1951 and 1957, and went to the Western Region, the LMR and the Southern. As with 73000, I have used a view that is out of period, as it demonstrates the versatility of these attractive engines. Standard Class 4 No 75002, was a Western Region engine, but in common with the 73000, was to move around in its last years. Shedded at Swindon at the start of 1960, it was transferred to Gloucester (Barnwood) in January 1960. In 1961, No 75002 travelled south to the former Somerset & Dorset shed at Templecombe, but moved to Bristol (Barrow Road) in June 1962. With progressive dieselisation, her stay was short lived, and by September 1962, she had

reached Machynlleth on the former Cambrian section, where she shared duties with the ex GWR Manor class 4-6-0s. In 1963, the Western Region sheds were recoded, following their transfer to the LM Region, Machynlleth becoming 6F in September 1963. Garbed in BR lined black when new, the 75000s on the Western Region benefited from Swindon's decision in later years to paint as many engines as possible in lined out passenger green, one of the engines so treated being 75002. As a WR engine, she also received the traditional coloured GWR route availability disc on the cabside, below the number. When I photographed 75002 on an Up excursion of Southern Region stock, at Brockenhurst on the Bournemouth – Southampton line at Easter 1966, she had strayed a long way from her home metals. Dieselisation of the Cambrian section was completed by December 1966, and 75002, by now an LM loco, moved to another former GWR shed that had been transferred to LM control, Croes Newydd, which was on the triangle serving the Minera branch, south of Wrexham. Her stay was brief, as Croes Newydd closed in March 1967, and 75002 was without a home for the second time in less than a year. The old North Staffordshire Railway shed at Stoke became 75002's last depot before withdrawal in August 1967. Was Riddles' decision to build the Standards correct? In 1948, government policy was in favour of steam, as it burned indigenous coal, and kept British miners in work. Without using US technology, which was politically and economically unacceptable, reliable main line diesels with adequate power output were several years in the future, assuming each stage in the development process went well. The railway workshops were equipped to build steam, and an abrupt cessation of steam construction would cause unemployment, as production could not be switched overnight, even if reliable designs were available. Finally, the railways needed motive power in the short term, rather than in 10 years time, so some steam construction was needed. The construction of steam during Riddles' term of office from 1948 to 1953 was justifiable, and any alternative would have put train services, employment and the survivability of the railway workshops in jeopardy. Whether a group of new classes was justifiable is less clear-cut. With hindsight, it was not, but Riddles had envisaged an orderly transition from steam to electric traction, with steam playing a diminishing role over a number of years. Had this logical plan been adopted, it is likely that the results would have been better than what actually transpired. It seems hard to blame Riddles for events that took place after he was forced from office, and which substituted an illogical and extravagant policy for a more rational one, that also saw hundreds of diesel locomotives produced and discarded as quickly. Were the Standards justified in terms of the numbers produced of each type? Out of the twelve types of Standard locomotives, eight were built in quantities of 40 or above. If these quantities were not justifiable, then the Stanier 'Princesses' and 'Duchesses', the Bulleid 'Merchant Navies', the Maunsell 'Lord Nelsons', Gresley 'A4's, the Collett 'Kings' and Hawksworth 'Counties' and dozens of other celebrated designs from outstanding CMEs were also a mistake.

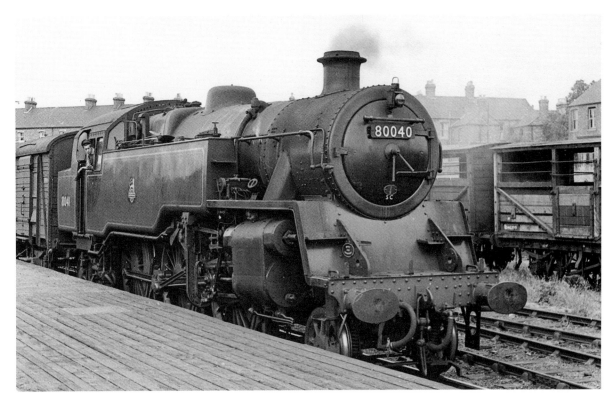

Above: The 80000 series 2-6-4Ts were envisaged as a BR version of the Fairburn LMS 2-6-4T, but Cox found that the 19⅝ ins cylinders of the LMS engines were too wide to fit the L1 loading gauge. WIth 18ins cylinders, boiler pressure had to go from 200 to 225psi to retain sufficient power output. The Class 4 tanks were also given a new treatment visually. Instead of the usual vertical tanks they had a curved profile, creating a stylish modern look. The first ten engines came from Derby in 1951, and went to Scotland, later deliveries going to five of the six BR regions, the exception being the Western, which preferred its own large Prairies. They were versatile, capable of everything from shunting to local passenger work. 80040, one of five consecutive engines sent to Bletchley, is at Banbury Merton Street on a Banbury - Bletchley local in 1953. Within a few years, branch line duties were crumbling in the face of closures and the spread of DMUs, but the last 80000 tanks survived on other work until 1967. The first of the Bletchley engines to move away from her original depot, 80040's later career revealed how the Standard tanks migrated. By 1959, she was at Chester, moving to Ashford, Tonbridge and finally Exmouth Junction prior to withdrawal in May 1964. Her sisters migrated similarly.

Opposite page top: With five classes introduced, 1951 had been a busy year. In 1952, three more Standard classes appeared, but instead of being 'new' designs, they were based on Ivatt classes of 1946-47, using BR standard components as recommended by the standardisation committee set up by Riddles. Mechanically, the Class 4 Moguls were the Ivatt class 4 of 1947, but with the draughting arrangements improved following tests carried out at Swindon. The Ivatt

engines (see page 156) were starkly functional, and Cox tidied up the design, with a sloped drop end and an edging to the footplate. It transformed an ugly duckling into a neat locomotive, as this Southern region engine, No 76007, recalls. The initial twenty Class 4s emerged from Horwich in 1952-53, and with another 25 Moguls turned out in 1956-57, were the last steam locomotives turned out at the former LYR works. The 115 Standard Class 4 Moguls mostly went to the Scottish, Southern, Eastern and North Eastern region sheds, as the LM had plenty of the Ivatt class 4s, but some of the 1956/57 deliveries went to the LM.

Opposite page bottom: The 78000 series 2-6-0s, power class 2, were the smallest Standard tender engines. As with the Class 4s, they were based on Ivatt engines built for the LMS. Sixty-five engines were built at Doncaster between 1952 and 1956, and went to the Western, Eastern, North Eastern, London Midland and Scottish regions, the first ten engines going to the WR. Machynlleth, (89C), with its sub-sheds at Aberystwyth, Portmadoc and Pwllheli, became a stronghold, with half the initial batch still there in 1960. The class leader, No 78000, out-shedded at Pwllheli, is at Barmouth Junction, on a Dolgelly – Pwllheli class K pick up goods. At Barmouth Junction, on the south bank of the tidal Afon Mawddach, the Dolgelly branch diverged from the Cambrian Coast line, and ran inland beside the river to Dolgelly, where it met the Great Western line from Wrexham, Corwen and Bala. Dieselisation meant that the Pwllheli class 2s were all reallocated between September 1962 and June 1963, their destinations including Nottingham, Wigan, Bangor, Gloucester and Crewe.

Opposite page top: The next two Standard classes were 2-6-2Ts, the Class 3 engines in the 82000 series appearing in 1952, and the class 2 engines in the 84000 series in 1953, at the end of the period we are covering in this volume. Both were sound designs, the Class 3 tanks being in effect a GWR Prairie with a domed boiler, but with BR Standard styling, whilst the class 2 tanks of the 84000 series were a BR version of the highly capable Ivatt class 2 tanks built for the LMS. Whilst the smaller engines did not have the deeper valance to the footplate, they received the drop front and other cosmetic improvements, together with the LYR style chimney that Stuart Cox, as a former 'Lanky' man, had set his heart on, and which as head of design, he was able to incorporate across the Standard range. Although masters of their work, and a marked improvement on the mixture of elderly tank engines of pre-grouping vintage that tended to run branch line and stopping passenger services, it was doubtful if there was any need for them when design work started, given the proven railcar technology that was already available. By the time construction began in 1952-53, any operational need had vanished, and many authors have said that resources would have been better spent on building DMUs similar to the AEC cars in use on the GNR(I) since 1950. Given that Riddles had adopted the diesel shunter, where the technology was already proven, why did the Railway Executive not adopt a similar policy with the class 2 and class 3 tanks? The only justification that can be advanced for building them was to maintain employment in the BR-owned works, rather than to meet any operational need, and this may well have been at the back of Riddles' mind. After 1952, construction of pre-nationalisation classes fell off sharply, and between 1953 and 1958, just 79 engines to the older designs appeared, of which 61 were pannier tanks built for the Western Region. Without the class 2 and 3 tanks, the workload at Swindon, Crewe and Darlington would have been meagre indeed. If workshop capacity was going to be needed when new types of motive power were built, it may have made sense to keep skilled staff employed in some way until new designs were available, and the works had been converted to diesel construction. Given that the Dundalk works of the GNR(I) had successfully mastered diesel railcar technology, it might have made more sense to have progressively switched from steam construction to diesel railcars, but given the different skills involved in railcar and locomotive technology, this option could have presented problems in the short term. It may well be that continued building of steam, although by no means ideal, was the least undesirable option open to Riddles and his colleagues, a point that most commentators seem to have overlooked. No 82001, one of the initial batch of ten class 3 tanks built at Swindon in 1952, has arrived at Leamington Spa General with a local service in 1952. The closure of many branch lines and the rapid spread of DMUs meant that they were amongst the least useful of the Standards, 82001 being withdrawn from Bristol Bath Road in December 1965, having been moved six times in a space of five years as work dried up. *H J Stretton-Ward*

Opposite page bottom: Apart from being responsible for 20,000 locomotives, Riddles' 'empire' also embraced running sheds, locomotive, carriage and wagon workshops, and a number of committees were set up to establish best practices, and senior officers moved from one works to another, to facilitate the process. Unlike much of the railway industry the workshops were a closed world, inaccessible to the outsider, but in the Fifties, British Railways ran a number of trips to Crewe and Derby works, two celebrated trips being to Crewe in 1952 and 1953. The South Erecting Shop, with its tracks grouped in threes, and locomotives in all stages of disassembly and refurbishment, was the high spot of any tour, and we see a 2-6-4T and Black Five 45068 being admired by a group of visitors under the watchful eye of a Crewe guide. The tracks at right angles in the foreground are for the traverser that served the north and south erecting shops. To modern readers, used to high visibility jackets, hard hats and the other trappings of the Health and Safety era, the drab work overalls and cloth caps will seem strange, but this was the world of the railway workshops for more than 125 years. I was privileged to meet men who had worked at Swindon, Crewe, Inverurie and the forgotten LNWR works at Rugby. They were skilled men, proud of their calling, with a fund of memories. At the bigger works, it was more impersonal, but at Inverurie or Rugby, the boss knew most of his staff by name. Lew Walton, who served his time at Rugby, where he knew Robin Riddles as a young man, recalled how the works manager walked through the erecting shop, without seeming to glance right or left, but if you were not doing something right, he would unerringly stop beside you, tell you what was wrong, and even show you how to do it. They were the days when works managers had come up the hard way, and could do the job themselves. Some commentators claim this produced inward looking managers, lacking in managerial skills and un-progressive in attitude. There may be a germ of truth in this, but it also produced men who were not afraid to take off their coats and show how it should be done, and who seldom had the wool pulled over their eyes, though they also knew when to turn a blind eye. To gain an idea of the importance of Crewe works, a few figures are in order. The first part of the works opened in 1843, and completed its 1,000th new locomotive in 1866. The 5,000th locomotive was turned out in 1911. Under the LMS divisional scheme, Crewe maintained 2,779 locomotives by 1947, but despite this massive maintenance load, and constructing 161 tanks for the army during the war, Crewe produced its 7,000th engine, an Ivatt 2-6-2T No 41272 in 1950. The first diesel locomotive to be built at Crewe was D3419, a class 08 0-6-0 in 1957, and the last steam engine to emerge from the works was 9F class 2-10-0 No 92250 in 1958.

Above: Although there had been considerable progress in Ireland, the Railway Executive was bogged down in too many other issues to make serious progress over diesel railcars, but after Frank Pope joined the BTC, Hurcomb was able to bring more pressure to bear on the RE, which set up the Lightweight Trains Committee, which reported back in 1952. The lack of progress had frustrated AEC and Leyland, both of whom had entered the railcar field before the war, and increasingly felt that the lack of home orders harmed their reputation and export chances. In 1946, these two rivals formed British United Traction, or BUT, to combine their trolleybuses and railcars interests. Although usually known as AEC, the Southall based company was actually called 'The Associated Equipment Co'. In 1948, it became a holding company, and was renamed Associated Commercial Vehicles, or ACV. Vehicle manufacturing was transferred to a subsidiary company, which took the short title of AEC. Using the BUT name, ACV and Leyland decided to apply pressure to the RE, and built 11 lightweight four-wheeled railbuses as a private venture. They were 37ft 6ins over the body, and there were 8 power cars, fitted with an AEC 125hp diesel, with a Wilson 4-speed mechanical gearbox, four being driving motor seconds, and four also having a brake compartment. There were also 3 trailer seconds, so they could run as 1, 2 or 3-car sets, a 3-car set weighing 40.5 tons, and seating 110 passengers. Commonly referred to as BUT cars, they were also known as ACV cars because of their engines. During trials in 1952, they worked out of Birmingham Moor Street, and around Gerrards Cross. They also appeared on the Harrow-Belmont branch and on the Watford-St Albans line. A

BUT set is seen at Watford Junction. After evaluation, they were taken into BR stock, but had little impact on BR thinking, and were withdrawn in 1963, after a period of disuse. *H J Stretton-Ward*

Opposite page bottom: Although the Railway Executive moved slowly over the introduction of diesel railcars, electrification made better progress, given the constraints on steel and other supplies. Apart from the comprehensive Southern electric network, the LMS and the LNER both had a number of electrified lines scattered about the country, whilst the LNER had announced plans to electrify the former Great Central route from Manchester to Sheffield, via Woodhead tunnel in 1936. The line was to use the 1500V DC overhead system, which had been recommended in a report prepared for the Ministry of Transport in 1927. Lineside equipment and locomotives were ordered shortly before the outbreak of the war, but work was suspended for the duration, and just one Bo-Bo Class EM1 electric locomotive was completed in 1940. It was used for trials, and then stored. One of the first acts of the new Railway Executive in January 1948 was to get the project moving again, and the first of 57 production locomotives, which were developed from the original Gresley Bo-Bo of 1940, appeared from Gorton works in 1950, the initial deliveries being sent to Liverpool Street for testing on the newly opened Liverpool St – Shenfield electrified system, which had been opened, using 1500V DC overhead, in September 1949. EM1 Class Bo-Bo No 26013, seen on an RCTS special that toured the electrified sections in South Yorkshire on 7th June 1953, had been completed in May

1951, but as test running started in the Wath area in 1951, had not been sent to London for trials. Stage 1 of the Woodhead electrification, between Wath and Dunford Bridge, came into use on 4th February 1952. A new tunnel was required at Woodhead, which ran parallel to the old 1850s bores, and when this was opened in June 1954, through working between Manchester and Sheffield became possible. Although the RE had developed this LNER project, Riddles' personal preference was for the 50Hz 25kV AC system. This required considerable development work, and Riddles championed converting the former Midland Lancaster-Morecambe-Heysham lines as a test bed, a project that was completed in 1953 shortly before the RE was abolished. Experience showed that Riddles was right, and the 25kV system eventually became the national standard, the Shenfield system being converted in later years, whilst the Penistone lines were eventually de-energised on the closure of Woodhead as a through route.

Right: Regular maintenance work is needed on any electric overhead system, and although tramways, working at 600v DC had traditionally been worked on live, this was not safe or feasible with 1500V DC. Careful isolation procedures had to be set out, with the areas that were to be switched off defined precisely in writing, so that staff coming on duty after an engineers' possession had started did not accidentally re-energise a section that men were working on with fatal results. A number of different forms were prepared and an isolation could not be terminated until Part 3 of the form was returned to the Control Room on conclusion of the work. Even with these safeguards, overhead line workers will tell you how scary it was the first time they worked on HT equipment.

FORM C.
PERMIT TO WORK ON OR NEAR OVERHEAD LINE EQUIPMENT

Issued to........................ Department ....

PART 1.
The following overhead line equipment has been isolated and earthed for your work :—
(State below exactly on which sections of overhead line equipment and between which limits it is safe to work).

....

....

....

This permit is to be cancelled not later than.............. a.m. p.m.

..............................Date.

Message number....................Issued by....................

Date..............Time..............Received by ....

PART 2.
I am now in charge of the work under this permit :—

	1	2	3	4
Signature				
Signature of person relieved...				
Date				
Time				

PART 3.
The work for which this permit was issued is completed, all my men and materials are clear of the overhead line equipment. I hereby cancel my permit to work.

Signed........................ Department ....
Contractor

Date..............Time..............

What was the overall legacy of Railway Executive policy on motive power after 1948? Some writers have castigated Riddles as a reactionary steam diehard. Do the facts support this charge? Riddles had no doubts that steam shunting engines were obsolete, and took the LMS 0-6-0 diesel electric shunter as the basis of the legendary class 08 shunter. The first engines were ordered during his tenure of office, and with over 1,000 built, it was one of the most numerous and most successful designs of all time. Riddles ordered the first of the Drewry 204hp diesel mechanical shunters, which later became class 04 under TOPS, and formed the basis of the BR class 03 shunter. Both were successful designs, and their demise was due to the massive changes in the rail network that took place after Riddles had retired. The RE went ahead with the 1500V DC Shenfield and Woodhead electrification schemes, although Riddles preferred the 25kV system. He was undoubtedly right, as experience throughout the world has demonstrated, but given the need for experimentation before the AC system could be introduced, and that altering the Shenfield or Woodhead projects to 25kV would put them back by many years, the RE took the right decision to proceed with the less technically advanced system. As the 25kV overhead is of much lighter construction than the 1500V DC, as the lower voltage system required a higher current, and heavier overhead wires to deliver the power, it is possible to convert 1500V overhead structures to 25kV use, as happened with the Shenfield electrification. None of the prototype diesel locomotives built from 1947 to 1954 were satisfactory, and unless the RE imported General Motors engines from the USA, which was politically and economically unacceptable, several years of development work was needed. Riddles was right not to invest heavily in main line diesel locomotives, as the result would have been to waste millions of pounds on technically unsatisfactory designs. However, a more aggressive testing policy was needed, but the RE was haunted by media reaction to the Leader project, which was not of their making, but inherited from Bulleid.

The most obvious failure was the lukewarm approach to diesel railcars. The GWR, UTA, and GNR(I) had blazed a trail, and the GN cars of 1950 entered service with few problems. If the smaller GN had the confidence to order 20 cars by 1948, there is no reason why the RE could not have followed suit. The cars were an immediate success, and instead of waiting until 1951 to set up a committee, the RE could have ordered cars from Park Royal and have started construction of these simple vehicles in their own workshops by 1952. Instead of introducing the first DMUs in 1954, and having to rush the program later on, hundreds of diesel railcar trains could have been in operation by then.

The greatest criticism levelled against the RE was its policy of building steam locomotives, which resulted in the delivery of 1,538 steam locomotives of pre-nationalisation design and 999 locomotives to BR design by 1960. As we have already seen, none of the main line diesels delivered prior to the demise of the RE was acceptable for mass production, so the options were to continue with an ageing and rundown steam fleet or to replenish stocks. To have abandoned steam construction would have seen a serious motive power situation deteriorate alarmingly. When the decision to abandon steam was taken as a result of the 1955 modernisation plan, it took five years, before steam construction ended in 1960, during which time no fewer than 533 steam locomotives were turned out, and many commentators suggest that the transition period was too brief. Had Riddles and his colleagues taken that decision in 1948, and kept to the same tight schedule, it would have been 1953 before steam construction could have ended, by which time over 1,400 engines to pre-nationalisation designs had been turned out. Abandonment of steam production any sooner would have led to unemployment at BR works, as no reliable diesel types were yet available for mass production. The decision to build standard steam classes is also condemned. Steam was an unavoidable stopgap, and existing designs could have been multiplied, but Riddles envisaged a longer transition from steam to electric traction than was eventually the case. Under the Riddles' plan, steam would have been moved from area to area as required. The unpopularity of Western or Southern engines when moved to foreign territory, suggests that such transfers on a large scale would have been unpopular. The Britannia Pacifics, and the class 4 and 5 tender locomotives met their design objectives, and their later careers showed how readily they could be moved about, as dieselisation took root. The class 4 tanks may or may not have been necessary, but the smaller class 2 and 3 locomotives were borderline when design work started in 1948, and construction plans should have been shelved in favour of simple DMUs by 1950.

Riddles and the RE made mistakes. There is no doubt of that, but set against the constraints of the day, the unworkable structure that the politicians and civil servants had foisted upon the railway industry, and the major decisions that they got right, such as the 08s, or 25kV electrification, the contribution of the RE in mechanical engineering was positive. They provided sound foundations on which their political masters and successors could build with confidence. That this did not happen is a matter of historical record, but the RE cannot reasonably be blamed for the failure of others to capitalise on what they had started.

13 · SERVICES WILL BE WITHDRAWN

In the eyes of the politicians who forced the 1947 Act through parliament, private enterprise and capitalism were dirty words, and meant that the interests of staff and customers would be disregarded in the scramble for profits for the bloated capitalists. Workers could expect to be laid off at the drop of a hat, and if a service was unprofitable, axe it! Nationalisation would safeguard the worker's job and ensure better service for the public. Neither premise was valid. One paradox of the company era was that railways developed a public service ethic that was alien to the majority of businesses where the profit motive is and always has been paramount. Even on the LNWR, which was ruled by an arch capitalist in the form of Sir Richard Moon for many years, this philosophy took root. Moon drummed into his officers that they were officers and gentlemen, that a promise was a promise, so you should be careful in what you promised, and having promised it, you must perform it. By the 1920s, the railways were feeling the pinch of rising wages and road competition was starting to bite on rural lines. Logically, the Big Four should have reviewed their minor routes, and axed hundreds or even thousands of miles that had no prospect of breaking even. They closed a few hopelessly uneconomic

Above: Coalport lies in the picturesque Severn Valley near Ironbridge and Coalbrookdale, two names that became famous at the birth of the industrial revolution. It was on the northern section of the GWR Severn Valley line, a few miles north of Bridgnorth, but was also served by an LNWR branch that ran north to Hadley, where it joined the LNWR line from Stafford to Wellington. Its stations were all close to busier stations on other routes, and with unification, the former North Western line was an obvious candidate for closure, passenger services ending on 2nd June 1952, although freight continued until 5th December 1960. The nearby GWR station closed three years later, removing Coalport from the rail map entirely. A branch line closure was sad, but this portrait of 40005, a class 3 Fowler 2-6-2T, recalls a 70 ton tank locomotive, with a tractive effort of 21,488 lbs, on a one coach train that will gross under 30 tons. The locomotive is over twenty years old, and the coach is from the LNWR, so the equipment is elderly, but even so, a single decker bus could carry the passengers at a fraction of the cost of the coal that 40005 will burn, without requiring a driver, fireman and guard. A smaller steam locomotive, similar to the GWR 48xx auto tanks, would be more economical, but crewing costs would stay the same, and the only realistic option would be a small four wheel railbus of the sort illustrated earlier. Operating costs would have fallen, but would be unlikely to match an ordinary bus. *H J Stretton-Ward*

lines, such as the Lynton & Barnstaple, or the Leek & Manifold Valley Light Railway, but showed little enthusiasm for widespread closures. At the start of World War Two in September 1939, services were suspended on a number of lines 'for the duration', a process that invariably turned into permanent closure, but with the need to conserve fuel and rubber for military needs, closures were infrequent after this initial phase. This hiatus continued into 1946-47, as fuel rationing was acute, and motoring had not resumed to any great extent. As a GP, my father, needed fuel to visit his patients, and recalled how he had to eke out his ration coupons, and how one patient who was some distance out of town and was taken seriously ill, requiring repeat visits, threw all his computations out of gear. As fuel rationing eased, a few closures took place, but railwaymen remained reluctant to close lines except as a last resort.

By 1948, railway operating costs were rising steeply, and with increasing financial pressure, this had to change, or railway finances would have gone out of control, but until 1953, railwaymen remained convinced that closure was an admission of failure, rather than a useful management tool. Apart from a worsen-

ing financial climate, nationalisation introduced a new factor into the equation. The Annual Report of the British Transport Commission was no longer the results of private enterprise, but of a government body, and was published by order of the House of Commons, and printed by His Majesty's Stationery Office. Before 1948, the Minister of Transport could fulminate about the shortcomings of the railways in answer to any criticisms in the House. Thereafter, he might fulminate, but he was the ultimate boss, with power to make things happen, as MPs and their constituents soon realised. When government agencies incur losses, the Treasury gets nervous, and Ministers start to worry. Instead of providing better job security and ridding the railways of capitalist commercial pressures, nationalisation meant that the politicians had to do something, rather than just complain. Time was to reveal that political expediency was far more ruthless than capitalist self-interest, though in fairness to the politicians, the crisis that was emerging meant that much of what happened was inevitable, irrespective of who was in charge, as we shall see later. This section examines a few of the lines that lost their passenger services between 1945 and 1953 to recapture the feel of this era.

Opposite page top: Between Barnt Green and Ashchurch, Midland trains had a choice of two routes, travelling via the main line and negotiating the 1 in 37 of the fabled Lickey incline just south of Barnt Green, or running over the single track route through Redditch, Alcester, Broom and Evesham. The Evesham-Alcester section was opened in 1866, and the line north to Redditch in 1868. This area, on the border of Warwickshire and Worcestershire, was also the frontier between the Midland Railway 'Birmingham & Gloucester' route, and the GWR line from Birmingham to Oxford. The GW inspired Alcester Railway was authorised in 1872 to build a 6½ mile branch from Bearley on the Stratford-upon-Avon branch of the GWR to Alcester. The AR opened on 4th September 1876, GW trains sharing the tiny Midland station at Alcester. To facilitate train working, a diminutive loco shed was provided on GWR property a few yards beyond the divergence of the two routes. The Alcester Railway closed in February 1917, the track being lifted and sent to France for military railways serving the Western Front. Unlike some closed lines, it was relaid and re-opened between Bearley and Alne on 18th December 1922, and from Alne to Alcester on 1st August 1923, but closed again as a through route on 25th September 1939, the shed closing on 27th October 1939. Its allocation consisted of one GWR 0-4-2T. In this 1955 view, the Midland line to Redditch is on the left, whilst the GWR Alcester Railway branch to Bearley passes behind the water tank.

Opposite page bottom: The principal intermediate station on the Alcester Railway was at Great Alne. Although the line had closed as a through route in 1939, it had not been lifted at the time of the German blitz on Coventry. This resulted in the Maudslay lorry factory being relocated to Great Alne, and unadvertised workmen trains were instituted in July 1941. They ran from Leamington Spa, making connection with main line services from Coventry and Birmingham, and continued until 3rd July 1944, when they were replaced by buses. The Alcester Railway was thereafter used to store crippled wagons, until it was officially closed on 1st March 1951. By the time this view of Great Alne was taken in 1955, the track bed was heavily overgrown. In the early fifties, an abandoned station was still unusual, but in less than a decade, the country was to be littered with closed stations, some of which had a further lease of life in residential use, but others fell prey to vandals and were eventually demolished.

Below: An obscure line called the Stratford-upon-Avon & Midland Junction Railway meandered across country from Broom Junction, near Evesham, to Ravenstone Wood Junction near Northampton. Except for Stratford, it served no large communities or major industries. The first section of the original East & West Junction Railway opened in 1871, and by 1873, reached from Stratford in the west, to Towcester in the east. Receipts were depressing, and as with other companies, the E&WJ decided to build itself out of failure with extensions. Given the poor results of the E&WJ, a separate company, the Evesham, Redditch & Stratford-upon-Avon Junction Railway was incorporated to build from Stratford to Broom, completing it in 1879. By then, the E&WJ had suspended its own passenger services, and did not resume them until 1885. However, it worked the ER&SJ, but did not actually pay that company anything, so the ER&SJ went into receivership in 1886. The companies limped on, a re-organisation in 1908-1910, and a dynamic new boss, helping. The line was absorbed into the LMS in 1923. About four passenger trains were still running each way as late as 1938, but wartime economies cut this to one train, and this meagre service was suspended on 16th September 1947. Bidford and Binton, the two intermediate stations, were temporarily closed. The closure was made permanent on 23rd May 1949. Through freight services ceased in March 1960, and the line was lifted. The goods shed, which is depicted in this 1951 scene, was beyond the platform at the west end of the station. What should the LMS or BR have done? Binton village is on a hill some distance away, so the appearance of buses and cars robbed it of any appeal it might once have for local people going to Stratford to shop. The concept of living in the country and commuting to the city is a product of the motor age, so offered little prospect in the 1940s. A more intensive service might have generated more traffic, but the 7¾ miles from Stratford to Broom was worked as one block section, and allowing for freights, an intensive service was not practicable, and it is doubtful if it would have covered costs. Lightweight railbuses, of the type illustrated

earlier, could have cut costs, but a conventional road bus could go into the village. Oddly enough, the LMS did run a railbus on the SMJ east of Stratford, but this was to take tourists from the West Coast Main Line to Shakespeare-land, rather than for local passengers, and suffered from such mechanical problems that it was abandoned after a few weeks.

Opposite page top: The Leicester & Swannington Railway is commonly credited with being the oldest part of the Midland Railway. In 1830, the City of Leicester contained some 40,000 people, and was 'well stocked with jails', as William Cobbett noted. Good coal measures lay a few miles northwest of the city, but with transport confined to packhorses, the coal owners could not compete with the more remote Derbyshire coal that came down the Leicester Navigation canal. The Leicester & Swannington Railway was incorporated on 29th May 1830, with Robert Stephenson as engineer. The 16 mile line was built from West Bridge terminus at Leicester, to Swannington, the first section opening between Leicester & Bagworth in 1832, and being completed the following year. The MR bought the line in 1846, to create a through route between Leicester and Burton. The southern end included the small bore Glenfield tunnel, which precluded normal sized stock, so an alternative route was laid in to join the MR main line in Leicester. The northern end included the Swannington incline, so a new bypass route was built by the Midland from Coalville to Burton. Swannington passenger station was on the new line, opening in 1849. The gable roof on the right is part of the original 1849 station house, which was extended in 1860 to provide a waiting room. The wooden shelter on the Down platform dated from 1871. As new pits opened and older pits closed, activity in the coalfield slowly drifted away from Swannington, which became a sleepy country station on a secondary line. The station, which is illustrated on 24th July 1949, retained its LMS Hawkseye signs, still in LMS yellow and black, and LMS poster boards, but fell foul of the policy of closing wayside stations on minor routes where traffic did not cover wages. It was closed on 18th June 1951. Passenger services on the Leicester-Burton line continued until 7th September 1964.

Opposite page bottom: Oxford was on the GWR main line from Paddington to Birmingham and the Mersey, and was also the terminus of the LNWR cross-country route that ran from Oxford by way of Bletchley and the WCML, to Cambridge. At the start of the 1850s, relations between the broad gauge Great Western, which had reached the town first, and the standard gauge LNWR were so bad that any hopes of a joint station vanished, so the Buckinghamshire Railway, which was an offshoot of the LNWR, built its own station adjacent to, but not connected with the GWR. Exchange sidings were finally laid in during the 1860s, but it was not until the impetus of war, that a running connection was provided in 1940, so that freight traffic from the LMS could gain access to GWR. Passenger trains continued to use Rewley Road terminus, any through passengers walking the

short distance to the GWR station, which was visible from Rewley Road platform. The cost of maintaining a separate passenger station was considerable, and with company barriers dissolved by nationalisation, BR sensibly transferred passenger services to the nearby GWR station from 1st October 1951, Rewley Road thereafter serving as a freight depot, until it was redeveloped in modern times. We are looking at the station forecourt, with its cast iron port cochere or covered porch for carriages in 1951, a few months before it closed to passengers. *H J Stretton-Ward*

Above: Oxford was renowned as one of the places where it was possible to see LMS stock at Rewley Road, GWR stock in profusion at the Great Western station, and Southern locos and SR or LNER coaching stock on through trains via the GC, but few people realise that for some years, it was possible to see Great Eastern engines at Oxford. As with the closure of Rewley Road, the reason was nationalisation. Cambridge was a major station on the former GE section of the LNER, with its own large motive power depot, coded 31A by BR. In pre-grouping days, the LNWR had a small loco depot at Cambridge to provide motive power for the Bletchley services. It could accommodate four engines, but in 1935, the LMS closed their shed, using the nearby LNER facilities instead.

LMS engines continued to handle the Bletchley services, but with nationalisation, there was no longer any need for LM region engines to do so, and from 1st October 1950, former GER D16 'Claud Hamilton' class 4-4-0s began to work through from Cambridge to Oxford. A Cambridge shedded D16/3, No 62571, backs out of the platform at Rewley Road, having arrived with a stopping train from Cambridge in 1951. If James Holden, the Locomotive Superintendent of the GER at the time the 'Claud's' were introduced, was looking down from the loco engineer's Valhalla, he must have been pleased, as he had been carriage & wagon superintendent of the GWR prior to taking the top job on the Great Eastern. The 'Claud's' reign at Rewley Road was short-lived, for exactly a

year to the day from the start of 'Claud' operations, passenger trains were transferred to the GWR station, so Holden's engines henceforth rubbed shoulders with Swindon designed engines at the GWR shed just north of Oxford station.
H J Stretton-Ward

Opposite page bottom: The 15 mile Tanat Valley Light Railway was authorised on 4th January 1899 under the Light Railways Act 1896. By the 1890s, British agriculture had been in recession for over twenty years due to cheap imports of beef, lamb and grain, and Parliament finally realised that the costly requirements of the Board of Trade, though vital on busy main lines, were ludicrous on remote branch lines where there might only be three or four trains a day, and ensured that such lines were not built. The Light Railways Act dispensed with such frills and offered a cheap way to obtain powers to build a line, and was responsible for a final spurt of railway building. If the idea was to serve remote rural areas, then building rails to Llangynog, with a population of just 547 people, must have been what parliament hoped for. The TVLR opened on 5th January 1904, and was worked by the Cambrian Railways. Freight traffic was tolerable, but passenger traffic was poor, and the line was soon in financial trouble. It passed into Cambrian ownership in 1921, and in 1923 became part of the GWR. It survived into BR days, but passenger services ceased on 15th January 1951, and freight services over the western end of the branch ended on 1st July 1952. For all but the last four years of its existence, it was home to some 2-4-0Ts that had belonged to Thomas Savin, the contractor who built much of the Cambrian Railways, and provided motive power in its early days. Cambrian Railways No's 57-59 were the last engines ordered by Savin, and came from Sharp Stewart in 1866. After working on various branches, they moved to the Tanat Valley in 1904, and although No 57 vanished in 1929, the other two survived as GWR 1196 and 1197 until withdrawal in April 1948. No 1196 is seen at Llangynog on 15th July 1941. Except for the short bogie coach that is partly obscured by the station buildings, the remaining stock is 4-wheeled. The spare rake in the siding includes a dia T.47 brake 3rd, with two passenger compartments. The second vehicle is a 5 compartment all-3rd, whilst the remaining coach is a 4 compartment all-1st, the greater space allowed between each compartment to provide more legroom being obvious. The train in the platform consists of a 4 compartment 1st, another two compartment brake-3rd, and a vehicle with a much lower roof line. The droplights, or door windows, are smaller than the

windows that flank them, whilst the ventilators above the doors are rounded. It is one of the 5 compartment S17 all third 'Holden' coaches built for the Hammersmith & City services worked jointly with the Metropolitan Railway. James Holden had been manager of the Carriage & Wagon department at Swindon, and principal assistant to William Dean, before being appointed Loco Superintendent of the GER in 1885. Of the two wagons in the yard, one is GWR, whilst the nearer wagon is LMS, a point that branch line modellers should remember. *R E Tustin*

Below: The London & Southampton Railway was incorporated in 1834, but changed its name to the London & South Western Railway when it obtained powers for a line to serve 'Portsmouth' in 1839. The original 'Portsmouth' station of 1841 was actually on the west side of the harbour in Gosport, passengers continuing by ferry to Portsmouth itself. Gosport station was the work of a notable 19th century architect, Sir William Tite, the designer of the Royal Exchange. It included a magnificent Portland stone Tuscan colonnade in 14 bays, with pavilions at each end. Although the station was

outside the fortifications that protected Portsmouth naval base, the military insisted that the station be of modest height in order not to mask fire from the forts ringing the harbour. Given the crushing superiority of the Royal Navy over the navies of the rest of the world in the 19th century, this obsession over base fortifications was strange, as a First Lord had icily put down a questioner during the Napoleonic war, saying. 'I do not say the enemy cannot come; all I say is that he cannot come by sea'. Eclipsed in importance when the direct LSWR & LBSCR joint line was built to Portsmouth Town and Portsmouth Harbour a few years later, the Gosport line became a quiet backwater, served by just a few trains each day. The station is seen on 3rd May 1953, a few weeks prior to closure to passengers on 8th June 1953, Gosport becoming the largest town without direct passenger services in the UK for a time.

14 · THE RAILWAY EXECUTIVE YEARS, MYTH AND FACT

The 1947 Act created a labyrinth, headed by the Minister of Transport and his civil servants who directed national policy. Below them, and subject to their directives, was the British Transport Commission, headed by Sir Cyril, later Lord Hurcomb. The BTC was responsible for the co-ordination of road and rail transport, inland waterways, numerous docks, hotels and other enterprises. Attempting to digest, let alone to co-ordinate, such a diverse mix of interests was a mammoth task, and although Lord Ashfield had offered the BTC the use of two floors at his beloved LT headquarters at 55 Broadway, the office space and headquarters staff were woefully inadequate for such a task. Overworked and understaffed, it was bound to be cumbersome in its deliberations, and Hurcomb's civil service background, in which minutes were drafted, rather than clear orders issued, meant that the BTC appeared dilatory and obscure. To men used to clear and prompt board decisions in pre-nationalisation days, this was frustrating, and the various Executives, such as The Railway Executive, the London Transport Executive and the Road Transport Executive, found it was easier to get on with their own work, and ignore 55 Broadway as far as possible. The Railway Executive faced a particularly daunting task, as their remit included unifying the Big Four, which necessitated a policy role. Friction arose between the BTC and RE over where their respec-

tive powers ended, and the BTC seemed incapable of laying down precise guidelines. This was bad enough, but periodic BTC meddling on what the RE regarded as its own turf, meant relations rapidly deteriorated, the RE producing one set of condensed minutes of its meeting for circulation to the BTC, and a more detailed set of action notes for its own use! The BTC, on its part, sent a series of letters to the RE suggesting policy ideas, most notably on diesel traction. The RE officers, frustrated by the generalising that emerged from their masters on the upper floors of 55 Broadway, found it simpler to stonewall, or to ignore such missives. The BTC Annual Report for 1948, covering its first year of operation, spoke of an Ideal Stocks Committee having been set up by the RE to assess future needs for motive power, carriages and wagons, and noted that the RE had decided that 85,000 mineral wagons were surplus to needs by July. Bland statements were made that the RE was exploring diesel and electric traction, but as one reads the report, the impression is that Hurcomb and the BTC had become immersed in organisational detail, rather than in policy guidance.

Skirmishing continued between the BTC and the RE over the next three years, but in 1951, there were two important changes. Sir Eustace Missenden, weary of the strife with the BTC, decided to retire from chairmanship of the Railway Executive. The man that Hurcomb wanted to succeed him was Frank Pope, whom we have met on the LMS NCC, and later as head of the Ulster Transport Authority. Pope was tough and ruthless, rejecting the public service mentality of many of his colleagues. He believed in diesel multiple units, and in slashing uneconomic lines. The other candidate was John Elliot. Another Southern man, he had been Missenden's deputy, and after Missenden left the Southern, on his appointment to head the RE, Elliot became Acting General Manager until 1948. He had then served as Chief Regional Officer on the Southern Region. Elliot was capable and strong willed, but had a gift for managing a team, and had experience of running the busy Southern Region, whilst Pope, despite his LMS pedigree, had been in Ulster for three years. Despite Hurcomb's backing, Pope lost out, Elliot being appointed to head the RE on 1st February 1951.

Both candidates were men of outstanding ability, with much to bring to the RE. Although Lord Hurcomb was remote from the empire he notionally presided over, and his ideas were often visionary, rather than practicable, it is likely that his nominee, Pope, would have been the better choice. Hurcomb believed that pruning the railway network was essential, and in Pope, he would have found a forceful ally. As chairman of the RE, Pope would have pressed for a more vigorous pruning of hopeless lines than the RE had in mind, but it is unlikely that the draconian measures that he inflicted on the UTA, closing half the system in less than a year, would have been necessary, or would have gained the endorsement of his colleagues. RE meetings might have been lively, but Pope's ruthlessness and the more traditional 'public service' approach of other RE members, would probably have produced a reasonable balance. Pope's experience with diesel multiple units would have been a benefit to the RE, which had become too preoccupied with providing diesel shunters for yard work, and main line steam until electrification was possible. As a result the branch line issue had been neglected. This was a mistake, and Pope's experience in driving through the DMU programme on the Ulster Transport Authority would have led to a more balanced motive power policy. Thwarted in his choice of chairman for the Railway Executive, Hurcomb told the Minister of Transport that there was a need to strengthen the BTC with someone of 'wider experience than that of the present members'. His choice was Frank Pope, who joined the BTC on 1st May 1951. Hurcomb now had a long serving, high-ranking and very tough railway officer on his team, who was well versed in dieselisation, and in railway

Opposite page: Earlier in this book, I have recounted how I was taken in my pram to Rugby station by a retired engine driver, who had been a patient of my father, and his father before him, to see the trains go by. I was less than a year old when the visits started, and my mentor returned home one day with the news that 'Master Robert has seen the streamlined engine'. I wish I could remember it, but it is nice to know that I really did see 46243, *City of Lancaster*, much as it appears in this 1948 view, taken from the spot where my guide took me. Childhood memories of the Wisbech & Upwell Tramway, or of a Garratt on the Midland main line, and of one of the Holden Intermediate 2-4-0s at Cambridge shed, flood back as I think of the railway system I knew as a youngster. In writing this book, I have relived many of those memories, and shared some of them with you. Before I began researching this book, I had read many accounts of the fascinating era from 1945 to 1953, and at times the accepted story seemed at odds with the evidence. As I brought the threads together, I realised that British Railways has always been a pariah. It was disliked by most enthusiasts, as it stifled the identity of the familiar and much loved Big Four. Later on, enthusiasts hated it because it replaced beautiful steam engines with boring diesels and electrics, and closed thousands of miles of line. Politicians and civil servants hated it because it 'lost' money, and they had to do something to avoid being blamed. Although most enthusiasts resented the loss of the old, the politicians hated it for not getting rid of the old order fast enough, and when modernisation came at a rush as a result of the 1955 plan, hated it even more when things went wrong. Dr Beeching came, and everyone hated him. The only people who didn't hate BR were the media, as they had a bad news story that could run forever. As I read contemporary accounts and turned the pages of countless official documents, I concluded that if one fact that does not agree with the accustomed story, it may be an aberration, but when all the facts do not support it, then the story itself, rather than the facts, may be suspect. In this closing section, I have committed the ultimate heresy for any author, of suggested that 'The Railway Executive', the men who actually ran British Railways from 1948 to 1953, have been much maligned. I am writing these words, almost exactly fifty years after the Railway Executive was consigned to the dustbin of history. I think it is time they were given their rightful dues, as men who undoubtedly made mistakes, but had been placed in impossible circumstances, and who avoided making the even bigger mistakes that many of their critics urged upon them.

re-organisation. Although this strengthened Hurcomb's hand in fighting the Railway Executive, the existence of the two rival candidates for the chairmanship of the RE in the corridors of power made for a piquant situation. One way in which the new power structure made its presence felt was in the pace of closures. Hurcomb was a keen advocate of pruning the rail network, and at his behest, the RE had been obliged to set up a Branch Line Committee in March 1949. Composed of regional and RE representatives, its remit was to examine un-remunerative branch lines with a view to closure. During Missenden's chairmanship from 1948 to 1950, the Railway Executive had been reluctant to embark on widespread cuts, and had closed just 343 route miles to passenger traffic. Spurred on by Hurcomb and Pope, and aware of the pressures that were being applied to eliminate the RE, Elliott felt compelled to accelerate the rate of closures, shutting 1,077 miles to passengers between 1951 and 1953.

There were political problems as well. The Labour government of 1945 had made nationalisation and austerity its key policies, but the electorate had grown tired of tightening their belts, and at the 1950 general election, its majority was slashed from 166 seats to just six. It collapsed within months, and the Conservatives, under Winston Churchill, were returned to power on 25th October 1951. To the Conservatives, Hurcomb's BTC was an anathema. They had promised to sell the road haulage business back to private enterprise, and reorganise the railway into regions, each with a sense of identity. Ideally, Churchill would have liked to recreate the Big Four, but as Eric Gore Browne had said, 'Once Eggs are Scrambled, I defy any cook to unscramble them'. After Elliot's appointment to head the RE, Hurcomb and Pope decided that the three-tier structure, with the BTC, the RE and the Regions, should be replaced by a two-tier system, eliminating the RE. In support of this, the BTC presented a reorganisation plan to the new Conservative Minister of Transport in December 1951. This envisaged combining the Railway Regions and Road Haulage Executives into regional transport authorities, similar to the Ulster Transport Authority, which operated trains, buses and lorries. With the new government's wish to return road haulage to the private sector, this was stillborn, the government issuing its own White paper in May 1952.

Although the Railway Executive had friends in high places, who felt that it, rather than the BTC, should survive, they were a minority in the government, and the fate of the Railway Executive was sealed when the new Transport Bill received its first reading on 8th July 1952. It provided for the abolition of the Railway Executive, and after revisions, became law in May 1953. Meanwhile, Frank Pope had been drawing up plans for the new structure minus the RE, but before these had been finalised, the Minister of Transport ordered that the Executives, except for London Transport, were to be abolished with effect from 1st October 1953. As a result of these upheavals, the cast list changed dramatically during 1953. Lord Hurcomb and Sir William Wood, who were both 70, retired. R A 'Robin' Riddles and V M Barrington-Ward, who were both strong believers in a central administration led by the RE, rather than a regional structure, were forced to retire, but most of their colleagues on the now disbanded Railway Executive became members of an enlarged BTC, which moved from its cramped offices at the top of the London Transport offices at 55 Broadway to the premises just vacated by the Railway Executive, which was the old Great Central Railway Station Hotel at 222 Marylebone Road. General Sir Brian Robertson, GCB, GBE, KCMG, KCVO, DSO, MC, a distinguished soldier who had worked under Montgomery in North Africa, and was a talented administrator, with a knack for dealing with people, was appointed to head the revitalised BTC. From October 1951, when the Conservatives returned to power, until October 1953, when the new structure came into effect, the RE and the BTC had existed in limbo, not sure what the future would hold, and not for the first or last time, railway managers found their time devoted to re-organisation, rather than managing their railways.

It is popular to portray 'The Railway Executive' years from 1948 to 1953 as a period when Britain's railways lurched into crisis, due to inept management from the RE. Generations of writers have accepted this unquestioningly, and a 'fact' once it is in print, takes on a life of its own. Whether it is true or not, becomes irrelevant. When I started researching for this book, I shared some of those prejudices, though a background knowledge of what was happening on other railway systems in the British Isles meant that I was not wholly convinced that railway officers who had done a good job in the traumatic years of World War Two, suddenly deteriorated into the buffoons that some writers would have us believe. As facts started to emerge, they had an inconvenient habit of not supporting the popular version of events. If one fact did not support the approved story, it could be disregarded as an aberration. If two were out of line, then there were two aberrations. If virtually every fact was an aberration, I had to ask if the story I had accepted all my life was right or wrong?

We have traced how Britain's railways changed between the outbreak of war in 1939 and the abolition of The Railway Executive in 1953. In concluding this section, we will look at some of the figures. The reader will then have the data from which he can draw his own conclusions.

Table 1 examines the motive power situation, train miles and staff employed on the railways as at 31st December 1947, and at the end of each succeeding year up to 1953. Standard Gauge steam locomotives stood at 20,023 at the end of 1947, rising to a peak of 20,211 locomotives a year later. Apart from the appearance of Thompson and Peppercorn Pacifics and Thompson B1 4-6-0s ordered prior to nationalisation, and the multiplication of Ivatt, Fairburn and Stanier engines ordered by the LMS, plus modest numbers of new Southern and GW locomotives as well, the decision to acquire 533 of the Wartime Austerity 2-8-0s to supplement the 200 engines already in stock from the LNER, pushed up the loco fleet, despite substantial withdrawals of older engines. The purchase price, of £2,929 each was a fraction of the cost of a new engine, and although the RE has been criticised for adding relatively crude machines to stock, the bargain basement price meant that they were far cheaper than building new motive power, even if steel shortages, and government policy had permitted it.

In 1949, the number of steam locomotives in stock dropped by over 400, and by the end of 1953, the steam fleet had declined by 1,439 engines compared to 31st December 1947, a 7.2% reduction. Between 1947, the last pre-nationalisation year and 1953, train mileage rose by 8%, from 351m miles to 379m miles. Electric locomotives rose from 16 in 1947 to 65, but this apparent rise of 49 engines masks the true state of affairs, for 10 of the 1947 locomotives were the long disused North Eastern Railway Shildon electric engines, and the solitary 1922 NER main line electric. The 1953 total was dominated by the new 1500V electric locomotives for the Woodhead route. Diesel locomotives had increased five-fold, from 53 in 1947 to 256 engines. They included several prototype main line diesels ordered by the Big Four prior to 1948, only one of which was in service by the end of 1947. None were satisfactory, nor did they provide a springboard to widespread main line dieselisation. Most of the increase was in diesel shunting locomotives, primarily the 350hp English Electric 0-6-0s, which had been developed for the LMS and then adopted as a standard for BR. Some 1200 were to be built by the early sixties, and many survive today. Coaching stock had increased slightly, but the 1947 figure reflected several years of minimal construction by the Big Four due to war conditions, and until 1952, passenger traffic remained substantial. On the freight side, wagon stock had been reduced from its December 1947 peak of 1,223,634 by over one hundred thousand vehicles, a drop of some 8%. During that time, as we shall see in Table 2, Freight Ton Miles rose from 21,505m miles to 22,766m miles, a 5.9% increase.

More train mileage was being worked, providing a better service to the public, and after allowing for the increase in diesels, the locomotive fleet had been cut by over one thousand engines. Freight traffic had risen, but wagon numbers had fallen. Staff numbers had been cut from the 641,046 employees on vesting day by almost 50,000, a 7% decrease. Rolling stock figures, train mileage and staff levels all suggested useful, if not dramatic progress. Had steel not been rationed in the early years, higher levels of productivity would have been possible.

Year	Steam locos	Electric locos	Diesel locos	Gas turbine	Petrol locos	Narrow gauge	Service locos	Coaching stock	Freight stock	Train miles 000s	Staff
1947	20,023	16	53	0	2	7	47	56,425	1,223,634	351,053	641,046
1948	20,211	17	67	0	2	5	50	55,666	1,179,404	365,572	648,740
1949	19,790	17	100	0	2	5	53	56,418	1,113,143	381,172	624,528
1950	19,598	10	125	1	2	5	53	58,222	1,104,965	384,109	605,455
1951	19,103	33	145	1	2	5	52	57,989	1,109,233	376,396	599,890
1952	18,859	58	207	2	2	5	51	57,672	1,120,118	376,398	601,381
1953	18,584	65	256	2	2	5	52	57,291	1,122,044	379,166	593,768

TABLE 1   MOTIVE POWER, ROLLING STOCK, TRAIN MILES AND STAFF 1947-1953

The figures in Table 2 are official figures taken from the Annual Reports of the BTC, and contemporary press releases. Occasionally, the basis on which some figures were calculated was adjusted. The changes were trivial, but means that official figures can differ. For example, freight train takings per mile in 1948 are sometimes given as £1 10s 7d instead of £1 10s 9d, as 'on company service' movements were recalculated, whilst passenger miles were 're-estimated' in 1952 and 1953. The revisions were minor, and can be ignored for practical purposes. What did the traffic statistics suggest? On the freight side, the number of loaded wagons forwarded had dropped by over 4%, but tonnage, average haul in miles, and the important net ton miles had all risen, the latter by 5.8%, showing that more freight was being moved a greater distance by fewer wagons. These were the kind of figures that were needed, and freight revenue per train mile had gone up by 40%, from £1 10s per mile to £2 2s per mile. This was due to increased freight rates, the reduction in the number of smaller low capacity wagons, and better loading. Passenger journeys fell by just 1% from 996m to 985m, so the situation also appeared stable, but a closer study revealed problems. Revenue was more important than mere numbers, and passenger takings per train mile had dropped from an average of 11s 1d (55p) to as little as 9s 1d (45p) in 1950, before climbing back to 10s (50p) due to fare increases. The average figures masked very different results, with some main line express services grossing many pounds a mile, whilst some branch line trains brought in a few pennies a mile, or in some cases, nothing at all. In March 1952, the Lightweight Trains Committee reported that a steam local train cost 7s 3d a mile, whilst a DMU would cost about 2s 2d a mile. As running costs were rapidly increasing, whilst receipts per mile had fallen, it was clear that urgent action was needed, if a crisis was to be staved off. The first steps towards creating the BR multiple unit fleet were in hand before the autumn, although the first Derby Lightweight unit was not to appear until 1954. Table 3, reveals how changing traffic patterns and rising costs affected BR finances.

TABLE 2 BR TRAFFIC STATISTICS 1948-1953

Year	Passenger journeys	Passenger miles (est)	Pass takings per train mile	Freight tons originating	Average haul in miles for coal	Loaded wagons forwarded, 000s	Net ton miles 000s	Freight takings per train mile
1948	996m	21,259m	11s 1d	273.2m	55.97	36,273	21,505,609	£1 10s 09d
1949	993m	21,138m	9s 9d	280.2m	56.30	36,220	22,010,195	£1 09s 10d
1950	982m	20,177m	9s 1d	281.3m	56.49	35,750	22,135,378	£1 12s 01d
1951	1,001m	20,793m	9s 5d	284.8m	58.32	35,496*	22,901,793	£1 16s 05d
1952	989m	20,690m	9s 10d	284.9m	56.32	34,978	22,391,143	£2 0s 6d
1953	985m	20,810m	10s 0d	289.3m	56.87	34,760	22,766,194	£2 2s 7d

* new basis

Table 3. The standard story is that BR did badly from the start, and the situation got steadily worse. Alas for the story, the figures do not tell the same tale. In 1948, the ratio of expenditure to receipts stood at 92%. After a lurch to 96% in 1949, it dropped as low as 90% in 1952, before climbing back to 92% in 1953, the year that the Railway Executive was disbanded. Despite average weekly wages rising by over 40%, and retail prices by over 30% over the six-year period, the Railway Executive held the operating ratio steady, with an average figure of 92%. To say that the RE had actually done rather well, or that BR was not any worse off in 1953, than in 1948 is rank heresy, but any other conclusion has to ignore too many facts.

Although the overall figures were good, a close study shows strengths and weaknesses. Freight had held up well. Although merchandise and livestock traffic had fallen by 7m tons between 1948, and 1953, mineral and coal tonnages rose by over 21m tons, and receipts had soared from £181 to £263m, a 45% increase. This was comfortably in excess of the retail price index, which rose by just over 30% over the same period, though in line with industrial earnings. As wages were a major part of operating costs, it meant that freight operations had held their own. These figures were welcome, but masked a less satisfactory situation on the passenger side. Passenger traffic had declined slightly by 1950 due to road competition, though the effect was not yet serious. However, government directives had kept fares artificially low in the run-up to the 1950 and 1951 general elections, by which time inflation stood at 20%. By 1951, fares were 10% below 1948 levels in real terms. Had fares risen in line with inflation, passenger receipts would have stood at over £180m by 1951, instead of £140m. Fare increases usually drive away some traffic, but with petrol still rationed, the potential loss was small, so a £30m increase in net revenue was feasible. The Conservative government relaxed the controls on fares, which enabled the RE to recoup some lost ground by 1953, but the end of petrol rationing meant that the market was more sensitive to price rises than it had been in 1948-51, so this could not be made up too quickly, without driving away too many passengers. Allowing for a 1% drop in passenger journeys over the six year period, passenger receipts should have reached £197m, had fares kept pace with 30% inflation, but were actually £153m. Had the government permitted a more realistic fares policy in 1948-51, much of this shortfall of £44m could have been avoided. As the annual operating surplus on BR varied between £12.7m and £39.6m, the impact of restricting fares for political ends exceeded the entire annual surplus. Had the Big Four remained in existence, they would have been subject to some government regulation, but not to the same extent as the Railway Executive.

Earlier in this book, we looked at several Irish systems. These included the ineffectually run CIE, and the Londonderry & Lough Swilly Railway, that had decided it wanted to scrap its trains in favour of buses in the 1930s.The railway results for both were poor. We also looked at the County Donegal Railways Joint Committee, the line that pioneered diesel railcars in the British Isles, and the Great Northern

Railway Ireland, the company that provided the technical backing for the Donegal, and introduced the first fleet of DMUs into day to day service in the British Isles. Both companies were well run, and in 1948 the GN was taking delivery of new steam locomotives and ordering diesel railcars. By 1953, it had to be rescued from collapse by a government take-over. The Irish railways, as Joseph Tatlow had so rightly commented, (see page 97) had a much smaller cake than their British counterparts, so the chill winds of competition and rising costs would hurt them harder and sooner than British Railways, but logically one could expect the same crisis, albeit delayed by two or three years.

Political interference in pricing policies clearly had a harmful effect on BR, but given the traditional story of how badly the Railway Executive performed, I had expected to find that time ran out for BR, just as it had run out for the CDRJC or GNR(I). As I studied the Annual Reports of the BTC, the real reason for the 'collapse' of British Railways during the Railway Executive years became clear. It was not what I had expected. From the earliest days, railway companies had raised the finance they required to build their lines from investors. In Victorian times, just as in today's Hi-tech world, investors varied from the aggressive risk taker, who wanted a high return, but accepted a higher chance of losing everything, to the more timid investor who wanted security for his capital, and would accept a lower income in return for that security. The Railway builders realised that, and catered for all categories of investor. For the timid investor, to whom security was paramount, they offered Debentures. A debenture holder was not a shareholder, but had loaned money to the company, in much the same way that a building society

loans money to a householder on a mortgage. If the railway or the householder was unable to pay the interest on the loan, the debenture holder or the building society could 'call in' the loan. They were a secured creditor, which meant that if the borrower could not pay his debts in full, they received priority over non-secured investors. Debentures were a secure investment, but carried a low return. For the more adventurous investor, there were two types of shares, the Preference share and the Ordinary share. The Preference share carried a specified dividend, 4 to 5% being common. Once the company had paid its Debentures, the Preference shareholder would receive his dividend in FULL. Only when he had received his full dividend, was any money distributed to the Ordinary shareholders. If the company did well, the Ordinary shareholder might receive 6 or 7%, or even more in the case of some of the Welsh Valleys lines in their heyday. If the company did badly, he might receive a small dividend, or nothing at all. To provide even more flexibility, Preference shares could be divided into Pre-Preference, or First and Second Preference stocks, which took priority over one another, should the company be unable to pay its Preference shareholders in full. Ordinary shares could also be ranked, Deferred Ordinary being the lowest form of life. This complex structure, with Debenture interest, Preference dividends, and Ordinary dividends, was geared to attract different types of investors in Victorian times, and worked well. It also meant that so long as net income covered operating costs and Debenture interest, the company could survive a lean spell, as the shareholders would receive little or no income, but could hope for better times in the future. How did this work in practice?

TABLE 3 THE RAILWAY EXECUTIVE YEARS – FINANCIAL RETURNS 1948-1953

Year	Passenger, Parcels & Mail Receipts	Freight Receipts	Miscellaneous Receipts	Receipts	Expenditure	Net Traffic Receipts	Ratio
1948	£151,940,685	£181,696,313	£3,677,998	£337,314,996	£311,057,259	£26,257,737	92%
1949	£142,973,887	£178,716,683	£3,797,875	£325,488,445	£312,827,636	£12,660,809	96%
1950	£137,294,250	£198,681,823	£4,094,225	£340,070,298	£313,740,213	£26,330,085	92%
1951	£140,074,034	£227,857,830	£4,791,098	£372,722,962	£337,769,821	£34,953,141	91%
1952	£147,885,976	£250,536,733	£4,935,173	£403,357,882	£363,756,185	£39,601,697	90%
1953	£153,340,491	£263,083,075	£4,967,419	£421,390,985	£386,330,175	£35,060,810	92%

Table 4. Uses 1941 to show how railway finances had worked. The GWR paid its debentures, all its preference dividends at the specified rates, and a dividend to ordinary stockholders. The LNER shows nil for ordinary dividends, as the company could not even pay its preference shareholders in full, and the ranking system applied, the senior preference holders receiving the full entitlement, and the lowest-ranked preference holders, with a 4% Second Preference stock, receiving just 2⅜%.

What happened in 1948? The government did not buy out the shareholders in cash. Instead, it took away their shares, and gave them fixed interest 3% British Transport Loan stock. Having done so, it told the BTC that it had to pay 3% on its capital. Instead of a financial structure, where a railway could survive if it covered operating costs and could meet debenture payments, BR had to pay fixed interest on the whole of its capital. At no time in the century and a quarter of railway history prior to 1948, had any railway possessed such a lethal financial structure. The only company to come near it was the Manchester, Sheffield & Lincolnshire Railway, which incurred such heavy expenses in building Woodhead tunnel in the 1850s, that to attract fresh capital, it had to issue pre-preference stocks. The proportion of ordinary stocks fell relative to preference issues, driving down dividends on ordinary shares, making further preference issues inevitable. It was a vicious circle, and the London Extension added more pre-preference capital. However, the MS&L, or GCR, as it became, was a paragon of financial rectitude, compared to the capital structure foisted on British Railways under the Transport Act 1947.

TABLE 4. THE BIG FOUR, DEBENTURE INTEREST AND DIVIDENDS TO SHAREHOLDERS 1941

Company	Debenture Charges	Preference Dividends	Ordinary Dividends	
GWR	1,649,855	3,339,914	1,717,189	6,706,958
LMS	4,439,170	8,474,383	1,904,049	14,817,602
LNER	4,214,637	6,131,056	nil	10,345,693
SR	2,243,167	2,751,276	1,930,409	6,924,852
Totals	12,546,829	20,696,629	5,551,647	38,795,105

TABLE 5. THE FINANCIAL CRISIS THAT NEVER WAS

Col 1 Year	Col 2 Net BR surplus	Col 3 BTC stock interest & BTC central costs	Col 4 Balance after interest etc	Col 5 Net BR receipts	Col 6 Less 'Big Four' debenture costs	Col 7 Dividend capability	Col 8 Passenger fare factor	Col 9 Revised 'surplus'	Col 10 Dividend with passenger fare revisions
1948	£26.3m	£34.3m	(£7.0m)	£26.3m	£12.5m	£13.8m	£0	£26.3m	£13.8m
1949	£12.7m	£36.6m	(£23.9m)	£12.7m	£12.5m	£00.2m	£10m	£22.7m	£10.2m
1950	£26.3m	£37.5m	(£11.2m)	£26.3m	£12.5m	£13.8m	£15m	£41.3m	£28.8m
1951	£35.0m	£33.3m	£1.7m plus	£35.0m	£12.5m	£22.5m	£20m	£55.0m	£42.5m
1952	£39.6m	£34.8m	£4.8m plus	£39.6m	£12.5m	£27.1m	£25m	£64.6m	£52.1m
1953	£35.1m	£37.3m	(£ 2.2m)	£35.1m	£12.5m	£22.6m	£30m	£65.1m	£52.6m

Table 5 lists the BR net operating surplus for each year from 1948 to 1953, a total of £175.1m earned for the nation over six years. Column 3 shows the central expenses of the BTC, and the interest due on BTC stock, basing the BR contribution on its proportion of the whole asset base of the BTC, which ranged from £33m to £37m, depending on other items. Column 4 reveals that when the capital debt that was caused by the 1947 Transport Act is added, an operational surplus of £175.1m became a loss of £39.7m over the six years. What would have happened had the Big Four remained in existence? They might have done better financially than BR, or they might have done worse. Column 5 assumes that their earnings would have done no better, whilst Column 6 shows the £12.5m debenture charges that the Big Four would have been obliged to pay. With the exception of 1949, when there is a balance of just £0.2m, Column 7 shows that the Big Four would not merely have been profitable, but could even have paid their preference dividends in three out of the six years. The Big Four would not have been as vulnerable to the political pressures to keep fares artificially low, that cost BR between £20m and £40m each year from 1949 onwards. Column 8 must be conjecture, but assumes that less than two thirds of any increase in line with inflation would be retained, due to customer resistance. The

potential surplus appears in Column 9, and suggests that the Big Four could have not merely paid their debenture interest, but covered preference and ordinary dividends as well, and funded a higher level of modernisation than was actually achieved under State control.

In reality, the LNER was the weakest of the companies, and would have been struggling by 1950, but the GWR, the Southern and probably the LMS would have been viable. The financial crisis on BR was not caused by mismanagement by the Railway Executive. It was the result of the financial structure imposed on the railway industry by politicians and civil servants under the Transport Act 1947. Once the politicians and the civil servants had created that structure, and the BTC had accepted it, the industry's chance of survival had been grievously harmed, but astonishingly, it could have survived, had the government not restrained passenger receipts for political reasons. With this double onslaught on its finances, the railway industry was doomed to public odium, as it was portrayed in the media, and in parliament, as a financial albatross. The BTC could not meet its interest burden without borrowing from government, and as this pseudo-deficit was added to its indebtedness to government, and had to be financed with yet more interest, this created a vicious circle that made the problems of the GC look positively trivial.

The suggestion is sometimes advanced that having compulsorily taken over the Big Four, the State 'had' to obtain a return on its 'investment', so charging interest against BR was proper. If the state bought the railways because the Big Four were failing to provide a good service, as the government proclaimed in 1946-47, then its purpose was to contribute to the public good. Saddling BR with a worse capital burden than the Big Four had assumed under private enterprise, was the antithesis of contributing to the public good, as it could only weaken the railways financially. The Southern chairman, Col. Eric Gore Browne contended nationalisation could not be justified, given their outstanding record, and that political dogma, rather than public interest, was the real reason. If the State bought the railways merely to pander to political dogma, then saddling the railway industry with an enormous interest debt that could only be met by draconian cuts in services, was even less excusable, as it harmed the public interest. For decades, it has been fashionable to accept the BR interest burden as reasonable, and even to claim that the purchase terms were over-generous, though a study of the income stockholders received before 1948, and what they received after 1948 reveals how hollow that argument was, with the sole exception of the lower ranking LNER shares. If the reason for imposing a massive and unsustainable interest burden on BR was to 'protect the taxpayer', then expenditure on museums, art galleries, overseas aid, and many other worthy activities, is even less justifiable, for unlike the railways, which provide a basic public service, they are not a necessity to the community. Would anyone suggest that these expenses should be abolished? If not, why should an important national service such as the railway industry be treated in a worse manner?

The collapse of the Irish railways between 1945 and 1953 gave warning that British Railways had a brief spell to put its house in order, if it was to weather the approaching storm, as costs and road competition became more serious. The reduction in motive power and wagon stocks, the multiplication of diesel shunters, manpower cuts, and the limited closure program from 1948 to 1953, were steps in the right direction. They were not enough, for neither the RE nor the BTC were perfect, and the greatest 'Missed opportunity' was the failure to follow the GNR(I) lead in introducing DMUs in 1950, and producing economical light weight railbuses for lightly used routes. Had Frank Pope been appointed to head the BTC in 1948, or even the RE, as Hurcomb wanted, the DMU era would have dawned sooner. The Railway Executive has been condemned for its failure to invest in main line diesel locomotives, but none of the experimental British engines put into service between 1947 and 1954 were acceptable, and given the serious problems with 10000, the RE were right to cancel an LNER proposal to buy 25 unproven main line locomotives. However experimental work should have been followed up with more zeal, but the RE was wary of criticism from politicians and the media alike. If the railway companies wasted their own money in experiments, that was one thing, but now that the railways were nationalised, it was a different matter. The Bulleid 'Leader' had cost a great

deal of taxpayers' money, and not produced one useful locomotive, as the papers screamed. The RE opted to play safe, even though it meant that the research data that was needed was not being accumulated. They were wrong, but given the pressures they were under, it is hard to blame them, and I suspect that most of their critics would have ducked for cover had the positions been reversed.

Of greater concern than the alleged failings of the RE in not introducing main line diesel locomotives, was the baneful effect of the capital structure foisted on British Railways, price fixing for political reasons, infighting between the political parties, the bad relations between the BTC and the RE, a mass media that cared more about headlines than accuracy, and relentless pressure on railway officers to 'do something'. Collectively they ensured that 'the financial crisis that never was' became a genuine crisis. Although it takes the story beyond the period we are covering in this volume, it is worth recording that as in Ireland, the position continued to deteriorate. In 1955, on a turnover of £440m, BR turned in a surplus of £2.1m, and an operating ratio in excess of 99.5%. 1956 was worse, with a deficit of £16.5m, and a 103% operating ratio. Now, there was a real crisis, and as with the Irish railways, it rapidly worsened, and the deficit had trebled to over £48m by 1958. This was serious enough, but with the interest burden, and the rapidly accumulating arrears that carried interest, the situation had spiralled out of control. Whether the Big Four could have survived beyond 1960 is open to debate, and even if they had, their limited dividend capacity by then would have put them at risk from asset strippers. What is clear is that a decade of nationalisation, with a fatal capital structure from the outset, and mismanagement by civil servants, and their Labour and Conservative masters, had brought a once proud and well-run industry to its knees.

In case, some readers feel I have been unduly critical of the Labour government that forced the Transport Act 1947 through parliament, I would say that there were three fundamental pieces of railway legislation in the Twentieth century. The first was the Railways Act of 1921, which moved from the pre-grouping era to the Big Four. It was untidy and confused, contained serious financial and regulatory problems, and by merging the Midland and the LNWR into the same group, when a five group structure would have been better, created unnecessary problems. Had it not been for the 1947 Act, it would be a candidate for the worst railway act in the last two hundred years. It was the product of a Liberal administration. In the opinion of Eric Gore Browne and most informed observers, the 1947 act was the result of political dogma, rather than economic necessity. The baneful influence that this piece of Labour legislation had upon British Railways in the first six years after nationalisation is traced in these pages. In 1993, the Conservatives produced a new Railways Act. There is an old saying, 'third time lucky', and one would hope that after 1921 and 1947, that the politicians would finally get it right. Most analysts agree that the 1993 Act has led to the most fragmented rail system in 150 years, and has simultaneously maximised the cost to the taxpayer and minimised the benefits to the rail user or staff. Ten years into the latest piece of legislation, Railtrack has come and gone; safety, punctuality, investment and soaring costs have become headline issues. The experience of eighty years of legislation, suggests that instead of learning from the mistakes of the past, politicians have the unique ability to repeat the old mistakes whilst inventing new ones of their own.

I had assumed that these words would have been the concluding comments, but a few days after they were penned, the news was released that Great North Eastern Railway had been awarded an extension to its franchise to operate the East Coast Main Line for 10 years from May 2005. One of the terms was that GNER would invest £125m in the business, which is entirely reasonable, and would pay the government a premium of £1.3 billion, or ten times the investment requirement. In the 1930s, the politicians of the day finally agreed to abandon the ridiculous railway passenger duty that had merely pushed up costs to travellers and reduced the money available to the companies to improve their systems. The franchise imposed on GNER has created a massive stealth tax that will fall upon the hapless rail passenger at a time when government policy is allegedly to encourage us out of our cars and on to public transport, and suggests that the ability of politicians and civil servants to repeat the mistakes of the past, and to invent new ones, is indeed unique.

Above: The amalgamation of the Big Four into BR saw many changes. At Lincoln, the LNER predominated, but the Midland had a presence, and its own station and loco shed at St Marks, with trains running to and from Nottingham. They were handled by LMS 2P 4-4-0s, but early in 1953, the Midland depot was transferred to the Eastern Region, and the 2Ps were replaced by a batch of former GCR D11 'Improved Directors'. One of the engines that was transferred to Lincoln was 62666 *Zeebrugge*, which dated from 1922, and had spent much of the period from 1948 to 1953 in store, as turns for Directors on GC metals were dwindling with the multiplication of the Thompson B1s. From 1953, Directors appeared on services between Lincoln and Nottingham (Mid-land) station, a piquant situation, as the GC main line, which had been home to the Directors for so long, actually crossed over the top of the Midland station. *Zeebrugge*, which was named in memory of the celebrated amphibious assault in April 1918 to disrupt German U-boat operations, is seen at Nottingham (Midland) on a Lincoln service. The reign of the Directors on the Lincoln trains ended in 1957, due to their relatively poor condition, when they were transferred to Sheffield (Darnall) shed.

INDEX

Accidents 48, 145
Air Raids 12, 43, 91,
Branch lines 12, 13, 17, 55, 56, 70, 74, 82, 86, 103, 104, 159, 172, 175-181
British Transport Commission 30-33, 47, 50-57, 114, 115, 122, 123, 154, 161, 176, 182-190
Canals 57
Coaching stock 42, 44, 64, 72, 93, 148, 149
Coronation 192
Devon Belle 44, 45
Diesel traction 38, 39, 72, 80, 84, 85, 88, 90, 98-101, 103-106, 111, 157-162, 172
Electric traction 43, 54, 55, 69-71, 153, 173
English Electric 38, 39, 157-159
Festival of Britain Exhibition 163
Freight stock 72, 100
Gas turbine propulsion 162
Goat (1st class) 86
Golden Arrow 66, 67
Horse traction 122, 123, 134
Hump shunting 143, 157
Light Railways assistance 92, 93, 97, 110, 180, 181
Liveries 58-73, 79, 85, 86, 93, 96, 100, 102, 106, 110, 123, 133. 152
Locomotive Exchange Trials 152 -154
Middle East Forces 24, 25
Motive power policy 18, 19, 26, 27, 79-81, 152-174
Nationalisation proposals 3, 28-49
Oil Firing 47, 107
Omnibus Services 53-57, 84, 85, 94, 98, 99, 122, 123
Plant Centenarian 14, 15
Pre-war railways 16-20
Rugby Locomotive Testing Plant 140-143
Railway closures 55, 56, 81-86, 91, 94, 99-101, 115, 135-139, 175-190
Railway finances 20, 22, 31, 33, 42, 48, 55, 81, 83-91, 94, 97, 99-105, 108-110, 185-190
Railway Operating Division 24, 25
Scottish Region 114-125
Seals of Railway Companies 76, 77
Seat reservations 117
Shipping services 36, 37, 46, 116, 121
Shunting 36, 37, 44, 68, 96, 110, 119, 122, 123, 143, 144, 157, 159
Single Line Staff and Tickets 89, 110
Train formations 11, 16, 18, 42-44, 54, 64, 70, 80, 86, 88, 100, 114, 137, 149, 160
Tralee & Dingle Light Railway 110-113
Trams & Trolleybuses 50-53
War 7, 11, 12, 21-27, 45, 74, 90, 91
Welsh Railways 126-139
Wrong Line Order form 75

Locomotives
B&CDR 88, 89
BP&GV 36, 37, 130
Caledonian Railway 118, 119
Corris Railway 134, 135, 139
County Donegal Railway 95-97
Dundalk, Newry & Greenore 85
Glasgow & South Western Rly 120, 121
Great Central Railway 42, 190
Great Eastern Railway 140, 141, 180, 181
GNR 14, 15, 68
GNR(I) 86, 102-105
GNSR 41
Great Southern & Western Rly 107, 108
GWR 19th Century classes 19, 22
GWR Churchward classes 2, 16, 17

GWR Collett classes 11, 28, 35, 59, 64, 129, 132, 133
Harland & Wolff diesel class 90
Highland Railway 124, 125
LB&SCR 13
LMS Fairburn classes 128
LMS Fowler classes 62, 64, 67, 148, 149, 175
LMS Ivatt H G classes 38, 39 156, 157-161
LMS Stanier classes 18, 24, 25, 62, 66-68, 114, 143, 145, 148, 149, 151, 159, 182, 192
LMS NCC 78-83
LNER 20, 63, 116, 154, 155
LNWR 144
LSWR 17, 21, 23, 44, 45, 47, 48, 61, 65
Londonderry & Lough Swilly Rly 92, 93
Midland Rly 22, 23, 61
Midland Great Western Railway 109
Midland & South Western Jcn Rly 14, 15
North British Railway 115
North London Railway Crane Tank 40
Riddles MOS designs 26, 27
Riddles BR Standard classes 141, 147, 163-171, 174
ROD Robinson 2-8-0s 24, 25
SE&CR 60
SR Bulleid classes 44, 45, 66, 67, 71, 152, 153, 160, 161
Talyllyn locomotives 136-139
USATC 2-8-0 26, 27
Vale of Rheidol 2-6-2Ts 133

Personalities
Allen, W P 'Bill' 32, 155
Ashfield, Lord (born A H Stanley) 31, 33, 50, 55
Barnes, Alfred 30, 31, 141
Bingham, Major S H, USA 27
Brabazon, Lord 9, 15, 23
Bramham, Marcus 38, 39
Bulleid, Oliver 44, 45, 60, 68, 70, 71, 78, 152, 153, 160, 161
Cameron, T F 114
Churchill, Sir Winston 16, 23, 28, 184,
Cox, E S 153, 154, 163, 164, 167, 168, 170
Curran, B L 76, 77, 100, 101
Dalton, Hugh, 7, 11, 12, 35
Elliot, Sir John 183, 184
Forbes, Henry 77, 97-101
Gresley, Sir H N 20, 63, 141, 154
Gore Browne, Col Eric 29, 30, 46-49, 140, 184
Haydn Jones, Sir Henry 136-139
Howden, G B 90, 91, 99, 102-107
Hurcomb, Sir Cyril, later Lord, 23, 30, 31, 50, 55, 65, 182-184
Ivatt, H G 38, 39, 68, 156, 157, 160, 161
Little, S C 76, 77
Mais, S P B 70
Maskelyne, J N 15
Maunsell, R E L 21, 23, 44, 45, 61
Milne, Sir James 29, 37, 109
Minnis, W F 87, 88
Missenden, Sir Eustace 22, 32, 33, 45, 47, 58, 60, 182, 184
Morrison, Herbert, 23, 28,
Nelson, Sir George 38, 158
Pope, Major Frank 83, 85, 91, 183-184
Portal, Viscount 29, 31
Reynolds, A P 108-111
Riddles, R A 6, 25, 27, 33, 64, 67, 68, 152-174, 184
Robbins, R M 76, 77
Sheard, A M 34, 76, 77
Slim, General Sir William 32, 33, 64

Speir, Major Malcolm, MC 81, 83, 125
Stamp, Lord 19, 22, 30, 156
Stanier, Sir W A 18, 19, 25
Stretton-Ward, H J 40, 136-139
Tatlow, Joseph 86, 87, 97
Thomas, Edward 136-139
Walker, Sir Herbert 18, 43, 69
Watson, General Sir D. 76, 77
Whyte, James J W 76, 77, 94
Wood, Sir William V 31, 38, 184

Railway Administrations (excluding LMS, LNER, GWR & SR)
Belfast & County Down Railway 86-91
Burryport & Gwendraeth Valley 36, 37, 130
Caledonian Railway 118-119
Cambrian Railways 130-133, 180, 181
Coras Iompair Eireann 76, 106-113
Corris Railway 134, 135
County Donegal Rlys Jt Cttee 76, 95-101
Dundalk, Newry & Greenore Rly 30, 85, 86
Egyptian State Railways 25
Glasgow & South Western Railway 120, 121
Great North of Scotland Railway 41, 115
Great Northern Railway (Ireland) 76, 86, 102-106
Great Southern Railways 107, 109
Highland Railway 124, 125
Isle of Man Railway 76, 101
Londonderry & Lough Swilly 76, 92-94
London Transport 50-55; 76
LMS NCC 31, 78-83
North British Railway 114 - 117
Railway Executive Committee 22, 23
(The) Railway Executive 31-33, 35, 58-77, 182-190
Sligo Leitrim & Northern Counties 77
Ulster Transport Authority 77, 83-85, 91

Railway Locations
Aberdeen 41, 115
Abergynolwyn 138, 139
Aberystwyth 133
Adelaide 196
Alcester 177
Annascaul 112
Ballymena 80, 81
Ballymoney 82, 83
Ballynahinch Jcn 89
Banbury, GWR & LNWR Stas, 11, 74, 75, 166, 168
Bangor, Northern Ireland 88
Bangor, North Wales 126, 127
Barmouth 132, 133, 169
Belfast 78-80, 83, 84, 87, 104
Belturbet 104
Binton 178
Birmingham stations 72, 144, 160, 161
Bow 40
Bridgwater 36, 37
Brinklow 18, 152, 153
Brockenhurst 166
Bulaq Shed, 25
Bournemouth 65, 169
Carlisle 148, 149
Chipping Campden 74
Clapham Jcn 44, 45, 70, 71
Clifton Mill 38, 39
Coalport 175
Corris 134, 135
Crewe 64,171
Darley Dale 23
Denbigh 128
Derby 162
Dingle 113
Donegal Town 100
Dorchester 61
Douglas 101

Doncaster 155
Dublin 102, 107, 111
Dundalk 86
Edinburgh 114
Euston 146, 147
Exmouth Junction 44, 45
Forth Bridge 116
Georgemas Junction 125
Gosport 181
Great Alne 177
Hatton 19
Hayling Island 13
Hersham 71
Hoe St Crossing 12
Hurlford 120, 121
Kew Gardens 54, 55
Killarney 108
Kilsby Tunnel reconstruction 150, 151
King's Cross 14, 15, 20
Kyle of Lochalsh 122, 123
Larne 82
Leamington Spa stations 6, 16, 58, 59, 64, 171
Leicester 156
Letterkenny 93
Limerick Junction 107
Llanfair PG 128
Llangollen 22
Llangynog 180, 181
Londonderry 92, 93, 95, 96
Machynlleth 131, 135
Moreton-in-Marsh 28, 29
Mortlake 69
Newport (Mon) 129
Nottingham 190
Nuneaton 62, 143, 157-159
Okehampton 57
Oxford Rewley Rd 178-180
Paddington 35
Perth 118, 119
Peterborough 63, 68
Portland 17
Rugby 41, 61, 62, 66, 67, 72, 154, 160, 164, 182
Saida, Palestine 24, 25
St Pancras 38, 39
Seaford 70
Shrewsbury 26, 27
Sligo 109
Staverton Road 26, 27, 42
Stewart's Lane 66, 67
Stranorlar 96-98
Sunningdale 23
Surbiton 18
Sutton & Baldoyle 103
Swannington 179
Swindon 14,15, 130
Tamworth 148, 149
Thurso 124, 125
Towyn 131, 136, 137
Tralee 112
Waterloo 43
Watford Jcn 172
Weedon 145
Winchfield 21
Wisbech & Upwell Tramway 158, 159

On the 6th of February 1952, George VI, by the Grace of God, King of Great Britain and Northern Ireland, and the last Emperor of India, passed away. His eldest daughter, Princess Elizabeth, became Queen Elizabeth II, and the Coronation ceremony was planned for 2nd June 1953. British Railways celebrated the event with commemorative headboards. Vast crowds had flocked to London, and on the afternoon and evening of Coronation day, 2nd June, no fewer than 12 specials took visitors home from St Pancras. Another 36 special trains departed from Euston. Visitors who wanted a longer stay in the capital, crowded into north bound trains over the next couple of days. Stanier 'Jubilee' class 4-6-0 No 45688, *Polyphemus*, carrying one of the LM region 'Coronation' headboards, blows off on a Down express at Rugby on 4th June 1953.